HOPE
NOT
FEAR

HASSAN AKKAD

HOPE
NOT
FEAR

WITH REBECCA LEY

bluebird
books for life

First published 2021 by Bluebird
an imprint of Pan Macmillan
The Smithson, 6 Briset Street, London EC1M 5NR
EU representative: 1st Floor, The Liffey Trust Centre, 117–126 Sheriff Street Upper,
Dublin 1, D01 YC43
Associated companies throughout the world
www.panmacmillan.com

ISBN 978-1-5290-5981-6

CITY AND COUNTY OF SWANSEA LIBRARIES	
6000395444	
Askews & Holts	09-Nov-2021
325.21	£18.99
SWKL	

Visit **www.panmacmillan.com** to read more about all our books
and to buy them. You will also find features, author interviews and
news of any author events, and you can sign up for e-newsletters
so that you're always first to hear about our new releases.

CONTENTS

To the untold stories.

HOPE NOT FEAR

It starts with a feeling in my stomach. A watchfulness that stops me sleeping. A sense that something is coming and I'll need to prepare. All my senses on high alert.

After all that has happened in my life, I've developed a radar for danger. It's like my superpower. A software adaptation in my psyche.

I felt my early-warning system kick into gear as soon as people began posting memes on social media about the outbreak of a new virus in China, confident that such a thing could never reach the UK. I felt a creeping certainty that it would. As commuters streamed past *Evening Standard* billboards about Wuhan without a second glance, rushing home to hot dinners and Netflix, I wondered why they weren't panicking. I was.

I can see danger on the horizon. Indeed, sometimes it feels as if it is following me around.

The general reaction to what was happening in Wuhan reminded me so much of that other time, before, in my home country of Syria, when things were changing quickly, falling apart, but people clung to their everyday routines like some sort of security blanket. Back then, my radar hadn't yet developed. Instead I had a young man's idealistic conviction that everything would be all right. Sometimes I miss feeling that way.

I've changed a lot in the last ten years, but one thing has stayed constant. No matter what kind of danger I find myself confronting, I become overcome with an overwhelming desire to contribute as best as I can. To help. I don't know exactly where it comes from. But my first instinct is to question what I can do to try and make things better. To ask how I can personally contribute.

That's how it was in March, when Italy became the new centre of the coronavirus. I watched news reports of people sitting on their balconies, playing musical instruments and singing to one another. By then I was certain that the virus was coming to my adopted city of London and that it was going to cause untold heartache. I recognized the feeling, of previous certainties shifting under my feet. But I also knew the best remedy for coping.

I understood that there would definitely be ways to help. There always are. And in my experience, sometimes being there for others is the only way we have of taking control over difficult things.

That's why on 27 March 2019, sitting on my sofa in my flat in East London, I googled a simple question. 'How can I help the NHS?' Like everyone, I knew the health service was under great strain, that it might struggle to cope with the influx of coronavirus cases. An agency link popped up with a job listing for cleaners and porters. Next to the word 'cleaners' was another in brackets. *Urgent.*

I looked at the documentation required. It asked for a DBS check and a passport. I had already applied for the former for a previous job and I had my refugee travel document, which I'd received just over four years earlier, after claiming asylum at Heathrow Airport. It was all I needed. I put scans of the documents in an email and hit send. Two hours later a woman rang me.

She outlined the desperate need for cleaning staff. Her tone was calm but the gravity of the situation was clear. I asked whether I would be provided with personal protective equipment or PPE, a term I had only just become acquainted with from all my obsessive watching of the news. She reassured me that they would be taking all necessary precautions. But I was still unsure about whether I could find the courage to go through with it. Reports were coming out about how many frontline staff were becoming infected and dying. Was I really prepared to put myself in harm's way, just at a point in my life when I thought things were becoming easier for me?

Since claiming asylum in 2016, I had started to build myself a life beautiful for its ordinariness. Despite the legacy of PTSD symptoms – claustrophobia, a constant restlessness, nightmares and flashbacks – I was trying hard to make the most of the opportunity I'd been given and that so many other Syrians will never have the chance to experience. Weekends away, holidays to cities I had never seen before, walks in Epping Forest, nights out with friends, fulfilling work. A future I thought I might never get the chance to have.

I paused.

But the voice on the phone explained that there were five hospitals in dire need of help and one was Whipps Cross – the hospital just ten minutes from my house, that I walked past almost every day. The building serving the community I had grown to know – and love. My doubt evaporated. I knew I had to do it.

Two days later, I found myself standing outside.

Whipps Cross is one of the oldest hospitals in London. A warren of Victorian buildings, many of them out of use, it looks like an intimidating cross between Hogwarts and an asylum. It's a place where lives change. Sick people are healed and some of them die. On the day I arrived there were already twelve wards full of coronavirus patients, many of them gasping into oxygen masks, others unconscious and being kept alive by tubes running deep into their lungs. Helping to look after them and keep the hospital running, was an army of nurses, healthcare assistants, porters and cleaners, many working for less than the London Living Wage. In a just a few months, these frontline workers would become as dear to me as family members. People like Gimba and Albert and Pilar and Giby and Vittorio, to name just a handful.

But I didn't know any of that back then, standing at the reception entrance. All I knew was that I'd never been as terrified. Even when I'd had my bones broken. Or been shut in a windowless cell and told I would never leave. Or when I was in a leaking dinghy full of other Syrians, including many children. Or during those afternoons when I longed for my distant parents and siblings so hard I thought my heart might break. Perhaps it's strange to say, but none of those experiences rivalled the unadulterated terror I felt that morning.

I'd grown to fear hospitals after what happened to me in one of them in Syria. I vacillated, my heart racing, my throat dry. Could I? It would be so easy to walk away and pretend none of it was my problem.

Somehow, though, I found myself stepping over the threshold, powered almost unconsciously by my strongest belief: love triumphs over fear.

The Red Zone. When I first went upstairs to the ward, I didn't know what that meant. I only saw a red circle on the door. The colour of blood, stoplights, danger. Then it was explained to me that it meant that every single patient inside had coronavirus. Once you stepped through the door, you had to be wearing full PPE. This was dangerous territory.

Things had to be put on in a certain order. Clean scrubs. Then the thin blue gloves. Then an FFP3 mask, sturdier than a surgical one. A plastic apron, similar to those worn by sandwich makers in cafes, tied around the torso. Finally, the visor. That plastic shield was the only piece of the flimsy kit that didn't need to be disposed of as contaminated waste when you walked out again. There simply weren't enough visors to throw any away, so they were disinfected instead. Every layer was essential, but carefully rationed. Supplies would arrive every morning on a trolley – a precious cargo of two boxes of masks, three boxes of gloves, one box of aprons. The gear was scarce; they could never give us enough to last even the week. There was constant anxiety about whether it was going to run out. When I first started, we were told to put our face masks into plastic bags and re-use them. But then the news came that this was in fact extremely unsafe and we needed to use a fresh one each time. The rules seemed to change by the minute, along with the guidelines.

Behind the door, every bed was full. And not only with the elderly. Many patients were younger – in their forties or so. So many of them struggled to breathe, leaning back, the lower halves of their faces covered by oxygen masks, their eyes unobscured. I didn't know if their expressions were desperate or resigned – I couldn't bear to really look. For the first few days, I wasn't able to make eye contact with anyone. It was clear that I was face-to-face with the virus.

Sounds come back to me from that ward. The constant coughing. The squeak when you rolled a bed to one side to disinfect underneath it. A 'Hello' from Albert to one of the patients or nurses, in his Ghanaian-via-Hackney accent. The gasps of people trying to catch their breath, desperately trying to suck in oxygen.

After three or four days, I started daring to look at the patients a bit more. The first one that I had an actual conversation with was a sixty-year-old man from Cyprus. He looked a lot like my granddad. Every day, I would come and greet him.

'How are you, uncle?' I would say, as I cleaned. 'Are you looking forward to going home?'

'Yes. My granddaughters are so worried about me,' he would reply. He was very ill, it wasn't clear if he was going to make it. Talking to him, witnessing the relentless rise of the death toll, made me determined to do the job as well as I could. I would clean every last bit of his bay, his side table, the light switch on the wall next to his bed. I was trying to throw a protective ring around him, to keep him safe. To do what I could. Luckily, he recovered, but so many didn't.

Nobody apart from the staff was allowed onto the ward. But one afternoon, an Asian man in his thirties somehow managed to make it to just outside the door of the Red Zone. I don't know how as there were so many secured areas to get past. He was obviously distressed, breathing heavily behind his mask, gesturing through the panel of glass, loaded down with bags. I went out to see him.

'Please,' he said. 'My mum's inside. I just wanted to give her some of her bits.' I knew the elderly woman he meant. She was gasping for breath just feet away.

'Okay, I'll take them for her,' I said, reaching out for the bags of stuff. I wasn't sure I was supposed to but he was so upset. I called one of the nurses. She looked at me and at the upset man and extended her hands for the bags.

'Please . . . can I just come and see her. My mum? I need to see her,' the man said.

'I'm really sorry but that won't be possible,' said the nurse. 'You're going to have to leave. It's simply not safe for you to be here.'

'Please,' the man appealed to me. 'Can't you help me? I just need to see her. Even if it's only for five seconds. Please.' He had started crying, tears rolling down behind his mask, sobs heaving his torso, unable to stop himself.

I felt desperately sorry for him. It was so unnatural and cruel. And it reminded me of how much I wanted to see my own mother. The vast distance between us. The constant anxiety of hoping she was okay during such frightening times, not being able to be close to her in person. How hard that was to bear. I glanced at the nurse, but she shook her head.

'I'm sorry,' I said to the man, with heartfelt regret. 'You can't.'

As well as the vast scale of death, it was quickly clear to me how much the ward was held up by immigrants. Most of the porters, cleaners, healthcare assistants had come from other countries. It was like the United Nations. Immediately I felt like I belonged. I had spent the previous four years advocating for the rights of refugees and here I was surrounded by them, witnessing up close their vital contribution. We had so much in common. We may not have shared a language or cultural similarities, but what united us was that we had made Britain our home and were working in that ward as a unit, to combat the virus. Risking our lives and the lives of those closest to us, to make a difference.

At the points that I've felt closest to giving up, I've often been buoyed by unexpected acts of generosity. Time and time again, bright spots of goodness have helped me just when I've needed it most. Reminders of connection.

Despite the terrible things I have seen – from a prison cell in Syria to that ward in London – my story is one of hope, not fear. If anything, it is a simple example showing that if we unite in kindness and love – wherever we are from, whatever we look like and however much money we make – we can get through the darkest of days.

AN EDUCATION

In so many ways, life in Syria was sweet before the war. Now that I've lived in Britain for five years, I appreciate more fully just how strong a sense of community there was in my old neighbourhood in Damascus. Family underpinned everything and everyone knew their neighbours. I couldn't walk down the street without bumping into at least twenty people I knew, and anyone going through hardship could find so many people to turn to for genuine support.

Life was also extremely affordable. You could be comfortable without needing to be wealthy. There was a simplicity and connection in everyday existence that was deeply fulfilling. It's something I see many people around me looking for now, but we took for granted at home. I miss it.

But despite the many positives, fear was never far away, thanks to the authoritarian regime we lived under. Scratch the surface and there was an implicit threat of violence if you dared in any way to contradict those in charge. A favourite Syrian saying, still uttered by parents to this day, is *Don't sleep in the graveyard if you don't want to have nightmares.* Don't you dare go looking for trouble, basically.

Every family had stories about people who had dared to defy the administration in some way. We all knew about people who had disappeared one day and never come back. Older people remembered the brutality enacted by the regime during the Muslim Brotherhood uprising of the late seventies. Where I came from, there wasn't such a thing as 'human rights'. That was a completely novel concept, something I had to enter into a search engine when I made it to the UK. People's votes counted for nothing – after every election President Assad would win – again – with an overwhelming majority of the vote. It was a pantomime of democracy.

The secret police, or *mukhabarat*, helped to enforce the dictatorship. They brought terror and intimidation to every aspect of Syrian society because they were always watching. Wherever you went, however mundane your activity, you were never far from their gaze. They drove estate cars with tinted windows and the president's photograph on the rear windscreen. You needed their permission for every little thing – from opening a falafel shop to throwing a wedding party. And we were so scared about them listening to us that my friends and I would always put our phones away if we even skirted the subject of politics. We would never dream of mentioning politicians or *mukhabarat* when we spoke on the landline. The saying *the walls have ears* was another that was often repeated.

My family was loving but my parents, Rania and Imad, only knew what they themselves had been taught. And at school, all Syrians began a process of indoctrination from their very first day. Attempted brainwashing. Portraits of the dictator President Bashar al-Assad hung on every classroom wall and stared up from the first page of textbooks. He was watching over us at all times, monitoring our every movement. We had to wear military uniforms. Instead of nursery rhymes, we chanted the slogan of the Ba'ath Party, the only political party in Syria: *Unity. Freedom. Socialism.* As students, we were given two options: join as an active member or as an 'ally'. I became an ally, although I had no idea what any of the words in the slogan itself meant. Every morning in the playground, we belted out the national anthem, which started with the lines, 'Guardians of our homeland / Peace be upon you.' The message was underscored – those ruling us were doing so for our own protection. Almost every subject we learnt was politicized and from Year 4 until Year 12 we had a compulsory class called Nationalism. We learnt about the achieve-ments of the president and his father (nicknamed 'The Immortal Leader') from a thick textbook. We were expected to regurgitate their quotes during written exams. During most of our classes we would address our teachers and other party members as 'Comrade', a word I hate to this day. It was normal for teachers to beat their students and, sometimes, to steal from them. I remember my head teacher at primary school slapped my younger sister Ghalia and kicked me in the shin with her stiletto because we were a few minutes late. The pain from her high heel was excruciating. While at secondary school, my PE teacher stole my first phone from my kit bag and then flagrantly used it in front of me. My mum had sold a treasured gold bracelet to buy that phone, but there was nothing I could do. It broke my heart. He was in a position of authority and so he could do what he wanted. That's how it was.

I was only twelve when I was first taken for active military training. As schoolboys we were driven to a field outside Damascus and handed Czech rifles containing real bullets. The instructors shouted at the top of their lungs, telling us to fire at the targets they set up. It began to rain and the ground was slippery with mud. I remember being so frightened about falling. It's a miracle that nobody was injured. Militarization was a core part of our upbringing and society.

Corruption was rife at every level of our society, where the concept of *wasta* or influence was key. It was all about knowing the right people and bribery was commonplace. At school, I didn't much care for doing homework, so I'd sometimes pay my class-mates to do it for me. When I first borrowed my father's car as a teenager he told me not to worry if I got stopped.

'Just pay the policeman and you'll be fine,' he said. So, I did.

Our country was largely closed off from the rest of the world. We were told what to think and believe by an authoritarian regime. Being different was frowned upon and what we were force-fed led to some questionable attitudes.

There was widespread anti-Semitism, given that Syria shares a complicated past with its historic foe, Israel, which has occupied the Syrian Golan Heights since the 1967 Six Day War. Jewishness was conflated with being pro-Israeli. At school we were taught in lessons about how terrible the Israelis were, and the occupation was used as an alibi by the regime to further oppress its own people. We were told that our extensive and repressive secret police would help to keep us safe.

We were kept in place through a system of lies and intimidation. So perhaps it's no surprise that I haven't always thought I could make a difference. It didn't dawn on me that I had the capacity or the responsibility.

When I was a teenager, you might even have described me as a bit of a thug. I was a bit classist, a little racist, unthinkingly homophobic – in short, not the most pleasant guy. If you had met me back then, you wouldn't have thought that one day I was going to risk my life to help others or become an activist or would look out for people worse off than I was. Not at all.

Where I grew up, fights were commonplace, and I even kept a baseball bat in the boot of the car. I never used it against anyone, but I did once smash in someone's rearview mirrors. Shards of glass on the pavement of a side street. Running away quickly with my friends, blood pumping. I can't even remember what the argument had been about. Once my shoulder was dislocated during a scuffle. After another, looking to avoid retribution, I hid out at a friend's parents' farm in the countryside for a week.

Aside from scrapping, my hobbies included playing war video games, shooting people on the screen. My friends and I loved one called Counter Strike, in which we played terrorists. I frequently bunked off classes and usually had a spray can about my person, to graffiti slogans onto the walls of Damascus. Nothing political, but the names of my favourite songs like 'Cleaning Out My Closet' by Eminem. I just wanted to have fun. I didn't really care about much. I was a young man embedded in an environment which was a breeding ground for toxic masculinity, where the only acceptable form of emotions I could show were different shades of anger.

Like all my male friends, I was rather sexist. I had grown up knowing so much more freedom than my sisters. I was allowed out with my friends in a way that as girls they would never be.

I was also xenophobic. I made fun of the foreign students at the non-Arabic language centre at my university and complained about all the Iraqis who had fled the war in their country and come to my city of Damascus.

'Those Iraqis . . . why can't they just go back to their own country?' I'd say, completely unaware of what it would have cost those people to be in exile, the agony of leaving their homes, the terrible things that would force them to uproot a family. Or that one day I would be in exactly the same position.

I was often homophobic, too. It's shameful to admit, but it was totally normal. It was common to use 'gay' as an insult. When one of my American cousins came out as gay, I was profoundly shocked and bad-mouthed him to everyone.

I cringe now about my outrageous views from that time. But they were the norm in my social circle, where prejudices were allowed to flourish unchecked in our mostly insular society. Overcoming them has been a process, but I can testify personally to the fact that conquering prejudice is all about education. People are afraid of what they don't understand.

Looking back, it's clear how much I was just a product of my circumstances. Which isn't to excuse my questionable opinions as a young man, but to give you a context to why I held them. But when I was nineteen, everything changed, when I got my first teaching job. I began to truly understand that all human beings everywhere deserve the same rights and freedoms.

From an early age, I had been obsessed with learning English. In a sense, it was my first rebellion. I admired how cool my American cousins sounded when they came to stay with us and I loved American music, like Blink 182. For many years I'd memorized lyrics and watched films, managing to become reasonably proficient. I copied out pages of English phrases and stuck them to my bedroom wall. So, I found myself at nineteen at university studying English Literature. I already had a desire to go beyond my own culture and language. I had begun to realize that there was so much I didn't understand about the world and was hungry for different perspectives. My university lectures were so full of students, however, that I found it really hard to learn. Attendance wasn't compulsory so I decided to get a job on the side, as well. I still studied for the exams.

When I applied for a job as an English teacher, I didn't expect to get it. Teaching had never really crossed my mind until a friend told me about a job in a private school called Little Village and I decided to apply.

I was interviewed by Ms Tamra, the head of the English department, an American woman who had married a Syrian, converted to Islam and moved to Damascus. From the very start, she liked me. Most Syrian teachers wear smart clothes but I was still a bit rebellious and turned up in ripped jeans and Vans trainers. She overlooked my casual dress because she saw something in me. The chance she offered me changed my life forever.

From the first class, I could feel my perspective starting to shift. It was the first time that I had a true responsibility. I could see the children in my class literally looking up to me. So many of them were from my own neighbourhood or were the younger siblings of my friends. I realized that I could actually have a personal impact on these young people, potentially changing their perception of the world. I resolved to become the teacher I had never had myself.

I had a good role model in Ms Tamra. She was a natural-born educator and profoundly influenced my life. She was the very first person to tell me that she was proud of me. My parents were very caring but they didn't have the vocabulary to express it. It wasn't really done. Nowadays, they tell me they love me but growing up that wasn't something they would have thought to do. My dad was a typical Syrian father figure – a little autocratic and remote. As a teenager, I was always a little bit afraid of what he thought.

Ms Tamra was proud of me and said so. Knowing that I could make a difference was a remarkable feeling. Almost overnight, my view of myself and my character began to change. I didn't have to be a hustler after all. I stopped fighting, discarded my spray can and baseball bat, and resolved not to mess around.

I took my role seriously, planning lessons carefully, determined to make them as fun and engaging as possible. I'd ask my students to memorize a speech from films I loved, like *Braveheart* or *Armageddon*. I shared the tricks I had used myself to help them learn. Within a short time, I was very popular with students. I found it really rewarding. What's more, the school paid me well, much better than my previous jobs had. It seemed as if I had found the route to a worthwhile life and now I had a reason to be better.

If I needed a reminder of the brutality of the Syrian regime though, I only had to look out of one of the classroom windows. Right behind the school there was a disused military base that had abandoned rocket launchers and rows of trenches dug in it. This was all just metres from a playground. This wasn't unusual: Damascus is full of secret police stations, constant reminders of the measures that those leading us would go to.

When I was a student myself, my friends and schoolmates had made fun of my obsession with learning English, but it had paid off. And I found that it brought benefits in other unexpected areas, too. Sometimes I would speak it in shops and find that I was automatically treated better than if I'd spoken Arabic. On one occasion, I was pulled over by a police officer for not wearing a seatbelt when I was driving. I pretended not to understand him when he spoke. A bit of my former rebelliousness was still in place, after all. I rang my brother and told them to tell the officer I was his cousin, over from America, unsure of the rules. The policeman believed the story and let me go.

The message was clear to me: the fact I spoke English was a ticket to success. Autonomy. A different, better life.

Years later, standing anxiously in an airport queue, my palm curled around a shiny, new fake passport, my entire future dependent on my ability to pass myself off as European, I was to remember that earlier conviction. And it still held. My English skills were to save me again that day.

But as a young teacher, it wasn't about preserving myself. It was about trying to positively influence my pupils and help them understand the world. It was the first time I realized how much I liked helping others. In teaching them, I learnt so much.

If I could undergo such a radical change of perspective about my personal capacity to make a difference, I really believe anyone can.

HOME

There is a tattoo on the inside of my left forearm. A set of co-ordinates marked forever in soft flesh. It helps to obscure the scars I have there, that legacy of torture, and gives the location of a place that is often on my mind and always in my heart, although I doubt I'll ever see it again. My home.

Our three-bedroom apartment near Maysat Square in Damascus was a happy place. My parents had saved hard to buy it and they furnished it proudly with thick oriental rugs and elegant furniture, including a long dining table that we all sat around at mealtimes. My mum had her favourite ceramic vases in a wooden cabinet and a special stand for reading her beloved Quran.

The apartment was on the eighth floor and had balconies on both sides that looked out over the city. You could see Mount Qasioun, the mountain that watches over Damascus, then the low-rise buildings of the cityscape rolled out like a prayer mat, punctuated by minarets. At night it twinkled with lights, dots of green emanating from the mosques.

Over time, as the situation in Syria changed, so did the view.

It became a curse instead of a blessing. It was easy to bear witness to just how much destruction was being wrought upon the city we loved. I could see thick black smoke curling up from numerous bomb sites and hear the sickening thud of explosions. The air, once so sweet with the floating scent of gardenia and jasmine on summer nights, now smelled of burning. When the Russians got involved in the Syrian conflict and the violence escalated, we knew that the civilian uprising was doomed. Somehow our gorgeous balcony view only highlighted everything that we were going to lose.

But I still love that place and miss it every day, which is why I got the reminder tattooed on my arm. It reminds me of a time when my family was happy and together. It was the last place we were all under one roof: my father Imad, mother Rania, my brother Bassel and sisters Dania, Ghalia and Ranim. We haven't been reunited since 2012.

Family means everything in Syria. There is no welfare state but you never see homeless people. They would be looked after by their relatives. People tend to live with their parents until they get married themselves and sometimes even afterwards, too.

I was close to my brother and sisters, but we also enjoyed winding each other up, as all siblings do. Bassel always played the eldest brother's role to bossy perfection, while Ghalia was annoyingly obsessive about keeping her room tidy. I used to go through her stuff and mess up her neatly made bed. As the youngest, Ranim was always a little bit spoiled by our parents. But Dania, who is only two years older than me, was almost like our second mother. She is very loving, with the kindest heart of anyone I've ever met.

It's weird to think that nobody lives in that place now. Those rooms, that were full of the sound of us talking, the smell of my mother's cooking, the sound of the TV, lie empty and silent. They must be covered in dust.

There are so many memories of us together there. If I shut my eyes they come rushing back in. My mother sending me up the road to the local market to buy dinner. Twenty pence bought twenty pieces of falafel, the Syrian ones with the palest yellow insides rather than the greener Palestinian ones. I would always munch on a couple on the walk home.

Talking to Bassel in the bedroom that we shared, the cotton curtains moving slightly in the breeze, their pattern lit up by sunlight, the notice board covered in our sketches and notes, the shelf stacked with hundreds of DVDs. Pirated versions of *Die Hard*, *Lord of the Rings* and *Terminator*.

Sitting in the living room, on my parents' smart sofa, underneath a treasured print of a verse from the Quran in gold lettering called Al Kursi. It is regarded as one of the most powerful verses and those who recite it daily are believed to be under the protection of Allah.

The walk from our apartment to the swimming pool around the corner, where we had swimming lessons every summer. The ability to swim well was something I was grateful for later, when I found myself swimming alongside a dinghy, trying to push it into Greek waters.

Driving to the orchards close to Damascus for *serans*, or picnics, a Syrian tradition. The countryside in the ring outside the city so lush and hilly, studded with fruit trees and springs which overflowed with the sweetest water I have ever tasted, so icy from the ground that my hands would almost freeze as I cupped them to drink.

Crates of fruit from those orchards. Apricots and peaches sweeter than anything I've ever tasted in Britain. We never described produce as organic – everything simply was.

Dressing up in fancy dress with my siblings on one of our many birthday parties. One time as the Backstreet Boys, we all drew on moustaches and danced for hours.

The smell of my mother's cooking coming from the kitchen. Vine leaves. Chicken and rice. *Foul mudammas* – fava beans with garlic, olive oil, tomatoes, parsley, onion, lemon and salt – the traditional breakfast before Friday Prayers, so that everyone in the mosque had garlic breath.

The music of Fairuz, the famous Lebanese singer, which we would always play in the mornings while getting ready for school. Across the Arab world her songs are fundamental, often touching on the specifics of village life in the mountains of Lebanon, with lyrics about fig trees, nightingales and drunken neighbours, but also carrying a universal and inspiring message of hope. Morning coffee and Fairuz always go hand in hand. Her delicate voice is played on every radio station and so formed the backdrop of our morning routine.

My mother bent over her sewing machine mending or making clothes. Or cutting relatives' hair – everyone in the extended family used to come to her to have it done.

The long runs I got into the habit of taking as a teenager, inspired by the Canadian athlete Terry Fox, who embarked on a long fund-raising run after his own cancer diagnosis.

My father coming home from the pizza restaurant he owned – named Pizza Roma and branded to look as much like Pizza Hut as possible – with sweets and juice boxes for us children. He had taken on his own restaurant after years of working in Saudi Arabia to save up.

Walking through the souk. Spice stands stacked with cinnamon, cardamom and cloves. Silk rugs, soaps from Aleppo, Syrian sweets, bright textiles.

The supper I had for my graduation, to which I invited all of my closest friends. My mum cooked a feast and we ate and ate. A photograph of the night shows our faces shining with youth and optimism.

The day I packed my bag to go, I knew that I was probably leaving for good. By then I had been put in the position of making a straightforward choice. Leave or die. Part of me was hopeful that one day the crisis would be over and I'd be able to go home. But I knew deep down that it was unlikely.

How do you decide what to pack from a life? There were things I left behind that I wish I hadn't. Like the shoebox full of old mementoes in my wardrobe. I think about that box often. It had cinema tickets and love letters in it, flyers, a bra from an ex-girlfriend. Fragments of the life of a young man.

There were also photographs I'd taken of my friends. Photography was a passion of mine from a young age. I just had an instinct for it. In Arabic they say, 'You have the eye.' I inherited it from my dad. On a trip to Lebanon, I bought a Canon camera with my savings, a semi-professional one with a good lens. I became the go-to person among my friends for anyone who wanted a new profile picture for Facebook. But what I really loved was street photography, especially photos of people going about their everyday lives. I would often go to the old city of Damascus looking for subjects. I also took many pictures from the balcony of our apartment. Of the mountain, the gleaming compound of the presidential palace, all the buildings running up towards the horizon. I had an urge to document things.

It's the same impulse that a few years later saw me take out my smartphone and film the protests that I went on. Or later still, keep the lens of my GoPro fixed on the dinghy that was slowly but relentlessly letting in seawater, panning around the frightened faces of people who were risking their lives because they didn't have an alternative. Recording their expressions, the sound of a baby crying, the uneven, indifferent sea. Unsure if I was about to drown, but still keen to pay close attention. It has always seemed important to me to really observe what is going on around you, to try and bear testimony to events.

Perhaps my tattoo springs from this same instinct. It's a testimony of where I come from. Who I am.

I never imagined that the situation in Damascus could unravel as quickly as it did. Thanks to my teaching job, I was starting to build a life that I really enjoyed and even better, becoming somebody that I was proud to be.

I knew we lived under a dictatorship. I comprehended how corrupt many Arab regimes were. But I was living a good life. I hadn't had direct experience of what was happening in the dungeons of my city – although everyone had heard rumours. On the surface Damascus was flourishing. You could walk through the ancient souk, which led to the Umayyad Mosque, and see tourists sitting in cafes, alongside women in headscarves and those with their hair uncovered. To an outsider, it seemed to be a model of tolerance and diversity. The new world layered upon the ancient one. But so much lay behind this romanticized image of the city of jasmine.

In Syria we were ruled by fear. The president's father, Hafez al-Assad, had been a famously hardline despot himself, who demanded nothing less than absolute devotion to the state during his almost-thirty-year tenure. Under his rule, the presence of the *mukhabarat*, or secret police, increased in Syria and, by the time he died, all political opposition had been effectively crushed. His successor was supposed to be his eldest son, Bassel, a preening, macho figure who was groomed for the role. But Bassel died in a car accident in 1994, so the succession fell onto his younger brother Bashar, a gawky ophthalmologist who had previously been working with children at a London hospital. This mild-mannered man seemingly advocated modernization and the internet. He flirted with reform after taking power in 2000, promising extensive changes, including updating the economy, tackling corruption and launching – laughably – 'our own democratic experience'.

He released hundreds of political prisoners and allowed the first independent newspapers for more than three decades to begin publishing. But the 'Damascus Spring', as it became known, was fleeting. Just a year later, the press was clamped down on. The country's long-running Emergency Law, which came into effect in 1963 and suspended most constitutional freedoms remained in effect. Any economic reforms brought in appeared to benefit only the elite and its allies. We all knew that criticizing the regime was still extremely dangerous. The *mukhabarat* was everywhere.

I'd even chanted in support of Bashar al-Assad at a demonstration in 2006, following the assassination of the Prime Minister of Lebanon, Rafic Al Hariri. He had been part of the anti-Syrian opposition in Lebanon and was killed in a bomb attack in Beirut. His death was a win for Assad and I took to the streets, along with many other Syrians, shouting in support of our president, hoisted up on someone's shoulders, the Syrian flag spread across my back like a superhero's cape.

Among the various different religious groups in Syria, Sunni Muslims like my family form the majority, but there are also Alawis (which President Assad and his family belong to), a sizeable proportion of Christians, Shia Muslims and the Druze. Growing up, the religious differences between us didn't much matter to my family and friends. We were all Syrians, first and foremost. One of the most awful things about the war has been how Assad has deliberately stoked religious sectarianism, creating divides in Syrian society that didn't previously hold much significance.

For example, one of my closest friends as a teenager was a boy called Sammy. We met at secondary school, where we would bunk off together. We both appreciated American pop culture and loved playing basketball. The girls liked us because they thought we were cool. We would save up our money to buy milkshakes in the cafe with the English-speaking TV channels playing. We hung out on a street down by the river that we nicknamed 'The Beehive' because of how narrow it was. We had so much in common. For a couple of years, I didn't realize he came from a Christian family. It simply wasn't an important thing.

For a long time, he was my partner in crime, but these days we no longer talk. He went into the army and became massively supportive of Assad. When I started to speak out against the regime, we argued and eventually went our separate ways. It's sad, but this kind of thing is not unusual. My father's side of the family were generally pro-Assad and I don't talk to most of them now. What happened in Syria has split up so many friendships and divided families. I simply think of it as 'the time before' and 'the time after'. Everything changed.

Although I parted ways with Sammy, I am still very close to my other closest teenage friends Redwan and Aghiad. Like me, they were both against the regime and also later had to leave Damascus, fearing for their lives. Both made the crossing to Europe as well. Redwan went first and then I travelled with Aghiad and another man called Alaa. I speak to them all the time. I've even visited Redwan in his adopted city of Cologne dozens of times. It's so good to be in touch with those who knew you before your whole life was uprooted and who can understand what you went through as well as the pressures of a life lived in exile.

Redwan was on my degree course although, like me, he also worked throughout rather than attending lectures regularly. While I was teaching English, he was behind the desk in a computer shop. Before exams we would push each other to study – he is probably the main reason that I passed my degree despite working full-time. I felt comfortable telling him everything, even the doubts I had about religion. My parents are extremely devout and really pushed me towards religion. They pray five times a day and find great comfort in their relationship with Allah. But I never felt a true connection. Instead, the constant sense that my sins would be met with hellfire only resulted in a deep-seated sense of shame.

During Friday Prayers, when the imam gives a half-hour sermon, I would often find myself so bored and unmoved that I would pinch my arm, just to feel something. Everyone around me seemed to find it so meaningful, but I didn't. Although I've always loved listening to the call to prayer and can objectively see that much of the Arabic in the Quran is beautiful, the religious feeling never truly ignited in me. I worried that there was some- thing deeply wrong with me, and I found solace in discussing these fears with Redwan. He told me that he felt the same.

We trusted each other implicitly, which allowed us to push at the borders of what was forbidden. I had my first alcoholic drink with Redwan, watching a film at Cinemacity in downtown Damascus. Nobody in my immediate family drinks alcohol. It was taboo when I was growing up. Redwan and I loved going to Cinemacity to watch films and there was a shop selling cocktails next door. One evening we dared each other to try a drink. We went in and casually asked for vodka Redbulls, but the owner could tell we probably hadn't drunk before and made us something weaker. I still don't know what it was, but I loved the loosening feeling it gave me, the warmth of the alcohol radiating through my body as we watched the film.

To some extent, like many teenage boys, I had a secret life that my family knew nothing about, albeit underpinned by shame and fear. There were girls, although I never actually slept with them because I had been told that adultery was sinful. But we found ways to have fun. There was driving around in the car I borrowed from my dad, blasting out Avril Lavigne, feeling as if I'd really arrived.

I had no idea just how much everything would change, in just a few years. That the life I took for granted would one day be so far out of reach.

After everything I've been through, I don't scare easily these days. But the idea of being back in Syria terrifies me. If I spoke openly there about some of the things I reveal in this book, I would be tortured and then killed. But my story is important. Although it's the account of just one man, it stands for so many other Syrians.

EVERYTHING CHANGES

They reminded me of my own students, those children in Deraa. When the news first emerged, all I could think of were the open faces of my pupils. Their laughter, their trust. The way they looked to me for answers and leadership.

Deraa is a dusty, unassuming city close to the border with Jordan. It wasn't somewhere I had ever really thought about, but in the spring of 2011, it began to assume a huge significance in my life – and in that of all Syrians. By then I'd developed a good reputation as a teacher and was also tutoring on the side; I was doing really well by Syrian standards, especially given my age.

The uprisings of the Arab Spring were spilling across North Africa. The Tunisian street vendor Tarek el-Tayeb Mohamed Bouazizi had set himself on fire in December 2010 as a protest. The fruit and vegetables he was selling had been confiscated by the police because he didn't have the required permit; in desperation he had doused himself in petrol and self-immolated. It became a catalyst for the Tunisian Revolution and wider demonstrations against autocratic regimes and economic hardship. I watched this phenomenon ignite, reading about it obsessively in the news – beginning a process of keeping myself as politically informed as possible, which continues to this day. I began to wake up politically for the first time, to question what we had been told. We had so much in common with those countries agitating for change. But I knew in my heart that if such a revolution came to Syria, it would be really complicated. I wasn't entirely convinced that the benefits would outweigh the costs.

But then came Deraa. As for so many other Syrians, it changed everything for me.

In February 2011, catching the breeze of disenchantment sweeping the Arab world, and with heartbreakingly youthful idealism, a group of Deraan schoolboys graffitied the walls of their school with revolutionary slogans.

They had picked up many of these slogans from watching satellite television. Phrases that had been repeated on the streets of Cairo and Tunis, such as, *The people want to topple the regime* and the simple but emphatic *Leave*. But there was also that special Syrian note for Assad: *Your turn is coming, Doctor.*

In a finishing touch of courageous naivety, the boys signed each slogan with their names.

For the regime, such a display of youthful insurrection confirmed their worst fears about the Arab Spring coming to Syria. It had to be quashed. And the manner with which they went about it provided a chilling precedent for future state response to the uprising.

The boys were taken and tortured in detention, their fingernails ripped out.

When their families went to plead for their release, they were brutally told by Atef Najib, the local head of political security and a cousin of Assad himself, 'Forget your children. Go sleep with your wives and make new ones or send your wives to me and I'll do it.'

The people of Deraa, mostly Sunni Muslims, had traditionally supported the ruling Ba'ath Party. But like so many ordinary Syrians, they had suffered as life became increasingly hard as a result of decades of neglect and lack of investment. This was compounded by an influx of climate-change refugees, a wave of people from rural areas hit by the widespread drought of the previous years. But the town's people would never have risen up if it hadn't been for the shocking abuse of the schoolboys, compounded by Najib's casual insult.

On the 18th of March, a crowd of several thousand gathered in front of Deraa's Omari Mosque, demanding the children's release and the resignation of Atef Najib, as well as the city's mayor. The police responded with water cannons and live ammunition. At least four people were killed, the first deaths of the uprising.

The next day, the funeral for the victims turned into a mass demonstration. More were killed. In a tactic that would later be used widely, security forces occupied the local hospital and anyone who arrived there was detained or shot.

Briefly, the regime adopted a conciliatory tone. On the 20th of March Assad sent a delegation to offer condolences to bereaved families. On the same day, however, thousands gathered again at the Omari Mosque and more people were killed.

Finally, Assad ordered the children's release and the removal of Faisal Kulthum, Deraa's governor, from his post. But it was too late to erase what had happened. More protestors continued to gather at the Omari Mosque, its walls now chequered with posters of photographs of the dead.

The regime's violent response outraged Syrians. As a result, the protests grew in number and spread geographically, rippling out to other Syrian cities. A chain of events had been set in motion.

Alongside my family, I watched these developments with a mixture of fear and fascination. It felt like we were having some kind of collective identity crisis. Since our early school days, we had been systematically indoctrinated by the state, taught to sing the national anthem, to chant political slogans, to never speak ill of the regime.

But, in a flash, it became clear just what the people ruling us really stood for. Those leaders that we had chanted for and been compelled to glorify, were prepared to turn their rifles against us in a heartbeat. The scales fell from my eyes as I realized that we had been lied to all along. The understanding only took a few minutes to register, but it changed everything for me. It was profoundly unsettling, to have all my previous convictions over-turned in an instant.

Those Deraan schoolboys could have been my own students. They were just as vulnerable, as idealistic. No child deserved that.

I could tell that my parents were having a similar kind of reckoning. But they had the memory of what happened in the early 1980s when the uprising of an Islamist political group called the Muslim Brotherhood had been forcefully extinguished in a brutal massacre. They knew just how harsh the regime could be. As the events around Deraa unfolded, my mum cried constantly as she watched the news. She was terrified for our future but hoped, as she always did, that Allah would look after us.

I found no succour in such thoughts. Instead, I made a decision. I would have to join the protests. I felt a deep conviction that I needed to take part. I'm an impulsive person, it's true, but to me there were two sides: right and wrong. I wanted to be on the side of right.

My teaching job had shown me that there was fulfilment to be found in advocating for others, in trying to be a good role model and in leading by example.

But it was difficult, because I knew already what protesting would mean. I knew how frightened my family would be if they found out. None of them was participating and at that point, many of my friends wouldn't countenance it either. From the beginning, some chose to believe the state line – that the people taking to the streets had been influenced by western powers and that they were terrorists and insurgents.

Many people started making fake accounts on Facebook to post their support for the revolution. I took down my profile picture and changed my profile name to HassanAk but stopped short of completely hiding my identity. I don't know why exactly, but perhaps because I'm stubborn. Despite the risk, I didn't want to entirely conceal myself. Quite the opposite – I wanted to use my voice to stand up for what I believed in.

It was maybe fitting that the first protest I had the courage to attend was at the Umayyad Mosque, right in the heart of my city's old town. It was a destination for all Damascenes, a very spiritual place but bursting with inter-generational life. Redwan and I used to go there all the time. You would hear kids running after each other, spot a tired salesman in the corner, sleeping in the shade. It was one of my favourite places to take photographs.

The mosque's compound was (and probably remains, since it wasn't destroyed in the conflict) glorious. A huge, rectangular court-yard laid with pale marble, surrounded by a colonnaded portico on three sides. Along the southern side runs a vast prayer hall. There are three minarets. It is a site of huge religious significance, once home to the Roman Temple of Jupiter, which had been converted into the Church of St John the Baptist in AD 379. After the Islamic conquest of Damascus in AD 634, the holy site was shared between the Christians and Muslims of the city before the church was later demolished and a vast mosque constructed instead.

It is a symbol of Syria's multiplicity, its unique history and central geographical position. The cradle of civilization. A fulcrum of spirituality but also – certainly back then – everyday life.

The morning of the protest, I got ready without telling anyone from my family where I was going. It was set for Friday Prayers, which take place at midday. I dressed carefully in an abaya, which is a traditional long tunic worn over trousers, rather than the western clothes that I so often favoured. That was important to me. I parked my car in a square outside the old city and walked towards the souk, at the end of which the Umayyad is situated.

I was so anxious. My heart was hammering in my chest and I could feel sweat prickling along my back. I didn't know what I was getting myself into. But I knew that I had to do it. Walking past the stallholders, I told myself that none of the vendors knew what I was doing, that there was no reason to suspect me. I knew that I was about to step from one stage of my life into another. Despite trying to reassure myself, I couldn't help but think that the men peering out from their stalls seemed more vigilant than usual. It was as if the city was holding her breath, waiting to see what came next.

Eventually I got to the Umayyad and walked into the prayer hall. It was packed. I had never seen it like that before. More than 1,000 men had turned up. Some had come from Deraa, the city where the uprising had first taken root. They were all young, between twenty and forty years old. These were people who had watched the brutality in Deraa and were determined that there should be another way. They hoped for a better future for Syrians within their lifetimes. We protestors had clear demands, including the repeal of emergency law, which gave the security apparatus sweeping powers, as well as the release of all political prisoners, proper elections and a constitution.

As I walked in, it was obvious that something was going to happen. The air was so tense, everyone was watchful.

I sat down and looked around. By that point my nerves had begun to be replaced by something else. Resolution. There were so many of us. It was really happening. The imam began his sermon. He was obviously in Assad's pocket. He started to talk about the situation in the country. He was saying that we should look after our country, unite with one another against our enemies. Phrases fed straight from the regime. But then he added something shocking.

'The people who died in Deraa don't deserve the term of martyr,' he said, his voice ringing out in the mosque. Those innocent protestors, who couldn't endure the torture of children, were in his eyes casually condemned to hell.

There was a shocked silence. And then a man at the back of the mosque stood up.

'Those people *are* martyrs!' he shouted, at the top of his voice, his words ripping through the sanctity of the huge space. Then he added, contemptuously, '*Kool khara!*' which means, 'Eat shit!', which was profoundly shocking. Syrian society is so hierarchical, such things never happened. The imam held a position of profound respect – challenging one to his face, and so rudely, was unprecedented.

It was like nothing I had ever seen before, but it felt great. The excitement was unbelievable. The rest of the assembled crowd started chanting, over the attempts of the imam to take back control. 'Allah akbar,' we said. This is a phrase which has become associated with suicide bombers in the minds of many of those in the West, but it simply means 'God is the greatest.' We reclaimed those words in our protest.

But in that moment, God was actually beside the point. In that moment, those words were just an exclamation of something extraordinary. The sense of having a voice after decades of silence. Of developing views that differed from the ones we had been spoonfed all our lives. Later on, Assad and his cronies deliberately cast the revolution as a religious movement. It was part of a plan to sow sectarianism, to stoke inter-racial hatred and deny the revolution its legitimacy. Sadly, it worked, as the extreme religious groups took over. But it didn't start like that. It began as a civil and grassroots movement, across people of all sects, as well as many atheists, who were tired of tyranny. It was so spontaneous, springing up in different parts of Syria simultaneously. It was beautiful.

The whole mosque rose, still chanting. A mixture of 'Freedom!', 'Deraa!' and End corruption!' I moved as part of the crowd, back out towards the mosque's courtyard. Some people were carrying the Syrian flag aloft.

It was easy to spot the secret police, the *mukhabarat*, with their stupid shiny leather jackets and mobile phones which they were desperately speaking into, summoning help. They were already a feature of our lives, with offices in every district, including a street near my family apartment. I should have been frightened at the sight of them, but I was swept along in the moment.

The crowd swelled outside and started moving back towards the souk. I was filming everything on my mobile phone. I wanted to record what I was seeing because I'd never witnessed something like that before: freedom was echoing through the heart of Assad's Syria. It's in my nature to document things and I knew how important mobile footage was to spreading news of the uprising.

Looking back, my strongest emotion at that point was joy. Obviously, I had no idea about what was to come. The adrenaline took over. It was the first time that I'd had a voice. After all the years of indoctrination, I felt like a snake shedding its skin, emerging anew. One man was holding up the Quran. I linked arms with another. There was a sense of solidarity and companionship.

As we approached the souk, the crowd was funnelled into the main street and it became clear that all the side streets had been closed by the *mukhabarat*. There was nowhere to slip away to. Nowhere to flee. I consciously kept myself at the fringes of the crowd. I'm like that – even in the heat of the moment, I'll look around, wondering what to do if things go wrong. It's my hustler's instinct and it has served me well in the years since. With the alleys all blocked, we had no choice but to keep on walking through the souk.

As we emerged on the other side, a man jumped on a car and shouted 'Deraa' and then 'Syria!' We walked away from the souk, towards the square where I'd parked my car.

Once there, I could see that the police had stopped passenger buses. The *mukhabarat* were urging the passengers off. Their plan was immediately obvious – they wanted to load protestors onto the vehicles, so they could be driven away. As soon as I saw that, I knew that I had to leave the crowd if I wanted to avoid trouble. So, I turned back towards the old city, despite the fact my car was parked in the square that we had reached.

I didn't run. I knew it was essential not to draw attention to myself. Instead, although it took every ounce of effort not to move more quickly, I sauntered. At one point I was overtaken by two men. They were running, panting and sweating heavily. It was obvious they had been in the protest. For a second, I was tempted to run along with them but I stopped myself. It was an act of self-preservation because moments later some members of the *mukhabarat* started chasing them and they were caught.

Back in the old city, the police were moving through the pedestrians, looking to see if they could recognize anyone from the protest. I took out my mobile phone and pretended to speak into it. Once again, this action probably saved me. Despite turning up to the protest and being swept up in the emotion of it, I was very keen not to get myself in trouble. I had heard so many rumours about what the regime was capable of and I didn't want to be subjected to that.

By playing it cool, I managed to avoid being spotted and eventually made it back to my car and drove home. I was still vibrating with excitement, but by then the fear had started to creep back in. It had been so close.

At home, my parents asked me where I had been. By way of answer, I took out my mobile phone and showed them the footage. My mum was terrified.

'Why did you do that, Hassan?' she said. She wasn't angry exactly, but she understood – probably better than I did back then – just how dangerous it had been.

That night I went to see my friends. I felt so empowered. I told them what I'd done, showing them the footage as well. They told me that I should delete it immediately because someone could stop me and check my phone. So back home I did that, but backed it up on a hard drive first. My instincts as a filmmaker took over. The same impulses that would later see me smuggle memory cards inside my body just to make sure I didn't lose what I'd recorded.

The next morning, my parents sat me down to talk about what had happened. With loving patience, they explained that my actions had been selfish. That I was risking their safety, and that of my siblings, as well as my own. But my convictions were unshakeable. Revolutions had been successful in other countries, why not ours? My initial uncertainty had been completely abandoned by this point. The dream was to occupy the large and central Umayyad square, much like Tahrir Square had been occupied in Cairo. It contains several important buildings, including the Ministry of Defence, Syria's National Opera House and the headquarters of the Syrian Armed Forces. It also has the Damascene Sword monument, widely considered the symbol of the city. Our belief was that if we could occupy such a symbolic place, for a period of time, the regime would certainly fall.

Afterwards, I heard that the people they had managed to get onto buses had been taken to detention centres. And yet I still sincerely believed that would never happen to me. Of course, I'd heard stories about people being killed, but I believed I'd be all right, that I could outsmart the *mukhabarat*. Run faster than them. Despite everything, I felt a young man's sense of implacable safety. Stupidity, you might call it. I miss feeling that way.

I had no idea of the horror that was coming. In those early idealistic days, none of us did. We didn't know that our way of life was going to end. We didn't anticipate the constant barrel bombs, which were to raze almost every town in Syria to rubble. Or the chemical weapons used against innocent children. The genocide.

We didn't know the lengths to which the Assad regime would go, the levels of depravity.

Later, objective proof emerged of just how bad it became in our country. A former Syrian Government forensic photographer – known only by the code name of Caesar – risked his life defecting from the regime, and smuggled out thousands of photographs of detainees who had been tortured to death in Bashar al-Assad's jails. Unequivocal evidence of crimes against humanity.

Before the war, it had been Caesar's job to photograph crime and accident scenes involving military personnel. He was in one division of an extensive military police divided into dozens of departments.

As the conflict started, the nature of the photographs Caesar and his colleagues were taking changed. They began documenting civilians' bodies, many of them tortured. At first, the corpses were all named, but as the number of atrocities grew, they were simply marked with two numbers, written on sticky tape, or in felt-tip directly on the forehead or the chest.

His photographs proved how disgusting things became – they showed people with their eyes gouged out, with burns made from candles, broken teeth, lashes from cables used to start cars. They chronicled a repulsive litany of abuse.

Before the war, there had been torture in Syrian prisons, designed to inculcate fear and extract information. But after the uprising began, it turned into institutionalized murder. Caesar's pictures proved definitively that torture and death were indexed and archived by a regime that obsessively recorded and filed every scrap of information. They were irrefutable evidence of brutality.

Exhilarated as I was after my first protest at the Umayyad Mosque, I had no idea how close I was going to get to becoming one of those numbered bodies.

OH SHAME

As the unrest in Syria grew, Assad remained silent. The population didn't know his intentions. Some speculated that he might be planning to make concessions to those calling for change. Looking back now, after the years of brutality and horror, it seems absurd that we even considered it. But at the time we had no idea of what lay in store.

After all, this seemingly placid man had been an eye doctor in London, tasked with caring for children no less. Surely the brutality enacted in his name in Deraa would have been intolerable to him? Perhaps he might go to the city and apologize, get rid of the administration that had perpetrated such atrocities. We dared to hope.

On 30 March 2011, President Bashar al-Assad made his very first speech on the crisis unfolding in his country. Everywhere, across the nation, we Syrians tuned in, leaning forwards on our sofas, desperate to drink in every word. So much depended on what he had to say. Everyone had been waiting to hear it.

As he started speaking, I felt sick. It was nonsense.

'I'm speaking to you from the heart,' he said, in formal Arabic. Before adding that he understood the practical concerns of the people but would allow for change only on his timetable. He did not call for an end to the state of emergency law that conferred extraordinary powers on the secret police, as many of us had hoped. Instead he described those protesting as 'insurgents', implying that they were influenced by outside forces. He also described the growing trouble as a 'virtual war' waged through the media and the internet. It was bullshit.

And then, worst of all, he giggled. A soft, high-pitched laugh that revealed his contempt for those who had died, the children who had been tortured, the ordinary people who had risked their lives in the hope of justice. With that, we knew that things couldn't return to how they had been. There was no way.

Assad's MPs gave the speech a standing ovation, clapping like seals.

My dad pointed at the television. 'What is this? What is this?' he repeated, his disappointment etched across his face.

After that, the protests flourished. There was so much momentum. They would crop up in Damascus, mostly in the suburbs, lasting for perhaps only as long as ten minutes – like flash mobs. People moving together, to show their desire for something different, something new.

In the cities of Hama and Homs, tens of thousands walked the streets. Floods of people. It was so beautiful to witness on the news. There was this sense that things could change and get better. That they had to.

Then a larger protest happened in central Damascus, in an area called Al-Midan, one full of restaurants where we used to go to have *shawarma*. The demonstration was shown on the television, but the presenter said it wasn't a protest, rather that the crowd of thousands was thanking Allah for rain.

'They don't know our rituals,' she said, not mentioning that the crowd was chanting 'Freedom. Freedom. Freedom.' It was a blatant lie, propaganda from the regime.

At that point, the regime was putting out so much disinformation about the uprising. Insane conspiracy theories designed to obscure the fact that ordinary people were sick of living under its control. One was that Al Jazeera was handing out pills with Al Jazeera stamps on them, to get protestors high so they would protest. Another that men were being passed kebab sandwiches rolled in money, given to them so they would go and protest. The government narrative was clear – if you were going out on a protest, someone was pushing you to do it. Our reality was being denied, that we had come to these conclusions without outside intervention. That we weren't traitors at all, but ordinary Syrians who wanted something better for ourselves and our families.

Despite the groundswell of public support, I was the only one of my close friends who joined the protests. And within my family, while some were very much in favour of the uprising, many on my dad's side remained staunchly pro-Assad. As I've said, Sammy was not supportive and nor was Redwan at that point (it was only later, when he witnessed what they were truly capable of, that he changed his mind). They both thought I was insane. It was so painful. You are used to these people, they are your people. At the same time, it had become clear to me that the cause, the liberation of Syria from tyranny, mattered more to me than not offending them.

Not long previously, I hadn't felt much responsibility towards others. But now I had woken up. And so many others felt the same. You could walk around Damascus and see graffiti against Assad on the walls. The slogans of the Arab Spring. Deraa. Freedom. People want the end of martial law. The end of corruption. The *mukhabarat* would quickly paint over any graffiti with the disturbingly prescient, 'Assad or we burn the country'. But it would crop up again.

Around the same time, a song by the singer Samih Choukeir called 'Shame' was adopted by the revolution. Choukeir lives in exile in France. That song became my Holy Book. I listened to it on repeat through my earphones.

Oh Shame
The youth heard freedom knocking on their doors,
  so they rose up chanting for it.
They saw rifles and said, 'Oh Mother, those are our brothers,
  they won't shoot us.
Oh Mother, they shot us with live ammunition.
We were killed by our brothers.'

The song unified us. It became the anthem of our revolution.

I began attending protests around once a week. I found out where to go from Facebook. Social media played a key role in the uprising. Organizers would tell people where to go. Once there I'd film the protest and then share the footage with them. Citizen journalism was profoundly important for the Syrian uprising, in terms of disseminating information about demonstrations – and later, revealing to the outside world the atrocities Assad perpetrated against his own people.

Many of the protests were held outside mosques, after prayers. It made me love mosques even more than I had before. As already mentioned, I'd always had a complicated relationship with religion, not being able to find the comfort in it that my parents did, but I adored those buildings when they became a focal point for the uprising. They represented so much that was beautiful about Syrian culture and identity.

At every demonstration I attended, I seemed to have a lucky escape. By keeping my wits about me it seemed that I could participate without being caught.

That was, until the 5th of August in 2011, when my luck ran out.

I had seen on Facebook that a protest was planned outside Al-Shafi'i mosque in Al-Mazzeh, which is a smart area of Damascus, with wide leafy boulevards. It's where most of the foreign embassies are situated and isn't far from the presidential palace. The protestors wanted to move nearer the seat of power.

That day, I asked my friend Ghaith to drive me there. He was on his way to another protest, and didn't want to attend the one I was heading to since he considered it too risky. I dressed casually, in a black T-shirt, khaki trousers and running shoes. I intentionally left everything at home, including my phone, so all I had on me were my keys and a few coins. By then I knew the drill and I entered the mosque and started praying. From the start, that protest was different. Some women had attended, which was the first time I'd witnessed any at a demonstration.

It was Ramadan and so the imam led us in a series of what was supposed to be twenty consecutive prayers. But after the eighth prayer, we left the mosque and the protest started outside. We stood outside the mosque for around five minutes.

Someone shouted clearly, 'We want the execution of the president.' It was the first time I had heard anyone say that. It was shocking to hear it spoken aloud. We all knew that if the *mukhabarat* caught you saying something like that, it would be a death sentence.

We started moving away from the mosque and encountered some *shabiha* (thugs loyal to the regime). They tried to hit us with leather sticks, deliberately driving the demonstrators into a small alley. People started running and panicking. Then guards from one of the nearby embassies, who had come to investigate the disturbance, loaded their AK47s and shouted 'Stop!' at us.

That moment was when it dawned on me that perhaps it could happen to me, after all. Perhaps I wasn't wearing a cloak of invincibility. I could indeed be beaten, detained, or even killed. It was the first time that I'd truly countenanced that reality. Perhaps that sounds naive, but I'd grown up with state repression, whispers about what happened to those who dared to defy our ruler. And yet, we lived lives full of ordinary things, we became accustomed to pushing the whispers to the back of our minds, so even when I started protesting, it took a while for me to fully comprehend the danger.

People turned around and ran back in the opposite direction. In my terror, I made a mistake that I'll always regret. Some of the protestors had chosen to scramble over the wall running alongside the alleyway, beyond which lay a school. I decided to follow them and climbed up onto the roof of a car, dropping down into the yard of the Omar Bin Abd Aziz School. But the wall was much higher on that side, essentially making escape impossible.

I followed the other men who had chosen the same route. We looked around for a way to exit and realized with growing horror that there wasn't one. Our only option was to hide, so we huddled together in a corner of the playground like school children playing a game. Only it wasn't a game – we were trapped.

One of the guards from the embassies had spotted us jumping over the wall into the schoolyard. He called the secret police, the notorious 215 branch, also known as the 'raid squad' and feared for their extreme brutality.

We were still thinking about how we could possibly escape, looking around us, but it was becoming obvious that we weren't going to be able to. We heard the secret police getting closer and closer. They found another man in a different part of the playground who was hiding behind a water container and started beating him savagely. His cries rang out across the yard.

It was so frightening to be trapped, knowing that they were coming for us next.

I asked a man if I could borrow his phone and I rang a friend of mine called Bilal.

'Listen, I'm about to get arrested,' I said. The words had a sense of unreality. 'Will you tell my parents?' I knew how worried my parents would be when I didn't go home that day. All Syrian parents knew that if their sons disappeared they might never see them again. Bilal agreed to tell them and I handed the mobile phone back.

Shortly afterwards, the secret police approached us with their weapons. They were fully armed, strapped with both AK47s and pistols, as well as holding iron bars in their hands. Unlike the initial embassy guards who had called for their assistance, these were men who were trained to kill, you could tell it by their every movement. They were surefooted and lethal, stepping towards us with satisfaction.

They started beating us, going for our faces and chests. I held my arms up to protect myself as the blows rained down. I immediately felt I was being hurt, but then there was a more intense sharp, shooting pain. A crack within. It was the sensation of the bones in my forearms breaking. My left arm broke in two places and my right in one.

After that, I could no longer protect my face.

'You want freedom,' they shouted. 'Here's your freedom.'

By then I was on my back on the ground. One of the secret policemen focused on hitting me and every time he made contact the pain was excruciating. But it was worse than that. I felt violated on a level that was far deeper than just flesh and bone. Each blow that came destroyed a little more of what I had previously believed about my country and the police force. Our own intelligence forces. The people that the regime had always led us to believe protected us from our enemies. Those self-styled guardians of our homeland.

That night changed my life. The irony that such an atrocity happened in a school playground isn't lost on me. Emblems of civilization – such as schools and hospitals – became perverted during the conflict. Nowhere was safe.

The attack lasted for around twenty minutes. I became determined to stand up. It felt very important to me that I did. I used every bit of strength and determination to get off the floor. They ordered me to go back down but I refused. By this point, I felt sure I was going to die. And if I was going to die, I was going to do it standing. It was the testosterone pumping through my blood, combined with the terror.

A policeman went for my leg with the iron bar and started kicking it too, trying to make me lose my balance. Still I stood. So, he put me in a headlock and threw me on the floor before beginning to kick me again.

Eventually, after the frenzied beating, the military police led us out of the schoolyard. The shabiha were waiting. While the secret police wanted to detain us, to pump us for information about the protest, the shabiha wanted nothing less than to murder us. They would have done so, with only their leather sticks and their bare hands, if the secret policemen – who had been attacking us themselves just minutes earlier – hadn't shielded our heads as they took us to the military land cruiser that was waiting.

There wasn't room for us all to sit, so we were stacked up on top of each other, like sardines in a tin. My arms were excruciatingly painful as I was jostled by the other men. It was also hard to breathe and I started to have a panic attack. I couldn't catch my breath. The sense of unreality and terror rose up and engulfed me. I thought of my parents and how much they were going to worry. In theory, I had known that this was a risk since I had started protesting, but I'd never really believed that it could happen to me. The brutality of the detention centres was notorious, intentionally so. I knew where I was going. The horror that would await me.

We arrived at Carlton Street, in the Kafr Sousa area of Damascus, named after the Carlton Hotel found on it along with different branches for the security services. A forbidding street of tall, Soviet-style buildings. You were never permitted to drive up it but I'd walked along it many times in the past. Even then, I kept my eyes trained straight ahead, not daring to glance at the bleak buildings. Everyone in Damascus knew that you never wanted to end up inside.

Branch 215, known by many as the 'Branch of Death', was one of the main Assad-regime prisons where torture and mass executions were carried out on a daily basis after the revolution began. Detainees who had been released had spoken about the horrors carried out at 215. I was dragged out of the vehicle, panicking so much that I'd lost the use of my legs and couldn't walk. The other detainees were led upstairs, but I crumpled in a heap in the hall, unable to stand. Eventually, I was dragged into the lift by two of the secret policemen.

'Oh look, he is in trouble. He needs CPR!' shouted one of them, laughing. And then, where I was splayed on the floor of the lift, he jumped on my chest, over and over again with his thick-soled military shoes. The full force of his body smashing into my torso cracked several of my ribs, and the intensity of his movement shook the lift. I felt a searing pain, like nothing I had felt before.

I was the last man to arrive upstairs. Despite my injuries, my freshly broken arms, I was lined up with the others by the wall and handcuffed. All of us continued to be repeatedly slapped and punched. It was a free-for-all of abuse. One man came out of his office and slapped me so hard that I overbalanced and landed on the ground. Then he casually went back to his desk. It was sadistic but was also obviously habitual. All in a day's work.

As well as beating us, they cursed us. 'Fuck your mums and your sisters.' In our culture, your mother and sisters are your honour. It's the most brutal insult for someone to say these things. They also called us traitors and that hurt too.

'You traitors. You sons of bitches.' More punches. More slaps.

They began taking people into a side office to take down the details from their ID cards. I was the last one to be ushered in. The man inside shouted at me aggressively. I gave my name.

At the end of the corridor was a cage door that led to the detention area. Prior to being put inside the cell, they strip searched us. They made me remove my clothes and then squat. I felt close to sobbing, it was so degrading. Then one of the policemen asked me to put my underwear on my head. I hesitated and he shouted at me. I couldn't bear to be beaten again, so I did as I was told. I stood there totally exposed, my legs, arms and ribs throbbing in pain. Completely humiliated. The men started laughing and jeering. They were enjoying themselves.

I was then taken to the cell. They had ranged the newcomers in a circle. Someone was beating up the new people, while the previous inmates sat on the ground, trying not to watch. There must have been around thirty men in that room.

Many of the newcomers began vomiting from intense pain. I keeled forwards, about to fall, when another inmate stepped towards me, using his body as a shield so I wouldn't hit the ground. This man, Anas, would later become a friend. He now lives in Sweden, having also escaped from Syria. Back then, I was just grateful to this stranger who saved me from further pain, and moments later I blacked out. Later, I was told that one of the guards came and gave me an injection. I don't know what they gave me but I didn't come round for about six hours. I woke, groggily, to find myself on the cell floor, my body in a kind of agony I had never experienced before. I still live with the legacy of the physical injuries – but my mind was also never the same. The young man I had been was gone forever.

ABU YASEEN

The cell was wretched, thick with the smell of unwashed, terrified, angry men. It was lit by one single dangling bulb, and a glimpse of natural light from two tiny barred 'windows', in reality they were chinks in the wall formed by knocking out a couple of bricks well above head height. The paint on the walls was yellowing and flecked with dirt and blood.

It was high summer and unbearably hot in the confined space. There was no breeze at all and the floor was sticky with the inmates' sweat. The men themselves were friendly enough. They made room for us newcomers and introduced themselves.

In the cell next door to ours was a terrifying cautionary tale: two Lebanese men who had been there for at least twenty-three years. One had the nickname Za'atar, after the spice. They had a microwave and a fridge and beds – the cell had become their only home. The sight of them terrified me. I was so scared of the same fate. Once you are detained in Syria, anything is possible. Torture, death or never seeing daylight again. There is no access to a court or lawyers. For us, detention is different. There are no safeguards. There is no justice.

It was quickly obvious to everyone in that cell that I was the inmate with the worst injuries. I couldn't use my arms at all and was in so much pain that it was difficult for me to stand.

From the start, a man called Abu Yaseen looked after me. He helped me to drink and eat because I couldn't use my arms. The jailers brought in bowls of boiled vegetables and crusts of bread flecked with mould to be shared among everyone. Abu Yaseen always made sure something was saved for me, crushing the barely cooked potatoes so that I could manage them.

Abu Yaseen was a hustler from the streets of Damascus. He was a big, tough streetwise man, but he had an incredible spirit. He saw the state I was in, that it wasn't only my body that had been broken but also my spirit, and he tried to cheer me up. He was very chatty and – despite the desperate situation we found ourselves in – he refused to be crushed. He showed the very best of human nature, in the darkest of situations.

The jailers were brutal. They beat us constantly. Every time one of us wanted to use the toilet, which was adjacent to the cell, we would be attacked. Most of us submitted to it without retaliating, terrified of even worse treatment. But Abu Yaseen would curse them as they left. He waited until they were just out of earshot, and he did it consistently. His defiance was inspiring. I was still so frightened that I couldn't say a word. He shone so much light in that filthy, dank cell. He was an amazing human being. He kept talking, repeating that the day that they released him, he would go straight back to the protests. That wasn't something I could bring myself to even consider.

Abu Yaseen kept telling the jailers how bad my condition was. I couldn't use my arms at all, and my leg was purple. The wound on my calf was festering and it throbbed. I couldn't bear to look at it. I knew that, left untreated, it would cause me serious problems. Every inhale hurt because of my broken ribs. The temperature in the cell didn't help. I felt like I could never catch my breath.

After a few days, I saw one of the Lebanese men next door talking to the jailers. I could tell they were talking about me. It was obvious that my injuries were pretty bad.

A bit later one of the guards told me to come out. They put a bin bag over my head, then taped it around my neck, then punctured it at the nose so I could breathe, just about. They handcuffed me and took me out and down in the lift. Everything was bin-bag-black but I still knew my location. From the glimpse of the streetlights I'd got in the prison toilet, that glimpse of the outside world, I'd been able to locate my position on Carlton Street.

They led me to a car. Inside the vehicle, unable to see anything, I tried to picture the streets of Damascus in my mind. The city I was so familiar with, my home. I was trying to work out where they were taking me, but also to regain a sense of control, of agency. As if knowing my precise location would protect me.

I worked out that I was being taken to 601. A military hospital.

At that point, it didn't hold much more significance for me than that. I wasn't to know that 601 was the throbbing heart of a nationwide system of brutality, one which was only to worsen as the conflict went on. The facility, about half a mile from President Bashar al-Assad's palace, was not somewhere where people were looked after properly. On the contrary, it became a site for torture itself, offering a sick parody of care.

From the earliest days of the uprising, the regime used medicine and hospitals as weapons. Stories have emerged about pro-government doctors performing amputations on protestors for minor injuries, of wards packed with men left chained and starving, and of piles of bodies in bathrooms. These were not places where people went to be healed. Many were never to emerge again.

The testimony of one man in particular has been useful in revealing this systemic abuse of hospitals. Mohsen al-Masri was detained after taking part in a peaceful protest where he released thousands of colourful ping-pong balls, each one marked with the single word 'Freedom', into the street in Damascus. He was tortured and interrogated over a two-year period in four detention centres, but it's his subsequent account about his experience of hospital that was perhaps most shocking.

After fleeing Syria, he talked about the 'welcome party' of being beaten by guards and medical staffers on arrival at hospital. Detainees were blindfolded and shackled to their beds and not given bathroom breaks, left to defecate where they sat. He recalled one guard known as Azrael, or the Angel of Death, taking a lighter to a plastic bag and melting it drop by drop onto a prisoner's face until he died, apparently of a heart attack.

Such revolting acts, I can hardly bear to think about them. In a report published in February 2017, Amnesty International said that torture and forced starvation were standard procedure at 601. According to the UN Commission of Inquiry, a body set up to monitor the Syrian conflict, at least five branches of the Syrian security forces operated wards inside 601 since 2011.

But I didn't know that when I arrived there. I didn't know that entering 601 was one of the most dangerous things I have ever done in my life. I imagined only that I was finally going to get some treatment for my agonizing injuries. As I was led out of the car, I was subject to my own 'welcome party', with guards and men in white coats kicking and slapping me. Somebody spat in my face. I couldn't see it happen, but I heard the hawking sound, the faint splat as it made contact with the plastic sheathing my head. The malice and contempt could not have been clearer.

They took me to a waiting room, where they lifted off the bin bag that was over my face. Then they took me to be X-rayed. By this point, I was struggling to carry out their instructions. I'd been slapped repeatedly, my arms were broken, I'd been muffled up in a bin bag and I hadn't eaten anything aside from slops in days. I was in a state of shock and despair.

A white-coated man in his thirties wearing glasses – to this day I don't know if he was a doctor or a radiologist – asked me to put my arm up to be X-rayed but I moved hesitantly. Too slowly for him. He cursed in irritation and then, as I put my left arm on the scanner on the table, he slammed the panel on top of my broken arm. The pain was excruciating. White-hot agony fissuring my arm again. Later, I found out that he compounded the damage. If he hadn't have done that, it might have healed properly but he ensured that I was left with a permanent injury: the sub-standard treatment ended up costing me the full range of motion in my left wrist. The whole episode took little more than three seconds.

He X-rayed the right forearm as well and I was then taken to another room where another man was told to put a cast on my left arm but to wrap my right one up. Later, I was told that both arms should have been put in casts.

The man who treated me in that room was not as aggressive. He was the first official to show me a scrap of kindness since I had been caught. He advised me to calm down. I was already crying, but his humanity made me sob harder.

'You're going to be okay,' he said.

'Can I call my parents?' I asked him, imagining he had a phone. It was the first thing that came into my head. I knew they would be terrified for me. I'd managed to alert them that I'd been arrested, but they would have been imagining all sorts of things. Wondering if I was dead already.

'I'm really sorry I can't,' he said, looking at me kindly. 'I'm so sorry.' I understood. If they found out that he had let me, he could end up in exactly the same position that I was in.

After he had treated me, I was taken out to where the jailers were. They said we were about to leave to go back to the prison. I asked them about my leg. If anything, that was the injury that worried me the most. It was still bleeding and pus was seeping out of it. It was a suppurating mess and I knew that I risked sepsis if it went untreated.

The jailers called another doctor and he asked me to roll my trousers up. The look on his face was very serious. He tutted.

'This leg needs to go,' he said, gravely. 'It's the only option.' He called for someone. 'Get the amputation tools.' I think he winked at them because one of the other men restrained me as I lost control in panic. I began thrashing around, trying to hit the doctor. Lashing out in utter terror.

'Let's talk about this,' I pleaded. There was no way I was going to lose my leg.

'No, no. There is nothing to discuss. It has to go,' he said. I felt absolute despair. I'd attended the protest a few days earlier as a young man with his future in front of him. A runner, who always believed he could outrun the *mukhabarat*. And here I was, facing a different future. Tears coursed down my face; my shoulders shook. I had thought I was invincible, how wrong I'd been.

'Please. Can't we try operating? It needs an operation and some antibiotics, but please can't we try that first?'

'No, I don't think so,' said the doctor, shaking his head. 'It's going to have to be cut off. The only option.' I wailed in misery. It was my worst nightmare.

But then I noticed the doctor smiling, fractionally. The other men snickered. The whole thing was a joke. He didn't plan to amputate my leg. Or perhaps I just got lucky that day, since it later emerged that unnecessary amputation was a tactic used on those rebelling against the regime, who were literally hobbled for life.

'Stop complaining,' he said. 'Your leg is fine. Stop whinging.' His mood instantly changed from mockery to aggression. I knew my leg wasn't fine, but that was the end of that. He made it clear it wasn't going to be treated despite the obvious infection. I was put back in the car and taken to the cell.

Time went by incredibly slowly. The heat was unrelenting. One of the inmates came up with a trick where he would take off his T-shirt and saturate it with water from the dirty plastic bottles we were given to drink from. Then he would spin his T-shirt around above his head, moving the air around, spraying us with fetid water. A human fan.

At night, we would take it in turns to lie down by the crack under the cell door, gasping for a waft of air, trying not to listen to the cries and screams of people being brought in. I was always out of breath, especially during the nights. I don't have the vocabulary to describe how awful that place smelled. The spaces high up where the bricks had been hammered out were a tiny portal to the outside world and were so important to us. We used to lift each other up, to try and glimpse the streetlight outside. Seeing the amber glow of that sodium light was the highlight of my day, it classified as our entertainment. Outside that awful place, the world was still going on.

Sometimes they gave jobs to longer-serving inmates and there was a young man with long hair who swept our cell. He had apparently made a joke about the president's wife in Dubai and had been arrested at the airport on his return to Syria. Someone had informed on him and he had been locked up. For a joke. Occasionally the jailers gave him a cigarette to smoke. One time he shared one with me. I didn't even smoke in those days. I'd always been really anti-smoking. It was only later that I picked up the habit, after I had fled Damascus, when I was in a holding pattern, constantly waiting. Smoking became something to do with my hands. But even so I said yes and had a couple of drags. It was something from outside. A taste of freedom.

I thought about my parents, my friends, my brother and sisters. I also thought a lot about my exams, which I knew I was going to miss. It was my final year at university, and I knew it meant I would fail the year, which really hurt. I thought about all the mundane things. I even thought about KitKats. Somehow, I started remembering when my dad brought boxes of KitKats home for a treat. I would imagine them in detail. I distracted myself by dreaming of sliding my fingernail along the foil wrapper, of the delicious chocolate wafer within. Later, during the pandemic when I worked in the hospital, I cleaned the bay of an old lady who was longing for a Diet Coke. She would rhapsodize about raising the can to her lips, the fizz of bubbles as she took a sip. I wanted to get her one, but I couldn't. She was gravely ill, stuck in a coronavirus ward, but she fixated on that little pleasure. I knew exactly why. It had been the same with me and KitKats when I was in detention. When you are in such an awful situation, you fixate on the recollection of ordinary joys.

My dreams of this remembered pleasure, though, were pushed away by thoughts of my mother. She had always been so protective because she knew the history of our country. She had never allowed me to go on school trips outside of Damascus. I knew that she would be frantic with worry. Prior to my detention, we had heard terrifying stories about what they were doing with detainees. She was constantly on my mind. I knew I was still breathing, but she didn't.

Later, I found out that she was so distraught that she had to be heavily sedated, just to get through the days. She would wake up and sit, just crying and crying and crying all day. My dad was also incredibly distressed. He doesn't show his emotions as much but one of my sisters said that he would cry during prayer time, when he would really let go, shaking from his sobs. He was also taking action, trying to see what he could do to track me down. As I've explained, my father's side of the family were pro-Assad. His niece, my cousin Majd, was particularly well connected with the regime. She was the 'go-to' person for our family, whenever we needed something that only *wasta* (influence) could provide.

She was very different from my parents – an urbane, bleach-blonde woman who didn't wear the veil and actually had a drinks trolley in her apartment. I'd always thought she was great fun and although she was so unlike them, my parents liked and respected her too.

Majd was the only person that could help me. I later found out that on the outside, she was desperately getting in touch with all of her contacts to see what she could do.

In the cell, the talk was constantly about who might be released and when. We spoke of our families and how good it would be to see them. One of the men I was captured with in the schoolyard was the first to be freed from the cell. A jailer came and called out his name one morning. We were all so happy on his behalf. Everyone got up and we congratulated him. But inside, I felt so envious. I wished, more than anything, that it was me. My pain, it seemed to me, was growing worse. My cracked ribs meant I couldn't lie on my side, and because I had large haemorrhoids from the terrible, inadequate diet, it was impossible to sit down normally either. I spent interminable hours crouching on my knees, supported by my elbows so that I could hold my broken wrists up. To say that it wasn't a comfortable position is a vast understatement, but it was the only one that wasn't unbearably painful. For my last two nights in detention, I didn't get any sleep at all.

After eleven days, a jailer came to the door of the cell. He called me and told me to get my stuff. I couldn't believe it. Everyone congratulated me but I could hardly walk out of the cell.

They led me down in the lift and out towards a car. They put a black bin bag over my head again and that's when my heart sank. They didn't do this if you were going to be released. They drove me away in the dark and I became deeply disorientated. The car windows were rolled down and I was able to breathe normally for the first time in days, to savour the sweet night air of my city rolling in, that unique Damascene perfume making such a contrast to the stagnant air of the cell. This time, I wasn't able to map out where I was going. After the days in prison, which had been so static and shut away, it was as if my senses had stopped working properly. It was horrible, the worst feeling ever. At just twenty-three years old, my body felt like it was collapsing.

When we stopped, the guards led me into a compound and my sense of dread grew. I was escorted into a basement office and asked for my belongings, such as they were. It was in that awful moment that it dawned on me that I was being transferred. Until then, despite evidence to the contrary, I had nurtured some small hope that I was going home that day. The men in the cell had congratulated me, but within an hour all my hopes were dashed. I wasn't to be released after all.

I was taken to another cell. And rather than any kind of improvement, this was ten times worse than the first one. It was underground with no natural light and had 105 men packed into it. There wasn't even room for everyone to sit down so inmates would rest in shifts, something that was commonplace in many Syrian prisons. Honestly, the previous cell was like heaven in comparison, because at least you could occupy your own floor space. In the new cell, space was in such short supply that at night, the men would lie down next to each other, lined up on their sides, and then one of the big inmates, known as the 'crammer', would lean against the wall and push them all together with the soles of his feet, so that more could squeeze into the line. It was a common practice throughout Syrian prisons. To this day, confined spaces bring back the memory of that place and I struggle with claustrophobia.

When I arrived, the others could immediately see that I was in a very poor physical state. They helped me to find a tiny space, handling me like a suitcase marked 'Fragile'. My leg was hugely swollen, and I was holding my wrists out in front of me. I couldn't sit down properly.

The first question was, 'What have you done?' Class bias is rife in Syria. Your surname plays a massive role in determining your fate and life chances. I come from the kind of family that you wouldn't expect to see in prison. If I say the name 'Akkad' it affords me immediate respect. It's far more common to see people from the countryside and suburbs in jail. And there was also the way I looked then. I wasn't the type of young man who was normally detained.

The men in the cell were grouped by their regions. There was a cluster from every town and city in Syria. One from Zabadani, Homs. Aleppo, Deraa. It was a map of Syria, a map of resistance, their faces all exhausted but defiant.

'We are sorry for what has happened to you,' said a man, also from Damascus. A *Shami*. This is our word for a native from the city. I can't remember his name but he was kind to me that first night. I asked him where I was, and he told me that I had been transferred to the headquarters for the *mukhabarat*, the General Intelligence Directorate, branch 285, which is President Assad's chief instrument of repression and social control in Syria. I asked him what the other men had done and his response was deeply concerning. Some had been accused of carrying weapons. If I had been transferred to a cell with cases like that, it meant I was in deep trouble.

WASTA

On my first night in the basement jail at headquarters, another man was brought in. While my injuries were terrible, they were nothing compared to his. He had been beaten so badly that he was literally blue-black with bruises, from head to toe. Even looking at him was painful. It was obvious this was a man close to death. I knew then without doubt that the place I'd found myself was a slaughterhouse.

There was no room for me to lie down to sleep. The other inmates apologized but told me that I'd have to spend the night in the toilet, which was in a corner of the main cell. It was about a metre square and spattered with shit. They placed me there, gently enough, among the human waste. I couldn't sleep. All night long, I was splashed by men using the toilet.

The cell was also full of tiny white cockroaches, which started scuttling down my cast between my skin and the plaster, where I could feel the movement but couldn't itch them. I've always hated roaches and feeling them was terrible. I lay there, flecked in sewage, with insects beetling against my flesh, my leg still oozing pus, every breath painful because of my broken ribs.

Until that night, I had been praying constantly. Despite my ambivalence towards religion, I'd automatically turned to God. You know the saying? *You're only an atheist until the plane starts going down.* But that night, I became very angry. I kept asking why this was happening to me. I was trying to see the reason or rationale. And I stopped praying for release, instead I began to hope they would transfer me to prison. At least in prison there would be a bed and proper meals. This detention centre didn't even have those basics. Everyone in that second cell hoped for the same. Instead of talking about release, they talked about when they might be transferred to prison.

With no window in that basement cell, we couldn't even get the glimpse of the outside world that had cheered us so much in the other place. The jailers would come in intermittently and beat people up. I didn't sleep at all that first night. And at some point, it became clear that the man with the terrible injuries had died. It had been obvious that he would. The jailers came and took him away.

On the second night, a group of jailers came in with tasers and started walking around giving electric shocks to the men in the cell. It was hard to make out what was happening, until I was tasered myself, in my right leg. I groaned in agony at an intense shooting pain like being stung by a huge bee. After a while, one of the jailers left and returned with a colleague who asked one of the inmates, a barber in his former life, to start shaving the men's heads. I was already bald, but many others had full heads of hair and beards, which culturally and religiously mean a lot in our society. It was a way of dehumanizing us.

At some point on that night, I began to feel like I wasn't going to survive. My body started to shut down. There wasn't any food: they brought two boiled eggs and some raw vegetables to share among twenty men. Every part of me throbbed with pain. My infected leg. My arms. My bottom. In the morning, I started to struggle to breathe. I was gasping for air, my chest heaving, so the other inmates carried me nearer to the cell door. The waft of air coming from underneath was my lifeline. I lay on my side, wondering how long it would before I died in that place, like the other man had.

A couple of hours later, a jailer arrived. He was one of the more approachable ones. Most would punch you if you so much as said a word to them, but this man was a little more moderate.

'This person needs a hospital,' said one of the men, gesturing to where I lay.

'Don't worry. He's being released today,' said the jailer, casually, looking in my direction.

'What did you say?' I croaked out the words, my voice hoarse from lack of use.

'You're being released today,' he said looking at me. I remember it very clearly. I realized in that moment that I had to try and stay alive. It was a conscious effort. I felt so near to giving up, to drifting away towards death, but I persevered. Every minute dragged on forever, but I had a reason to keep going.

After a couple of hours, the jailers came back. I couldn't walk but two of them put my arms over their shoulders and helped me get up. They took me upstairs, away from the stinking hellhole where I'd been locked up.

There was a door and behind it an office. It had all the hallmarks of officialdom: a poster of Assad on the wall, tacky fake-gilt furniture, the sour reek of a thousand cigarettes. Behind the vast desk sat a man with white hair dressed in the regulation suit, huge belly straining against his shirt. A government man, accustomed to overseeing brutality. General Khedr. And sitting opposite him, looking at me with eyes full of love and concern, were my well-connected cousin Majd and her husband.

I was in complete shock. Civilians are never allowed in these spaces. That she had managed to get into the secret police HQ was truly remarkable. But I also felt overwhelming relief. Someone from my family. At last.

'Majd?' I said, starting to sob.

'Hassan.' She stood and crossed the room to hug me. She must have been alarmed by my appearance, but she didn't say so. Majd knew how important it was to be careful. There was a reason she had *wasta*. Instead she drew back and locked eyes with me. A look that spoke a thousand words. *I'm sorry. What have they done?* But also. *Don't tell me now. Behave. Be good. Don't complain.*

'What happened to you?' said General Khedr, looking me up and down. My left trouser leg was rolled up, to avoid the festering wound sticking onto the fabric. My arm was in a cast. I could hardly walk.

'Oh,' I said, Majd's silent injunction in mind. 'I fell over.'

'Oh, you fell,' he said, smiling at my clumsiness and then glancing again at my leg. 'Roll your trousers down.' He didn't want to see my leg. My rotting calf annoyed him. He didn't want evidence of the brutality happening a couple of floors down from his office. I did as he asked.

'You made a big mistake,' said General Khedr.

'Yes,' I agreed. 'An awful mistake.'

'They are manipulating you from the outside,' he said. 'Why would you listen to them?' At this, I was silent. I hadn't been manipulated by anyone. My desire to protest had sprung up inside myself.

'Listen, you're an educated man from a good family,' said General Khedr. 'A teacher, no less. You don't belong here. We're going to release you. I don't want to see you again.'

The relief rushed through my bloodstream like a drug. But, over time, these phrases have destroyed me. I've replayed what General Khedr said a thousand times. I was a teacher, from a good family. But what about those other men in those cells? Those who didn't have cousins with good connections? They might still be there now. Later on, in 2013, I found out that Abu Yaseen, who had shown me such kindness in that first cell, had been killed. After leaving prison, he had joined the armed rebels, known back then as the Free Syrian Army. He led a unit of rebels in Jobar, a rebel-held suburb in Damascus. In June 2013, Assad forces came up with a dirty, evil plan to get to the rebels. They released a woman from detention, shot her in the legs and left her as bait, half-naked, on a major road in Jobar. Four of the rebels tried to save her. The first three were shot dead by snipers but that didn't stop Abu Yaseen from attempting to rescue her. He was shot dead too and she bled to death. The guilt of having survived when so many died never leaves me.

I was taken to another office, away from Majd and her husband. There was another man in civilian clothes. A huge officer with a gun. He started talking.

'From now on, you're going to work with us,' he said. 'If you see anything you have to report it.' You can't say no in a situation like that, so I didn't. The man took out a document that said I would be working with the government and asked me to sign it. I didn't hesitate. I had no choice.

After this, I was taken back to Majd and we were escorted to the car park inside the compound. I was amazed that her car was parked inside. These are places that you don't enter as a civilian. The fact she had managed to get inside – that she had got to me – was testament to her remarkable charm and influence. It turned out that she had once had dinner with General Khedr. That had been enough to mean that he considered her plea when she was trying to find out where I was.

They laid me across the back seat. I still couldn't sit on my haemorrhoids. Once inside the car, with the doors shut, they started to show the emotion they had had to repress inside the office.

'What is this? What have they done to you?' said Majd. They debated whether or not to take me straight to the hospital. Majd's husband wanted to, but Majd knew how frantic with worry my parents were. They both knew that hospitals weren't necessarily safe places. Eventually they decided to take me straight home.

My father and brother were waiting downstairs outside our apartment as Majd's car pulled up. My mother and one of my sisters were sitting on the balcony upstairs. As I got out of the car, I heard my mother's scream of agony echoing down from the eighth floor.

'What have they done to you!' she shouted. In the two weeks I'd been gone, I had lost fourteen kilograms (more than two stone) and looked like a skeleton. My physical condition was so poor. Even with all the stories everyone in Damascus has heard about detention centres, it was still very painful for them to witness my transformation.

My dad had grown a beard in my absence, which was unlike him. He and my brother kept hugging me. My dad kept clapping me on the back, saying 'You raised my head' which means, 'You made me so proud'. It was the first time in my life that he had ever told me that I made him proud. I sobbed.

They took me into the lift, supporting me to stand. I felt so happy inside. Finally, I was out, reunited with my family. I'd missed them so much. Every minute that I'd been inside those terrible cells, they had been on my mind.

Once upstairs they opened the door. My mum looked at me for

a moment and then she came and hugged me tightly. She wasn't crying exactly, she was wailing. My sisters were crying, everyone was hugging me and they tried to sit me down. I explained that I couldn't sit. Then they realized how terrible I smelled. All the sewage and dried blood that clung to my clothes, that T-shirt and khakis I'd put on so optimistically two weeks earlier.

My parents took me into the bathroom where they stripped me as if I were a baby again, and both scrubbed me with soap in the tub. Half an hour later, I still smelled bad, so they carried on scrubbing. I could see them looking at my leg with worry. I always felt like I was my mother's favourite, just a little bit, and I could hardly bear the expression on her face as she tried to get me clean and took in the extent of my injuries. Eventually their crying eased, and I remember them saying, 'Thank you, God.' Despite what had happened to me, they were so grateful I'd been released. That I was still alive.

Afterwards they dressed me in fresh clothes and took me out to the sofa near the open door to the balcony, where I lay on my side. It was so good to be back in that place looking over the city, the breeze on my face. The family started debating whether to take me to hospital. They knew how bad my leg was, but they also understood it would be deeply risky. There were stories of people who had been captured by the *mukhabarat* from hospital and they knew they wouldn't be able to explain that I had just been released.

Instead, they rang my friend Bilal's father. He is a doctor and came straight to see me to check me over. First, he asked me to cough, to see which ribs were fractured. Then he looked at my wrists and explained that the right one needed to be put in a cast as well. He checked my haemorrhoids and prescribed lotions. Then he examined my leg and said it needed antibiotics and surgery. Throughout, he tried to calm me down, using soothing words. It was only when he had finished that he turned to look at my mum and saw her crying. He burst into tears as well, great racking sobs that he couldn't control.

We were all shocked because he was a doctor and they are supposed to be used to such things. But he was crying so emphatically that we all burst into tears as well.

'I'm so sorry,' he said, trying to regain control. 'I just . . .' He sobbed again. It transpired that his brother had been arrested in the 1980s and had never been released. He saw his brother in me. This just showed the level of pure evil under the regime. Everyone is traumatized. Everyone has suffered. And the layers of generational trauma run deep.

A week later, another doctor, who was friends with my uncle, came to our apartment to operate on my leg to excise some of the infected skin; fortunately, not a big job. Two weeks after that, I visited a local hospital to get my arms looked at. I was terrified to go, but I needed treatment. There they took off the cast from the military hospital and re-cast it, but by then it was too late to put a cast on my right one, so they gave me a plastic brace. As it was, my arms have never been the same again.

TRUTH TO POWER

My cousin Majd, who had been so instrumental in my liberation, was trying to help in her own way with the febrile situation in Syria. After my release, she tried to start a political party: the 'Syria Homeland Party'. It wasn't a true movement, but a farce that was tolerated by President Assad.

Majd's influence was such that she even spoke to President Assad directly about me. They were talking about the increasing number of protests and the situation in Syria, the discontent of young people.

'Maybe you shouldn't torture them,' she said to him.

'We aren't torturing anyone,' he replied.

'Well actually, that can't be true,' she replied. 'My own cousin Hassan was tortured in detention.' What happened to me had become public knowledge. I was a young, popular English teacher from a 'good' family and my students had talked to their parents about my disappearance.

At that point, in October 2011, Assad was still in the phase of pretending to care about what his people thought of what was unfolding in the country. He was making a great show of consulting with people from different groups – farmers, actors, doctors – to talk about their political views. He wanted to give the illusion of caring without enacting any real change. Meanwhile, protestors were increasingly being arrested and tortured in the cells. Just as I had been.

Majd told me that he was eager to hear from young people. She asked me if I wanted to go to the Palace. At first, I thought she meant the restaurant of the same name in Damascus. I couldn't believe she meant the real one. In Syria such things never happened. Under a dictatorship, the president becomes something akin to god, like an immortal figure.

But Majd was serious. She meant the actual Palace. Assad had asked her to bring her political party along for a meeting and she wanted me to come along too.

'This is the right way to try and improve things in Syria,' she said. 'Talk to President Assad about your experiences. Share your story and perhaps that will help.'

This was about three months after my detention. My broken arms were still wrapped up. I couldn't believe it was going to happen but I decided to try and make the most of it. An audience with Assad was a privilege, one only open to me because of my family. Maybe I could help open his eyes to how his people were being treated by their own police force.

My parents encouraged me to go. My dad even prepared a question that he wanted me to ask Assad.

I arrived in Majd's flat smartly dressed in a white shirt and met the group of about twelve others also going. Everyone was full of excitement and nerves about what they planned to say to the president.

'I'm going to tell him this is abject brutality and it shouldn't continue like this,' said one.

'We should give him constructive criticism; this is bad, but this is how you should do it,' said another.

We all had to leave our mobile phones at Majd's apartment and then we were led into a convoy of shiny black people-carriers. I couldn't believe that I was really heading to the presidential compound, which looms over Damascus, situated across the plateau of Mount Mezzeh to the west of the city, a hilltop fortress of white Carrara marble.

We arrived at the exterior gates and drove up an immaculate, curved drive flanked by date palms. Usually our roads are full of pot-holes and far from well maintained, but this tarmac was as smooth as silk. We arrived at another tall gate and then went down a straight drive, about a kilometre long, which led directly to the palace building.

As we approached, I was incredulous to find myself actually in front of that structure I had seen so many times glinting in the distance from the balcony of our apartment. There wasn't a blade of grass out of place, everything eerily immaculate.

They parked the cars and we got out. There were guards, but I was surprised that they were at a distance: we were being treated like guests. We didn't have to go through any scanner or security checks as we were ushered into a hall with gleaming marble floors. Everything was on an overblown scale. The incredibly tall ceiling was so high that there was a massive indoor tree planted in the middle of the room, stretching upwards. There were elaborate chandeliers and beautiful carved side tables, a thick red carpet underfoot, each giant door off the hall was made of pale wood. Apart from the carpet, all was bleached of any colour or nuance, like a corporate office lobby.

I was looking at everything as we were led to the left. I struggled to comprehend that I was where the president lived. It was so surreal. He was the person who was in charge of what had happened to me and there I was. It felt like going to meet your rapist.

We passed a doorway and I glanced in. Inside was a bank of TV screens, showing all the news channels from across the world. Al Jazeera. BBC World. Fox News. A woman was sitting in front of them, wordlessly watching them.

We were led on to another room. Assad was standing by the door. I was in the last quarter of the queue. He was shaking hands with everyone in our group. It was so weird. I hadn't known what to expect. I had grown up with pictures of Assad in my classrooms, in every official building I went to. I'd seen him on the news. And yet, it was an immense surprise to see him in the flesh. He was tall, with a long neck and was dressed smartly in a suit, a vague affable smile plastered across his face. Remember, this man had been a children's eye doctor in London; he didn't present as a psychopath but rather a kindly, respectable professional. He nodded and smiled at all of us.

And he spoke in informal language. On television he always speaks in *fusha* – formal Arabic. I had only ever seen him giving state addresses, but here he aimed to sound like an everyday person and the effect was quite disconcerting. With him, two glamorous women with clipboards also greeted us. They were beautiful and extremely well groomed. I later discovered that one of them was the daughter of Basha al-Ja'afari, Syria's then-ambassador to the UN.

Behind them were chairs arranged in a U-shape. The floor was covered in a vast yet intricately patterned carpet, an Islamic mandala. The ceiling was inlaid with carved wooden panels from which dripped yet more chandeliers.

We all sat down and were offered tea. The president invited us to start talking. A man at the front began. Back at Majd's flat, this man had told me that he was going to tell President Assad exactly what he thought of the current situation. I waited, expectantly.

'Mr President,' he cleared his throat. 'My mother remembers you in her prayers every morning.' I slumped back. Instead of speaking the truth, it seemed that we were here to praise President Assad after all. And so it went on, with each person being hugely complimentary to him. I was still resolved to speak the truth when it got to my turn. Part of me still hoped that maybe I could be the one to get him to change his mind. I could see Majd watching me with a nervous smile on her face, entreating me to be careful with her eyes, as she had done in the general's office, just months earlier.

'With all due respect, I didn't come here to say prayers for you . . .' I said. I could see immediately that I had grabbed his attention. He had been lazily swimming through formalities, but looking at me, he suddenly seemed to wake up. 'But if I speak what's on my mind will I be able to go back home?' I continued. It was a real concern to me. I knew that not far away from that palatial chamber, there were pockets of hell, full of people who had done nothing wrong.

'Yes, please do,' he said, emphatically. 'I actually really want to hear from people just like you.' All the people who had praised him so fulsomely looked on in slight surprise.

'I'm Hassan. I'm an English teacher. I was taking part in a protest and I got arrested. They beat me up. They broke my arms. They tortured me and hurt my leg so badly that I almost lost it. I'm just wondering, why is this happening? I went to prison not entirely sure I was on the side of the protests, but I ended up convinced by the brutality of this regime.'

'How much money do you make?' he asked in response.

'I make about 80,000 Syrian pounds,' I said, knowing full well that my teaching salary was very good for someone of my age.

'Why protest then?' he replied.

'That's not the point. I may be earning well but that's not the issue. The issue is what is happening to your people. Right this very minute. I only wish I had been taken to court if I'd done something wrong, but instead I was taken to a dungeon where I and others were beaten up and tortured.'

'That was an individual mistake,' he said, airily. 'We were not ready for a movement like this. We didn't have anti-riot police.'

'So, you shoot and torture civilians instead?'

'In Idlib they were carrying anti-aircraft weapons,' he said. 'These protestors.'

'I'm not talking about Idlib, I'm talking about here. Let's talk about the capital, Mr President.'

As we spoke, he would occasionally joke. When I first told him I had protested, he amiably called me a 'mondas', which means a kind of puppet or stooge.

'In the protests, what do you say? What are the chants?' he asked me at one point.

'I say what other people say,' I said. I was hesitant. It felt like total madness to actually say the phrases to his face.

'No. Tell me what the chants were,' he said. I think it was a power trip. He wanted to hear it. He wanted me to say it.

'Freedom,' I said. 'That's one.'

'Do you also say that "The people want the execution of the president"?' he asked, looking at me straight in the eyes. I paused.

'Yes,' I admitted. 'I have said that before.'

'Are you fully convinced you want that?' he looked at me, raising his eyebrows. Everyone in the room stared at me. I could feel Majd's concern radiating across the chamber.

'No,' I said. 'Not entirely. I don't want you to be executed necessarily but I do want the downfall of the regime.' Majd frowned. I couldn't believe I was saying such things to Assad's face. One of the aides holding a clipboard circled something. I later found out that she had a list of our names and she had highlighted mine.

Assad switched to English and started talking about the failures of the West and their democracies. Then I replied in perfect English and said, 'Mr President, we are talking about Damascus. Let's just stay with that.' He didn't like that one bit.

'I'm tired of description and description,' he said. 'I want a real solution.'

'It's a bit sad that I need to be your solution because I'm only an English teacher, but I think you should first stop killing and torturing. You could start with that. You are building your own enemies. A couple of days ago students were protesting outside the biology faculty of the university and they all got arrested. Why? It's a university. No regime that is acting like your regime has stayed in power throughout history. Downfall is imminent. But you can save it if you change what you are doing. It doesn't have to get that ugly.'

'We fought the Muslim Brotherhood for ten years and succeeded,' he said, with a smirk, referencing the brutal government crushing of the Islamic uprising.

'But you are killing your own people,' I replied. 'That is never going to end well. History will show you that. Nobody tortures their people and stays in power. You need to listen to them instead.'

'That's what we are trying to do. We are trying to have these conversations. Would you like to work with us?' he asked.

'No, I'm okay thank you. I don't want to work with you.' I glanced at Majd's concerned face. The rest of the group just smiled blankly. Since my detention, I was constantly on the brink of anger. The group knew that I was not ready to be lectured about how to speak to the president. They hadn't been in my situation. It was all right for them to say their mothers remembered him in their prayers – they hadn't been tortured.

Then I went on to ask my dad's question. The regime police have a habit of cursing Allah a lot. For religious people this habit is more than just annoying, it's deeply disrespectful.

'My other point is something that my dad asked me to say. It's quite discourteous that everyone in every government faculty curses god and religion constantly. The majority of ordinary Syrian people don't like that.' This definitely wasn't the top of my list of concerns, but I had to ask about it for my father's sake.

'Yeah, we should have a dialogue,' said Assad, in his dopey voice. We must have been talking for about half an hour. At one point as we were talking, an old man who was Assad's PA walked into the chamber and Assad had waved his hand, saying, 'Cancel the next meeting.'

After our conversation ended, everyone stood up and they grouped together for a photograph. I backed away thinking there is no way I want to be in that photo. It would be in the records and people will think I was working with the regime. But the president saw me trying to get out of it.

'Hey *mondas*, don't you want to take a picture with us?' he said to me.

'Yeah, sure,' I said, internally cursing. I have the photograph to this day. Everyone is dressed in their smartest clothes as we stand alongside that man who has been responsible for so much suffering. My expression is bemused. The whole encounter was entirely surreal, symbolic of the yawning chasm between the face of the regime and the vicious underbelly that I'd experienced.

When I left, I actually felt pretty good. I hadn't been able to change his mind on anything, I knew that. The idea that I would be able to single-handedly make him see sense had obviously been wildly optimistic. Nonetheless, I was proud that I'd told him what I truly thought to his face. I'd told him he was doomed to go. I hope that if that stuck with him for even twenty-four hours, it was something.

By early 2012, things were escalating in Syria. The balance of power seemed to be tipping in favour of the opposition side. There was so much solidarity among the people rising up; a collective awakening. It was profoundly exciting. We glimpsed freedom from the repression we had taken for granted for so long and it was dazzling.

Protestors began calling for a no-fly zone over Syria and the measure was considered by America and Turkey in August 2012. I was incredibly hopeful. I never wanted the West to send in troops on the ground but a measure that prevented Assad from bombing his own people would have enabled the opposition to consolidate its progress. Sadly, however, the Obama administration decided against bringing in a no-fly zone at that crucial stage. The illegal invasion of Iraq and the repercussions that followed had – understandably – made many in the West deeply disillusioned with foreign interference. But Western intervention can be successful, such as when NATO got involved in the Kosovo War. In Syria's case, targeted intervention could have made all the difference. Assad had all the power in the air and, as the conflict progressed, he used it to destroy entire cities, towns and villages which defied him. Regime forces dropped tens of thousands of barrel bombs, killing tens of thousands of innocent civilians and wiping out half of Syria's infrastructure. They also deployed scud missiles, which had never been used in a civil war before. These weapons are not smart bombs. They obliterate everything in their path. The aim was annihilation. Suddenly you could see society collapsing in front of our eyes. It was intensely depressing.

Assad also used besiegement as an illegal act of war to crush key rebel-held towns and suburbs including Darayya, the suburb of Damascus where Little Village, the school I taught in for three years, was situated. Shortly before my first detention, in the summer holidays of 2011, I had interviewed for a new role at the Syrian National School, located in more central Damascus. After three wonderful years at Little Village I was keen to test my confidence as an educator and stretch myself. I was offered the role, which was really well paid, meaning that after my first detention, I went straight into my new job. I was no longer travelling to Darayya each day, but the area I had once worked in was to take on a key significance in the following years.

During the early days of the uprising, Darayya had been regarded by many Syrians as a symbol of the peaceful movement against the Syrian government. A largely agricultural region, famous for luscious, cultivated grapes, Darayya had a reputation for civil activism even before the Syrian conflict, holding protests in solidarity with Palestinians and against the United States' invasion of Iraq. When the peaceful uprising first started, Darayya's residents were keen to be involved. In 2011, videos from Darayya showed protestors offering flowers and iced water to security forces. The flowers were met with bullets, and this beacon of non-violent dissent became a rebel stronghold as the conflict progressed, and in November 2011, the Assad regime decided it would seal the area, hoping to starve the local population into submission.

Darayya was also bombed repeatedly. During a single two-month period it was hit with 330 barrel bombs. With all food and medical supplies prevented from entering, the situation in the suburb eventually got so bad that the imams issued a disturbing fatwa, allowing people to eat dead cats to avoid starvation. The regime turned the area I had loved working in, which had been so optimistic about civilized change, into nothing less than hell on earth. Yet still, Darayya's extraordinarily brave activists tried to maintain hope. They even created a secret, underground library, a safe shelter for residents to gather and read, which became a haven of normalcy and education.

Despite enduring years of near-constant bombardment and shortages of food, water and power, the remaining rebel fighters and civilians were evacuated in August 2016. They were sent to Idlib, along with many others. The province, which sits on the border with Turkey is, at the time of writing, the last remaining area of Syria controlled by forces opposed to Assad and one of the most densely populated places in the world.

For three years in Syria, after the first pro-democracy protests erupted in March 2011, it was us versus them. But then, despite Obama's attempts not to get drawn in, it turned into a proxy war. It became mainly America, Saudi and Turkey versus Russia and Iran. The US was funding some opposition groups, but it was messy. On one occasion there was even a skirmish between two rebel groups, one funded by the Pentagon and one by the CIA. That's how chaotic it became. If the Americans had intervened more decisively earlier on, things could have been different. I felt massively let down by Obama. When he'd been elected, I had thought he was amazing, but he profoundly failed Syria. Then once Russia started helping Assad, the revolution became doomed.

Despite my new role at the Syrian National School, I found myself increasingly depressed as we moved into 2012. My personality had changed after my detention. I took everything very personally in terms of politics. I stopped talking to supporters of the regime on both sides of my family. There was a total schism. Later, that was one of the reasons that I found Brexit so difficult when I came to the UK. To see families falling out over politics was painfully familiar to me.

I started reading more widely than I ever had before. After what I'd witnessed first-hand, I understood that those carefully scripted textbooks I had been forced to memorize at school were nothing more than propaganda. I wanted to educate myself about the truth about our government. Memoirs written by others who had experienced detention became a lifeline; in the absence of a free press and factual history books, they helped me to learn. One in particular, *The Shell*, struck a chord. It is banned in Syria and is written by a man called Mustafa Khalifa. The book takes the form of a diary and tells the story of a young graduate, an atheist who gets falsely accused of being a radical Islamist and member of the Muslim Brotherhood, and is imprisoned for thirteen years without trial in Tadmur prison, one of the most notorious in the Middle East. It documents the acts of brutality he endures, and the book is extremely bleak, but also manages to pick out moments of humour and irony. It is seen by many in the Arab world as a symbol of the Syrian opposition in the current Syrian war and it really spoke to me. Not least because my mum's cousin had actually been detained in the same prison the book talks about. It was risky to be reading it. But I didn't care.

My mother sensed my growing discontent and had an idea. She has a theory that seawater cures everything. 'The sea absorbs depression' is one of her favourite sayings, meaning that you'll feel better when you spend time by the coast. After seeing me moping around, she suggested that I go away on holiday for a week. So, I went to Turkey with Bilal to stay in a hotel in early

March 2012. On the bus on the way there, we could see skirmishes happening around us. The war was unfolding in front of our eyes.

Nonetheless, it was a good week. I swam and ate good food and started to feel physically stronger again. I also took many pictures with my camera. Inch by inch, I was regaining myself. I didn't know – how could I? – what was lying just around the corner.

JUST FIVE MINUTES

There is a dream that I have at least once a week. In it, I'm back in Damascus. The city that I miss with every fibre of my being. But instead of being happy about this, I'm completely terrified and overwhelmed with the desire to leave. I know that if I don't, I'll be killed, but there is little I can do about it. I'm stuck. The fear sits in my belly like a stone, weighing me down.

I always wake up from this nightmare with a pervasive sense of loss. The city I loved had become somewhere profoundly unsafe for me. It happened incrementally, over a period of months, like when water gets hotter and you suddenly realize that it's scalding. After my first detention and even after being so frank with President Assad, I still thought that I had a future in my hometown. Until the day I knew for sure that I didn't.

On that awful morning, just a couple of weeks after I got back from my holiday to Turkey, the intercom of our apartment rang and my mother picked it up. 'Hello,' she said. 'How can I help?'

'Is Hassan there?' a male voice enquired.

'Who wants him?' said my mother.

'His friends,' said the voice with a confident sneer, perhaps expecting my mother to open up immediately. This was a man used to people doing what he asked.

What he hadn't realized – the idiot – was that our intercom had a camera attached. So, my mother could clearly see him and his companions. Four members of the *mukhabarat*. Thugs in shiny leather jackets, no friends of mine.

Her legs crumpled from underneath her and she sank to the floor, still clutching the intercom receiver. She knew what it meant, that these men were looking for me. The significance. All Syrian mothers would have done.

'He isn't here,' she managed, before ringing off and starting to sob. Then she rang my dad and told him what had happened. He immediately called me. I was midway through my morning of teaching, surprised by the call. Knowing how unlike my father it was, I told my students that I would need to take it quickly and stepped into the corridor.

'Drive your car to the border, Hassan,' my dad said, his voice ragged, the minute I picked up. 'Leave it there and go to Lebanon. Do it. Now.'

'Dad, what are you talking about?'

'They turned up at home looking for you . . .' But before he could explain any more, he rang off. The thugs had turned up at Pizza Roma, having headed there straight from our apartment.

Shortly afterwards, I got a call from General Khedr. The same white-haired, portly man who I had met when Majd organized my release.

'Your dad is with my men,' he said. 'Would you like to come and see us, Hassan?'

I was still standing in the corridor, next to the lockers. Overwhelmed, I smashed my head into the door of one of them.

The metal door buckled. One of those lockers, that I'd always coveted so much as a student myself, hallmarks as they were of all those American high school films I had watched with such fascination, that world of seeming freedom and fun, marked forever by my terror and frustration.

'Yes, I'll come,' I said, deliberately keeping my voice flat. His men were with my father. I knew I had no choice. If I didn't agree to it, they would take him.

'Would you like to come this evening, Hassan?' asked the general, calmly. 'It'll only take five minutes.' A mere formality, his tone suggested. A routine matter of events. Nothing to worry about. *If only.*

'Yes, I'll come tonight,' I said, my voice breaking. 'Just let go of my dad. Please, please just let him go.'

I drove back from the school in a daze. My heart was pounding, my throat was dry. I felt sick with terror. *Just five minutes*, he had said. That was all. But I knew that once I was back inside the detention centre, I was theirs to do whatever they liked with.

The look on my parents' faces once I arrived home told me the same thing. All the colour had drained from my dad's and he was haggard with worry. Yet still, he tried to reassure me.

'They said it would only take five minutes tonight,' he said, hugging me. 'Just a quick chat. That's what they said.' But he couldn't meet my eyes. We both knew, in our hearts, that it was unlikely to be that straightforward.

My mother spent the rest of the day crying, praying and reading the Quran. She looked for comfort in her faith, as she always does.

I left the apartment to see Redwan and Aghiad. I told them what had happened that morning and their faces dropped too. Everyone knew what the summons could mean. We had grown up with the stories of what happened behind closed doors. It was possible that they wouldn't see me ever again.

'You just have to go,' said Redwan. 'You don't have a choice. Insha'Allah all will be well.' He was right. I didn't have a choice.

That March in 2012 was freezing cold, winter still lingering over Syria, as if spring would never come. I will forever remember that day as one of the worst of my life. I returned to our family apartment, the scene of so many lively gatherings. Family meals around the long table. Afternoons when I'd sat on the balcony watching Damascus, taking photographs of the city that I loved spread out beneath me like one of the carpets sold in the souk. My home.

I dressed smartly, I remember that. It was important that I look presentable. Then we drove, my dad, my brother and I, in my brother's car, to the very same headquarters that I had been released from, just seven months earlier.

As we approached the headquarters, it was around 10 p.m. I felt like vomiting. All Syrians know these places exist, but we push them to the back of our minds. But I'd been inside this one, I knew what lay inside the compound. The casual and arbitrary horror. I was so scared that I had stopped talking altogether. With every fibre of my being, I didn't want to go back to that place. My mum had told me after the first detention that I should leave Syria. But I hadn't wanted to go. Despite everything, I couldn't see a life for myself out of Syria, away from my family. But I didn't want to be back there. Terrified is an understatement. My dad and brother were almost entirely silent as well. We parked the car and went to the gates. There was a booth, where two guards were standing.

'We're here because someone wants to speak to Hassan,' said my dad. 'For five minutes,' he added. We'd been told five minutes. If we said it out loud, kept repeating it, maybe it could make it so. The guard nodded. One of them picked up a handset, spoke into it and then nodded.

'Yeah, he can come in,' he said, matter-of-factly.

'Can we come with him?' said my dad, gesturing towards my brother. They flanked me. I knew that if they stayed with me then nothing too bad could happen.

'No. No you can't,' said the guard. So, I had to say goodbye, to my dad and my brother, I had to walk away from them, towards the compound. Beyond the gates, the path was rugged, lit by the streetlights that rose from the ground. I remember that one of them was flickering. I was led to the general's office. Back to that place where I had met my cousin before. Somewhere I'd hoped never to see again.

'Oh, it's good that you made it,' said the General Khedr, as if I were turning up for a dinner reservation. As if I'd had any choice about the matter at all. Outside it was night. I thought of my mother and my sisters, in our apartment. I thought of my father and my brother waiting outside.

'Of course,' I replied.

'We heard that you went to Turkey,' said the general. So, they'd got wind of my holiday. The one that I'd taken with Bilal, to try and recover from the after-effects of my first detention. At that point Turkey was a hub for the Syrian opposition, but it hadn't occurred to me that travelling there would cause me problems.

'Yes, I did,' I said.

'So, you're not denying it?' He looked at me.

'No, I'm not denying it.' Why would I? I hadn't done anything wrong.

'Here's a piece of paper,' he said. 'I'd like you to write details of every single thing you did while you were in . . . *Turkey*.' The last word spat out.

'Sure,' I said. I knew my holiday had been entirely innocent. I'd drunk juice with Bilal, we'd eaten *shawarma* and swum and talked about pretty girls. Two young men, trying to relax. I was led to another office, where I spent two hours writing down all the details. I filled A4 pages detailing the restaurants we had been to, who we had spoken to. I racked my brains for every last detail, hopeful that if I could just set it down, they would understand that I hadn't done anything wrong.

Eventually I returned to the general, who had been joined by another man. As I handed over my pages of notes, my hand trembled. The general took it and then sat there reading. Time seemed to move very slowly, it had already taken on the slow-moving quality that I remembered from my first detention. The hands on a clock were meaningless.

After what felt like forever but was probably only ten minutes he picked up my handwritten notes and ripped them down the middle. The tearing sound of the paper was one of the most terrifying noises I can ever recall.

The other man in the room cleared his throat. Smaller, younger. He spoke. 'We have our own reports about you,' he said. 'So, we know.'

Know what?

'However, we're not interested, and we aren't going to ask you any questions anymore.' His air was weary. 'But we know what you've done.'

I wanted to cry. I wanted to shout. I wanted to run. I wanted to enfold myself in my mother's arms. But there was nothing I could do. I was rooted to the spot, horror coursing through my body. They led me to another office, which held a different man. He wore a suit, huge biceps filling out his sleeves. He looked brutish but his voice when he spoke was spookily calm.

'If we hear anything from you,' he said. 'Anything at all, we'll beat you so hard your mum will *hear you bark.*' His soft tone made the threat even more terrifying. 'Take him,' he said dismissively. Two other men took my arms and led me to another desk where I was asked to hand over my belongings. On hearing that, I knew with utter despair there was no way I was leaving that evening. That I might never leave again.

They took my belt and my shoelaces, and emptied my pockets of my phone and money.

Throughout all of this, my dad and brother had been waiting outside the compound in the freezing darkness. Every hour, mindful not to annoy anyone, my dad had approached the guard and asked for an update. They had told him to wait, but it had become abundantly clear that the promised five minutes was a joke. After a while, it started to rain heavily, great sheets of water. After six hours of waiting it was very late, almost three in the morning, and my father approached the guards again, asking the same question about what was happening. They rang through.

'Your son Hassan is not here,' one of them said. 'It's time to go home.'

'What? But Hassan . . .'

'Go home,' they said, cutting him off. So, they did, for what else could they do? My brother later told me that in the car on the way back my dad kept repeating, over and over, 'I took him with my own hands. I took him with my own hands.'

A BUTTON AND THREAD

Inside I was led downstairs to a basement. At first, I thought they might be taking me back to one of the communal cells in which I had first been detained. If only that had been the case.

Instead, I was led to a solitary confinement cell.

It was two metres square, with a hole in the corner for a toilet. There were no windows at all. An abyss that I couldn't have come up with in my worst imaginings. It was a place where you couldn't tell day from night. A place where people gave up. The walls were scrawled with the messages of desperate men. One had written consecutive years – 1994, 1995, 1996, 1997 and then a plaintive, 'Please God, release me.' Someone else had written 'Mohammad from Homs'. Trying to assert an identity in that dreadful place.

Anguished graffiti, all written by people who were broken. Pleas for release. *God, release me. Just please let me out. Please.* Mixed in with the scrawls were sizeable blood spatters.

This time, the jailers didn't rough me up. But what one of them said was worse. 'We aren't going to lay a finger on you,' he said. 'There is no need for any interrogation. But don't ask us any questions about when you'll be released or what's happening, because you are going to live here forever. For the rest of your life.'

Right away, I knew that I couldn't do that. There was no way. I would rather die. It was literally the first time in my life that a suicidal thought had occurred to me. I'd never been depressed. And despite what had happened in my first detention, I always felt like I could recover, that life could be worth living. But in that awful cell, I lost my faith. It was hell on earth, the most frightening place I have ever been.

The jailer left and I was all alone. There was nobody I could talk to. I was destroyed. The first time I'd been detained, I had at least been protesting, but this had come out of the blue, for no apparent reason, just as I'd felt as if I was getting back on an even keel. Psychologically, it was unbearable. I was twenty-three years old and had assumed my life was stretching ahead of me, but as soon as I entered that place I lost my will to live. This is why I always feel embarrassed if someone calls me a hero. I know I'm not a hero because I could never do that. From that very first night, I started strategizing how best to kill myself.

I removed a button and thread from the fancy shirt I had put on in my apartment, carefully chosen to be as smart as possible, in the desperate hope that I might have been able to stay for the routine five minutes that had been promised. I played with them constantly, worrying them in my hand obsessively. And I started talking to myself. Guttural utterances that came from somewhere deep inside. I was losing it.

On the second day, they came and took my picture. Up against the wall of that solitary cell. I've never seen that image, but I imagine that I look hopeless, desperate. A man who has nothing left to live for.

Every single time the jailer came to the door with my food, rotting vegetables and dry bread, he would remind me that I was going to spend the rest of my life there, in that cell. That I'd never see daylight again.

Despite his cruelty, on the third day, I held his ankle and begged him to stay for a little bit. 'Please,' I said. I had never been so alone before. I was used to being constantly surrounded by my family and friends. I felt my mind fraying at the edges. I needed human company to remind me there was something apart from the horror of that cell.

He kneeled down next to where I was lying on the ground. For a second I thought perhaps he would talk to me. But instead he started touching me. Intimately. Stroking me. I froze. There was nowhere I could escape to. I didn't stop him. I just held so tightly on to my fists and waited for it to be over.

After that, he repeated the same thing every day. It made my resolve to commit suicide even stronger. I couldn't live there and continue to be subjected to that. I know that people have gone through worse, but that was my limit. I couldn't endure it further.

I had been raised in a culture that – despite its many supportive aspects – was saturated in shame. I was conditioned to behave, talk and live in ways that society dictated wouldn't bring indignity upon my family. While it is primarily upon women's bodies that shame culture is practised and enforced, men in Syrian society are also deemed responsible for upholding certain standards to maintain their family's honour. I had bent the rules here and there on certain occasions, such as trying alcohol with Redwan, or kissing girls I liked, but I was always cautious, constrained by an invisible fretwork of expectation. In a few moments, the abuse completely shattered the self-image I'd developed, as an Arab man, forever.

Until writing this book, I had never shared this aspect of my story with anyone. Not even Aghiad or Redwan. The sense of shame was still too deep. I was anxious that if people found out, my parents might feel ashamed. Just before my second incarceration, my dad had told me, for the first time, that I'd made him proud. More than anything, I didn't want his newly expressed pride in me to disappear. For years after the abuse, I still assumed it was somehow my fault. I told myself that if I hadn't touched my jailer's ankle, it would never have happened. I thought about it over and over again, and it always hurt. It caused me unbelievable anguish that I had been sexually abused by a man, before I had even made love to a woman.

So, back in that cell, I started to plan. I chewed the disgusting food they brought me and spat it onto the ground, making a retching sound once I had a pile in front of me. As a result, they started to bring me pills, three times a day. I don't know what they were exactly, but I reasoned that if I took enough of them I might be able to kill myself. The jailer would stand over me, trying to ensure I swallowed them. But I'd store the tablets in my cheek and then hide them in a twist of plastic that had been used to wrap the bread.

I waited until I had seventeen pills. I was sure that was enough to do the job.

In our culture, suicide is taboo. In religious terms it means you go straight to hell. I knew it was something that my parents, with their faith, would struggle to ever understand. So, I sat in the corner of the cell and started to talk to them. In my disorientated state, part of me was convinced they would hear me. That if I said the words aloud they would somehow listen. I made an emphatic case for why I should die. Then I swallowed the pills.

I passed out. I don't know exactly what happened but when I

came round I was no longer in solitary confinement. I'd been moved into another communal cell. It was full of men – there must have been around eighty-five inmates in there.

Every part of me ached. My body was so tired that I couldn't even lift my head from the ground. I was dehydrated, my mouth was completely dry and my head pounded. I hadn't died, but I felt as if I'd come close to death. I'd touched the edge of oblivion. I had survived but I was still lost.

In every cell, one of the oldest inmates is always chosen as the leader. This man had been asked to feed me. I referred to him as *Ammu*, which means uncle, and he was gentle in his work. He would tell me that I should believe in God and have faith, that everything is meant to be. But I couldn't believe those things. I think he knew that, could sense my disbelief radiating from me, but he was really kind. I'd hit absolute rock bottom, but he nevertheless treated me with dignity.

I was very quiet. I didn't say anything to anyone. I had shut myself down. They had successfully broken me. The abuse had taken the last of my self-esteem and fractured it into a thousand smithereens.

On the thirteenth night that I was in detention for the second time, one of the jailers came to the door of the cell. He was moving so fast that he banged into it.

'Where's Hassan Akkad?' he said.

I was on the ground, but raised my hand. He told me I was to go and see General Khedr and took me back upstairs. Once again, the general's entire demeanour had changed.

'Have you been eating well?' His first question.

'Yes,' I said. 'Very well, thank you.' I squashed down thoughts of the crusts and tired vegetables that had been all I'd had. To complain would have been a death sentence.

'Do you have your phone on you, so you can call your mother?' he said. As if I'd been left with my iPhone and could have rung my parents at any time. Every endless day bleeding into night, I had been tormented with how much they must have been worrying about me.

'No, I don't,' I said.

'Shall I ring her?' he asked.

'If you want to,' I replied.

'It's okay,' he said, waving his hand, as if at a trifle. 'We can do that later. Now tell me . . .' He put his hands in front of himself on the table. 'Tell me why you keep on getting yourself into trouble?'

I didn't reply. I couldn't. I just nodded my head.

'Don't worry,' he said. 'Tomorrow we'll release you. Now let the jailers take you for a shower.'

I was given a shower and then taken into another office, one within the maze of rooms in the compound. They put a blindfold over my eyes and a member of the *mukhabarat* started asking me a series of random questions. He told me that I was banned from travelling without permission and reminded me that I'd signed a piece of paper that said I'd work as an informant for the regime.

'Do you remember?' he said. I nodded. The blindfold I wore was pitched slightly high and I could see him through the gap at the bottom, a normal man. I had to pretend I couldn't. As part of the secret police, his day job could have been something mundane like a bus driver. He made me sign more pieces of paper. Sign. Sign. Sign. Many of them were blank. This is common practice. An insurance policy against being prosecuted for war crimes, in the event of which they could print something on it saying that I admitted to being an insurgent or carrying weapons or whatever. A way of obscuring the truth in their endless hall of mirrors.

He also asked me questions. Endless questions. I tried to answer everything. To tell them what he wanted to hear, in the hope that the promise of release was upheld. Eventually I was taken back to my cell. I told the old man who had been looking after me that I was to be released the next morning. He was overjoyed for me.

'Can I just ask you for a favour please?' he asked. This man from the port city of Latakia, who had brought food to my mouth when I had given up.

'Of course, *Ammu*,' I said. It was the least I could do.

'Will you please call my family for me? To let them know that I'm alive?' It was a simple enough request. One of the terrible aspects of such detentions is that the families on the outside have no idea what has happened to those who are detained. In his position, I would have asked for exactly the same thing.

'Of course,' I repeated. But I had no way of being able to write his home telephone number down. First, I tried carving it into the insole of my shoe with my fingernails, but it wouldn't work, no matter how hard I tried.

'It's okay, just memorize it,' he said. So, I did. Seven digits, repeated over and over again. The next morning at seven in the morning they came for me. It was winter and some of the detainees were only wearing their underwear; they had been stripped of all dignity along with their clothes. There were some loose rugs on the floor of the cell, which they wrapped around themselves, and as I left, I gave away items of my clothing. One man asked for my coat. Another got my socks. A third the thermal leggings I was wearing. I stumbled out with my trousers falling down, without socks or laces. It was obvious that I'd been in prison.

They nonetheless put me into a car and a man drove me to a busy roundabout, where he ordered me to get out. The banknote – 500 Syrian pounds, at the time equivalent to around 6 British pounds – I'd had in my pockets before my detention had been returned to me, so I hailed a taxi, asking for Maysat Square, aware that the journey would take about half an hour from where I'd been dropped.

I just wanted to write down that telephone number, as soon as I could. I asked the driver for a piece of paper and a pen, but he said he didn't have them so I asked if I could borrow his mobile. He agreed and I started to dial in the first digits of the Latakian man's number. Yet, despite my furious attempts to memorize it, it had evaporated from my head. I was never able to remember it, no matter how hard I tried. I thought and thought, but my mind was blank. The shame was unbearable. I still think about him now. He could still be sitting in that filthy cell, while his family has no idea if he is dead or alive.

FLIGHT

This time, I returned to our family apartment without a scratch on me. After trying and failing to remember the other inmate's telephone number, I rang my dad from the taxi to let him know I had been released. My sister Dania was waiting for me downstairs when I arrived and my mother was upstairs; the rest of the family hadn't had time to return home yet.

Dania was deeply relieved that I wasn't visibly wounded. Once inside, my mother hugged me so tightly and kept repeating, 'Alhamdulillah. Alhamdulillah.' But although I didn't have the physical injuries of my earlier incarceration, what I'd suffered had been even worse. I may have walked out with no broken bones, but my second detention was far more damaging.

Later, I found out that the sexual abuse I endured was a deliberate strategy, and one which had probably happened to many others. What seemed random was most likely anything but. The regime didn't like members of the opposition who were like me. Young, bright, dynamic, professionally successful. They set about systematically breaking us. Now, most young Syrians like me are either dead, still in detention, or they have fled Syria, part of the diaspora of seven million Syrians since 2011. Those who remain in our country face daily risks and uncertainties.

I still don't know the exact circumstances of my second release. This time Majd hadn't been able to do anything, despite frantically prevailing upon all her contacts. I later heard that one of my students who really liked me had told her family about my imprisonment and her uncle had been instrumental in my release. As I understand it, a large sum of money was paid as a bribe to liberate me.

After that second detention, there was no way my life could return to normal. Shortly after my release, the head teacher of the Syrian National School, who also owned it, told me she was going to have to let me go.

'I'm sorry, Hassan,' she said, her voice full of regret on the phone. 'They have told me that if I don't sack you, they will close my school.' I wasn't able to get another job either. I tried other schools but was rejected repeatedly. It was clear that I could no longer pursue the profession that I loved, that had fundamentally altered my approach to life.

I was heartbroken. Since Damascus didn't have a future for me, I made a plan to go to Beirut. My Syrian passport wouldn't easily let me go anywhere else. I was very angry and disaffected. Looking back, it wouldn't have taken much for me to have been radicalized at that point in my life. I was furious and looking for answers and if someone from an Islamist group had groomed me for it, I may well have fallen for it. That's how such things happen – groups like this approach people who have already lost everything, promising them a sense of security, purpose and, crucially, revenge. Young men subjected to the kind of things that I was in prison are understandably angry and embittered and I can see how joining one of these groups would be a way, albeit a misguided one, to channel the trauma. The groups also offered good money to recruits, which made them even more attractive to people with so few options. It was visible and talked about but, luckily, I never went down that route.

I got a room in an apartment in Beirut in the spring of 2012, but I couldn't find work in the city and so hated being there. I spent all my time on my phone watching the news about what was happening in Syria. At the time, I still had a desperate optimism that the international community was going to intervene. That Western democracies wouldn't allow Syrians to be tortured and massacred. That Obama would institute a no-fly zone or try and help after his supposed 'red line' was crossed and Assad used illegal chemical weapons against civilians. But he didn't. I kept scrolling. Hitting refresh. Addicted to the latest update.

Redwan came to visit me. He brought me some money from a teacher I'd worked with who had sympathy for my situation, and also some food home cooked by my mum. She had sent chicken, *kibbeh* and stuffed vine leaves. All my favourites, but instead of being comforting they just made me miss home more than ever. We discussed the situation and I felt the sting of my uselessness. I felt like there was nothing that I could do to help from Beirut. After three days, Redwan went back and I found myself more alone, disorientated and lost than ever, my head a storm.

And then came a skirmish in the area of Beirut that I was living in. There was a nine-hour shoot-out just three buildings away from mine. It seemed as if danger was following me around. My dad happened to ring me as it was happening and I answered from my hiding place, under my bed. I was so frightened. He told me to give up the room and flee as soon as it was safe.

So, I headed to Tripoli in north Lebanon to stay with a friend of mine who was studying at the university there. I lived by the sea for two months, which was pleasant, but I couldn't get a job and my mind was constantly elsewhere. I'd gone from being a popular and respected English teacher, to someone on the fringes of society, looking in from the outside. I posted a picture on Facebook and captioned it, 'Refugee me. LOL!' I was joking, but at the same time I wasn't. I was trying on the identity of Refugee for size. I couldn't be in my own country, so that's what I was.

It was in Tripoli that I took up smoking. I'd always been so against it, scolding friends who did it as an unhealthy habit, but the friend I was living with smoked and I followed suit. It was a ritual to keep myself occupied. I still smoke now.

I spoke to my family on the phone every day. And then, with the impulsivity that is such a feature of my personality, when my flatmate's mum came to stay from Damascus, I decided to get in the car with her and go home. I just knew I couldn't exist in a place where I couldn't work, with no real option for a future. I was terrified as we approached the border in her little car. When I'd left Damascus, I'd only had clearance to go to Lebanon for a day. But I tried to reason with myself that technically I hadn't done anything since then. I hadn't been on any protests. All I'd done was to keep posting on Facebook.

I handed over my ID and held my breath. The border guard glanced at it and I was let back in without any consequence. By then, the administration had more to worry about, in the form of the Free Syrian Army, a militarized opposition, than protestors like me. That's not to say that they wouldn't have detained me, but on that occasion I was lucky.

I was dropped in our neighbourhood, outside a restaurant where my mum was eating with her friends and family. She had no idea I was coming back and as soon as she saw me, she burst into tears and hugged me so tightly. There was so much she wanted to ask me, but she couldn't because we were in public.

We went home and for two days I was happy. It felt great to be surrounded once more by the people I love the most, my family. But then, the depression started again. It was triggered by the reality; I was terrified every time I drove through a checkpoint. The fact I had no job prospects made it worse and many of my friends had stopped answering my calls because I was too risky to be associated with.

And then, just days after returning, I got a phone call from General Khedr's *mukhabarat* headquarters. They asked me to report to them, giving a date three weeks hence. I agreed, but after what had happened to me before, I knew that there was no way I could do it. No way was I going to risk another detention. I had to find a way out.

At this point, in September 2012, my older sister Dania was living near Dubai in the United Arab Emirates (UAE). I rang her up and asked her to get me a visitor's visa. It was then still relatively easy for Syrians to get these two-month visitor visas.

Then I had to say goodbye for good. I spent an entire day in our apartment packing my bag. My mum sat on the door of my bedroom, tears streaming down her face. She kept trying to squeeze extra things into my suitcase, which is a real Syrian-mum thing to do. Sweets. Packets of nuts. My clothes. My dad sat on the balcony looking out over the city, smoking. We were all so miserable.

I found it hard to choose what to take. What do you select for a new life? The weight limit was only twenty kilograms. How can you fit a future into that? There were so many books and T-shirts and albums. I packed my sports watch but I left my shoebox of mementoes, there simply wasn't room.

The next morning, I had to say goodbye to my mum. It was one of the hardest things I've ever had to do. I buried my face in her chest and we both shuddered with sobs. I cried and cried and cried, holding her so tight. As she cried too, she prayed aloud, like an incantation. 'May Allah be with you. May Allah guide you. May you find happiness.'

Then it was just me and my dad in the car for the trip to the airport. We didn't really talk. I stared out the window drinking in every detail of the city I loved so much, that I feared I wouldn't ever see again. Pizza Roma. The souk. All the familiar parks, corners and squares. The city that I could navigate my way around with my eyes shut, where I couldn't wander down the street without bumping into twenty people that I knew, that I had taken my camera around so many times. I was trying to imprint it all in my mind. Then we joined the motorway, the rest of the journey featureless in comparison.

I had been to the airport many times to collect family members and friends. I had always dreamed of travelling from there myself, flying to Europe or America. Exploring the world. But I had never been beyond the arrivals hall. It seemed cruel that the first time I went inside, I was leaving my city forever. By then, a dense, dark terror weighed down every cell in my body. There was no way of knowing if they would detain me when they checked my passport, whether I had been put on a blacklist.

I said goodbye to my dad and walked towards the gate. When I looked back, tears were running down his face. My father had always seemed distant when I was growing up. But my detention – and then my having to leave – made me realize just how deeply he loved me. He had made me promise to call when I had passed passport control. *If I passed passport control.* Under my breath, I recited Al Kursi. That special verse of the Quran that was on the wall in our living room at home.

The hall was like any other government facility, like those offices above the dank dungeon where I was detained. It was full of queues of travellers, with policemen everywhere: both those in uniform and plain-clothes ones, eyeing each person that walked past. Posters of the president were everywhere, with him looking down, missing nothing. I felt fear ripple through my entire body.

Still, I queued. We moved slowly but eventually there was just one person in front of me. The official checked his passport and then radioed someone. The traveller ahead of me was taken away to a side room, something about his details raised their suspicion. It was the exact fate that I was dreading for myself. By then, my entire body was shaking. I stepped forward and presented my passport, trying not to let it tremble too visibly as I handed it over.

I was so certain they were going to take me. My name must have been on their lists. But almost without a second glance, the passport guard stamped it and I walked through.

I took my first proper breath in what felt like an hour. I rang my dad from the other side. 'Alhamdulillah,' he kept repeating, over and over, his voice catching. He sounded relieved, but also incredibly sad.

EXPAT EXILE

It is hard for every single person who has left Syria. As I said, before the war our society was deeply content in certain ways. We lived surrounded by a sense of connection, embedded in our families and communities, which promoted a certain security. Being uprooted from that lifestyle is very difficult and has a profound impact on the mental health of most of those in exile. While some manage to move on, many struggle in their new countries of residence, sliding into apathy and depression. Others turn to addiction, unable to moderate themselves after being raised in an environment with such different attitudes.

In my time in Dubai, I also lost myself. Although I didn't fall into addiction, I forgot my values, lost touch with what motivated me and what gave my life meaning. Those lessons I'd learnt when I'd started teaching which had begun to put my life on a better track. The beliefs that I remind myself of now, when things get difficult.

I was so angry. The stand I'd taken in Syria, for the values that I believed in so dearly, had come to nothing. I hadn't managed to change anything, and I'd had to leave Damascus, probably never to return.

Of course, when Dania met me at Dubai airport, I knew nothing about what was to come. It was a relief to see her, to be free from the constant worry about being picked up by the *mukhabarat*. Within a week, I had secured an interview at a private school to teach English. I had left my nationality off my CV. Syrians weren't being given work permits but I knew that if I could just meet them, I stood a chance of making an impression.

That's just what happened. After a trial class, they offered me the role, but when they found out I was Syrian, they were disappointed but said they would try and apply for a work permit. In the meantime, I started teaching. Five attempts to get the work permit failed and after two months, when my visitor visa expired, I had to leave.

I flew to Cairo where my good friends Redwan and Aghiad were both living. They had also been forced to leave Damascus because the situation had become too dangerous for them to stay. Redwan had fled conscription. While Aghiad, who had studied law, had had to leave because the regime was clamping down on those, like him, who worked in money exchange, claiming they were devaluing the currency. I landed and Redwan was at the gate. He looked so happy to see me. I was thirsty, so he offered me a sip of water from his bottle. I almost spat it out, it tasted so flat and terrible. He told me that was just how bottled water tasted there. It wasn't a good start but it was a sign of what was to come. My experience in Egypt was far from good.

Redwan had tried to seem upbeat, but when we got back to the flat he was renting on the outskirts of Cairo with Aghiad, he burst into the kind of tears I'd never seen him cry before.

'Hassan, it's shit here,' he said. 'Really bad.' He hadn't wanted to tell me because we had no other options. It was in a block that was still under construction and they didn't have any furniture. We had to sleep on the floor. Worse though, was the sense that we couldn't do anything. At that time, there were so many Syrians in Cairo. You could see them everywhere you went, but there were no jobs. We were just waiting and waiting. Biding time. For what, nobody was quite sure.

After twenty-one dispiriting days, I checked my Facebook account to find a message from one of my students in Dubai. The school was trying to get in touch with me. It turned out that – against all the odds – the final application for a work permit for me had gone through. So I said goodbye and went back to Dubai. I had extremely mixed emotions. I was excited to have secured a job, doing what I really loved, but I was really sad to be separated from my best friends again.

Dubai was to become my home for the next two and a half years, and it was then that I got sucked into a way of life that left me feeling empty. Without other options, I threw myself into Dubai's flashy, materialistic ex-pat culture. I worked out at the gym. I bought an American muscle car, a Chevrolet Camaro, to match my newly pumped-up body. I stopped following the news. I even started binge-drinking every weekend. I stopped believing that I could change things and make a difference. What was the point?

It was the first time I had made friends with people of other nationalities. The school had teachers from Canada, America and Britain. It should have made me happy but, despite teaching, I felt purposeless. I spent my weekends boozing and trying to flirt with women. Many disappeared as soon as I told them I was Syrian, so I started lying, trying on different identities for size. One night I was a marine biologist from Virginia. The next a doctor from Toronto. When I told such stories, the women I met were much more likely to stick around. Everyone had heard about Syria by then. The destruction and horror. Many wanted to avoid any association.

Aged twenty-four, I actually had sex for the first time in my life. After a boozy dinner I started getting intimate with a woman I'd been on a few dates with. But I was panicking. I didn't want to admit to her, someone I hardly knew, that I was a virgin; I felt too embarrassed. So, I went along with it. But it was a horribly disappointing experience. As soon as we finished, I felt overwhelmed with guilt and shame at my sinfulness. I was convinced that the short and deeply unpleasant encounter had doomed me and spent an entire month praying for Allah's forgiveness, convinced that I was going straight to hell. Back in Syria, I'd had the constant reminder that adultery was sinful. I'd tried to outsmart religion by reasoning with myself that as long as it wasn't full intercourse, it was okay. But the sexual abuse I'd endured during my second detention had only served to compound my sense of shame. After that first disappointing encounter, I got involved in other negative, short-lived relationships. I wasn't happy with myself or the person I'd turned into.

There was so much that had happened that I hadn't managed to deal with yet. I had no understanding or education about the concept of mental health at that time. Nobody had helped me to process the trauma that I'd suffered. So, I tried to numb myself with partying, exercise and spending money.

It just about worked during term time, but in the summer holidays, all my new friends would fly back to their home countries and it would hit me: I had no home to go to.

Dania was wonderfully warm, as ever, but she was also dealing with her own trauma. In Damascus, she had lived in a suburb called Harasta, about half an hour's drive from our flat. Despite getting married, she spent most of her time in our family apartment, especially after giving birth to my nephew Zaid. We all adored him and I've always felt a particularly close relationship to him.

When both Dania and I were in the UAE, an Al Jazeera report about the escalating crisis in Syria showed footage of her apartment in Harasta being bombed and destroyed. She called me, crying in pain and disbelief.

'Zaid's toys were still there,' she kept repeating.

Over time, my parents realized that they had to leave Syria too. They couldn't live with the bombing. It had become worse and worse. So, I sponsored visitor visas. First for my dad. Then my mum. My younger sisters. My brother, Bassel, was the last to leave our flat in Damascus, but by then, he couldn't get into the UAE, so he ended up in Erbil in northern Iraq where he lives to this day, working for the United Nations World Food Programme. Only my maternal grandmother and an uncle remain in Damascus now, both living in relatively quiet neighbourhoods and unable to countenance leaving, despite everything that has happened.

Although my family had joined me, I didn't see them that often. In my first year I had lived in the same building as Dania, but after that I moved into accommodation provided by the school. I cut myself off from my loved ones, which is so unlike me. Looking back, it seems obvious that I was depressed. But I couldn't articulate it. Eventually I started realizing that I couldn't make Dubai my home. It wasn't somewhere I could build a future.

After the difficulty of obtaining a work permit for my job, I knew it would be very difficult to get another one if I ever wanted to change jobs. My options were limited.

At the same time, my passport was about to expire. Renewing it would mean going to the Syrian embassy and I physically couldn't do it. The very thought made me feel sick. It brought back memories of being detained. There was also a good chance the Syrian Government wouldn't allow me to renew it. I knew I had to fly somewhere else while I still had time.

Redwan was also seriously depressed in Egypt. He rang me to ask if he should come to Dubai and I told him not to, since things weren't any better there for Syrians like us. Instead, he started to investigate boat-crossings to Europe. He went to Alexandria and found some smugglers who would take him for 3,000 US dollars. He asked me for help, so I gave him half the money. The crossing took nine days, during which he went totally silent. It wasn't possible to text him or call – I was so worried about him. But eventually, I heard from him. He'd made it.

The idea that I should try it too started to form in my mind. I would never have left Syria if I'd had a choice and by this time I'd spent years circling my home country, desperately unhappy.

You see, security isn't just about being safe from imminent death. It's also about having a future, options, the autonomy to build a life of your choosing. It became increasingly apparent to me that this wasn't going to happen for me in Dubai. I wanted to be somewhere I could live without an expiry date on my ID card. Somewhere I could be a citizen, an active member of society.

I tentatively told my family I was planning on leaving Dubai and trying to get to Europe. They could see how profoundly unhappy I was. I was so ashamed of who I'd become that I was hardly seeing them. They encouraged me to try. After I left Dubai, my parents went back to Damascus. They were so desperate to go home. Upon arrival, my dad was told by border control to visit the secret police for interrogation. He was terrified and was there for almost six hours. They asked him about why he had been abroad for such a long time and what he had been doing. They also asked him about my whereabouts. He told them that we hadn't been in touch for the last few years and they eventually released him. But the situation was untenable in Damascus and my parents returned to Sharjah in the UAE after a year, where they remain until this day.

By this point, Aghiad had also left Cairo and gone to Istanbul. I joined him there and together we started to investigate the idea of trying to get to Europe. We were joined by a young man called Alaa, the cousin of an old friend from Damascus, who had also washed up in Istanbul. There was nothing to do in Turkey. There were so many Syrians there too and there weren't any job permits. We all went on Facebook constantly, looking at groups with information about how to make the crossing, full of tips from people who had already done it.

I still had about 10,000 pounds sterling left of my savings. I offered to lend Aghiad enough for a crossing if we tried it together. Alaa had enough to pay for himself. The decision made, I bought a smart, light forty-litre rucksack from Decathlon. I had to purge my possessions once again, discarding the suitcase I'd brought with me from Damascus, but I felt excited. I was a man in search of a new home. And I was going on a quest with others. I wasn't alone. From the start, I felt supported by my friends in the endeavour. I knew we would do everything we could to look out for one another.

I packed the essentials: my razors, my sports watch and my favourite perfume. I knew it wasn't going to be easy to shower and I wanted to smell good.

While Redwan had headed to Germany and settled in Cologne, I always knew that if I tried to go to Europe, I'd head for Britain.

It was common knowledge among displaced Syrians that it was the most difficult country in Europe to get into but I wanted to give myself the best chance of integrating fully and for me personally, I knew that meant Britain. Thanks to my obsession with learning the language, I felt familiar with British culture. I had watched so many television programmes, listened endlessly to the BBC World Service, even studied English Literature at university. Besides, it was the Holy Grail for me, a dream nation where people could choose their own destiny. Or so I imagined.

At that point, I had no idea that Britain wasn't everything I hoped it would be. I had no idea there were food banks, or people living below the poverty line. You have to be here to know those things. All I knew was how it appeared to me from afar. I went in search of happiness and safety. I went looking for security.

A DINGHY AT DAWN

In Izmir, there were only two questions on everyone's lips: 'Where are you from?' and 'Where are you going?'

Everyone knew the answer to the latter. Most people said Germany, Holland or Sweden. When I said Britain, they would respond, 'Are you mad? It's so hard to get to.'

The town, on Turkey's Aegean coast, was full of people planning to try and cross the sea to Greece. They sat in the cafes on Basmane Square, clogged rooms in the cheap hotels, clustered on the sea front frowning out at the horizon.

On 1 July 2015, Aghiad, Alaa and I went there from Istanbul after determining to try ourselves. Like many Syrians trying to make the journey to Europe, we had formed a group with some others, including Aghiad's uncle and two cousins, another friend's mother and brother, as well as a man whose group had left him behind so he had joined ours. Of the nine of us, I was chosen as the leader of the pack. The others placed their trust in me. It was partly because of my English skills, but also because I like to take action.

People smuggling was an open industry in Izmir. I had thought it would be underground but it wasn't at all. Life jackets and floaters dangled outside shops. From the window of our hotel room you could watch people waiting to be picked up by their smugglers, rucksacks on their shoulders, holding bin bags containing these life jackets. It was quite obvious that the Turkish Government must have condoned it.

All you had to do to find one of the agents promising to connect you with a people smuggler was to wander into a cafe. It was discussed everywhere, in plain sight.

I found an agent quickly. There were agents of all different nationalities but he was Syrian. Very slim, with bad teeth and covered in tattoos. The kind that people give to themselves. A man from a rough neighbourhood. For 1,200 US dollars each, he promised a 'five-star' service with a maximum of forty people on a dinghy. There was a hierarchy of transportation, with three tiers offered for the crossing: 1,200 US dollars got you a dinghy, while 1,700 US dollars meant you had a boat and 2,500 US dollars ensured a speedboat. I opted for the dinghy option, since the others were too expensive. The agent assured me, with his tooth-less smile, that they hadn't had any cases of drowning. Not a man to put your trust in, but this kind of person was our only way out. Had there been a safe and legal route, we would have taken it in a heartbeat.

I returned and told the others the price. They all agreed to it, gave me their money and I went to a makeshift office to pay the deposit. There was a system: you deposited the money and then you got a code which you gave to the agent after a successful crossing so he could go and collect the money.

The office was on a side street. It didn't have a sign and stank of cigarettes. Downstairs people sat around on leather chairs, waiting in the heat. I was told to go up to the second floor where I encountered a man at a makeshift desk. Behind him was the biggest safe I had ever seen – full, no doubt, of desperate people's money. I gave him our deposit and was given the code in return.

Then we waited. I kept ringing the agent and asking when we would be taken on the boat. For three days he told me the sea was too rough, so I downloaded an app with the sea conditions, so that I could monitor it myself. The group was nagging me about what was going on. We ate together every evening, unsure if the next day would be the one that we risked our lives.

After three days the agent rang us and told us to get ready. We were put on a bus and driven to Marmaris, a little town south of Izmir. Everyone was excited and ready, but when we arrived after the four-hour journey, they told us they had booked a hotel for us and that we would have to wait a few more days. It was a crushing disappointment.

Marmaris is a resort town, full of tourists whooping it up on banana boats and jet skis. Our hotel even had a swimming pool. I remember walking the central strip with Aghiad, watching people throw back shots under the neon bar signs. I wished I could let my hair down, but we stayed sober. We were superstitious, not wanting to do anything that could potentially displease Allah. Even though I have never been drawn to religion exactly, I wouldn't describe myself as an atheist either and it didn't seem to be the moment to be taking a chance. To cross safely, it seemed that we would need some kind of luck, divine or otherwise. I badly longed to be one of the holidaymakers on the party strip, seemingly without a care in the world, rather than myself, stateless, waiting to get in a dinghy. We wandered among them, the contrast between us jarring. They were mostly young, just like us. Our lives were so different, only because of an accident of birth.

In the afternoons we busied ourselves by practising our swimming in the hotel swimming pool. There was another group who were using the same smugglers as us and it included children. One of the little boys, Omar, latched on to me in particular. He was nine years old and always sought me out to play games with him. I loved throwing him up in the air in the pool. I tried to push away thoughts of what it would be like if we ended up in the sea together. To an outward observer, our splashing around in the pool probably looked as if we were just on holiday, enjoying ourselves, rather than acting out what could happen in a nightmare scenario.

I spoke to my family every day. By then, they knew that I was planning to try and get into Europe, but I didn't tell them that I was planning to cross by sea, suggesting instead to my mum that I was going for a route that was largely over land. Although some people did this, it wasn't a real possibility for me, but I didn't want to worry her.

Since leaving Dubai, I had begun reading the news constantly again. I was dismayed to discover how much hate there was online. Articles from British newspapers calling people like us cockroaches and invaders. They questioned why we were carrying smartphones. It really shook me. The dehumanizing language was dangerous and there was so much ignorance. I felt so frustrated that people didn't understand why we were doing it and what we'd been through. If they knew just one of the stories of the people in my group, they would haven't said those things. It was reading those pieces that made me take the decision to try to film the crossing. There was such a huge gap in understanding that I felt I needed to document it to show the world what was really going on. Of course, then I didn't know that I'd be so successful in realizing this goal. It was just an instinct. I hadn't brought my beloved Canon with me as it was too heavy, besides I reasoned that I'd need to keep my hands free, so I invested in a GoPro and a couple of memory cards.

I knew the crossing was going to change my life forever. It was a milestone. And although I wasn't to know my journey would be so widely seen, I wanted to make sure I had a record of such a significant event in my own life. There was also an element of magical thinking. I had this idea that maybe if I kept filming, the camera would protect me. It was an instinct. Do this and it will make things better. The setting was so wretched. I knew that filming would help me to focus on one frame at a time, taking my mind off my miserable circumstances, even just a little.

After five days of waiting in Marmaris, they told us to get ready to leave that evening. I packed our passports in a plastic wallet. They put around twenty of us in a van and we drove for five hours. Eventually we stopped, and they told us that it wasn't going to happen that night, after all. There was no adequate explanation and we were all massively disappointed once more. We had no control over the situation.

We went back to the hotel and I checked my Facebook feed. On it was an article about a boat that had sunk the previous night, and five people drowned. I worried even more about the safety of our group, but didn't tell them about it. I didn't want to frighten them. I decided we should push ahead. What other life was there for us?

The next night, they brought five cars for us. Again, we drove for hours before pulling over into a layby at the edge of a forested slope, where we were met by members of the smuggling ring. A man holding a torch with a *keffiyeh* covering his face told us to go down the slope. In the gloom, I could just make out the pistol by his waist. His manner was very angry, not loud, but aggressive. I was frightened, but there wasn't time to think.

'Keep your voices down!' he hissed. 'Be quiet.' I didn't understand the need for secrecy when it had all been so open in Izmir but I wasn't about to argue with him.

The slope was difficult to navigate in the dark. Everyone was scared. I looked around, as I started to move, and saw others descending in a hurry. Some were covering the crying mouths of their children and almost everyone was stumbling because of the rocks on the ground. At one point I tripped, cracking the cover of the GoPro.

All of the members of our group got to the bottom and huddled together. There were a lot of people waiting by the water, at least a hundred altogether. I thought to myself surely there would be three boats, at least, for so many of us. When they started to blow up the dinghies, however, it quickly became evident that there were only two. Surely there was another one somewhere?

With that realization, I began to feel like I had in detention, my senses submerged under fear. I had unleashed a train of events, but I had no idea where I was going to end up.

The reality of my displacement confronted me. I was the persona I had jokingly tried on for size on Facebook when I'd been living in Tripoli. Back in Damascus, there were Palestinian and Iraqi refugees and as previously said, I'd even moaned about all the Iraqis, displaced by war, seeking sanctuary in my home city. Now I was in an even more precarious position than they had been since I wasn't technically a refugee yet. I was a traveller, still on the move and hadn't yet got to a destination where I could claim asylum. It would only be after arriving in the UK that I would officially became an asylum seeker and then finally, a refugee. These distinctions are important because there are millions of people in the world who are displaced. At that moment, it was very difficult to process and accept the reality that I was one of them but, sitting there in the dark, there was no avoiding it. Only four years earlier, everything had been going so well for me, but now I was in this desperate position. An 'illegal immigrant' being smuggled. I remember feeling profoundly disappointed in that moment. It was so far from how I'd expected my life to turn out.

We all put on our life jackets. I saw the parents of a one-year-old toddler holding him, each on one side, to put on his tiny jacket, both crying as they did so.

The people smugglers started loading people onto the first boat. They got about forty people on and it set off. I had been praying to be chosen for that first vessel, but the smugglers didn't pick our group. Everyone else was left to get on the second dinghy, which meant there were at least sixty-five people.

It was mayhem as we piled on. There were people sitting on the sides, perched on top of each other. I was so afraid but there was no arguing with those men with guns.

I thought one of them would come onboard to steer it, but they just showed one of the passengers how to turn on the engine. That was it. We were on our own. Facing the sea in darkness with no knowledge at all of how to operate the dinghy or of the body of water ahead of us. If something were to happen to us, there would be nobody there to help.

The boat was so crowded that when the engine initially chugged into life, it stayed stationary from all the weight. Then, very slowly, it started to move forward in the water. Creeping into the Aegean Sea.

As the sun rose, I discovered that I was sitting next to two university professors, an electrical engineer, a belly dancer. There were eight or nine children, the youngest only a year old. A heavily pregnant woman. There were people from almost every city in Syria. The last time I'd met such a diversity of Syrians had been in the prison cell at the *mukhabarat* headquarters. I really felt like Syria itself was on that boat and it broke my heart. I felt so sad that this had happened to us, after the protests had started in such a spirit of optimism. All those people were innocent, but we had been completely dehumanized.

We moved forward slowly but after only about half an hour, it became clear that we weren't going to make it. The engine wasn't operating properly because of how overloaded the dinghy was and water was seeping over the edge.

We were quite a way from the shore by then and while I didn't necessarily think *I* would drown, I couldn't say the same for the children, like Omar, or the older members of the group.

We started to pray in our terror. Muslims have a Dua for everything, and we started to say the Travelling Prayer. Everyone calmed down a bit through praying, but I felt so angry at the state of us. As a group we'd spent more than 60,000 pounds on a boat that was sinking. It was the epitome of how badly humanity had failed. People had sold their land and property to afford to pay that money and it was going directly into the hands of the smugglers.

I was furious with Assad, the international community and the smugglers. We had been let down so badly. My rage was a force that rippled through my body, prompting action. Praying wasn't enough.

I decided that we should all throw our bags away, to try and keep the dinghy afloat. Around fifteen people did so, including me. That rucksack, into which I had packed all that was left from the twenty-seven years of my life thus far, floating away. It hurt, getting rid of the last things I had left from my life in Damascus. My passport. My beloved Terry Fox T-shirts from my marathons. My perfume. A prayer that my dad had written out for me by hand. Some prints. A couple of favourite books. Packets of cheap Turkish cigarettes. Fragments of a life.

I wasn't that bothered to be losing my passport. It was effectively useless anyway, since hardly any country in the world would let me in on a Syrian passport, and there's no border control on a dinghy crossing. I still had my ID card, proving my nationality. I was unbelievably fed up about my personal possessions, especially since the sacrifice made little difference and the water sloshed in relentlessly. It was clear that there was no way our craft could make it to Greece. I still had my phone, which I'd kept in the separate plastic bag. So, I WhatsApped my friend Hiba who lives in America, explained the situation to her and dropped a pin showing our precise location, so that she could alert the coastguard.

I gave the bag of phones to Alaa and jumped into the water, along with several of the other young men, to try and reduce the weight in the boat.

As I swam alongside the boat, the boy Omar kept making eye contact with me. Just the day before we had been goofing around together. I knew he trusted me as someone who would be able to look after him

'Help us, Ammu Hassan,' he kept saying. 'Please help us.' I didn't know what to say in response. I dreaded the boat sinking and being left with the very worst of decisions about who to try and get back to shore.

Then, alerted by my friend, a coastguard boat appeared in the distance.

'What's the flag?' asked some of our group, hoping against the odds that it was a Greek boat. But I knew it was Turkish. Alongside, the coastguards began helping people onto their boat. The wind had picked up and the waves were then quite big. There was a scramble as there was such desperation to be rescued that people were losing themselves. I shouted that it needed to be women and children first. Eventually we were all on and the boat started returning to Turkey.

Alaa had also jumped in the water and all our mobile phones were broken. My GoPro had got water in it and stopped working, but I took out the memory stick and wrapped it in a piece of plastic. Then I hid it in the only hiding place I could think of – slipping it into my bottom when nobody was looking. This might sound a bit extreme, but I didn't know if we would be searched and, after everything we'd just been through, I didn't want to risk losing what I'd filmed. I had an instinct that the footage I'd got was important. I was right, because it was later used in BBC2's film *Exodus: Our Journey to Europe*, which won me a BAFTA and changed my life. It showed the world the reality of what refugees were going through, repudiating all the upsetting narratives about cockroaches and scroungers.

Of course, I knew none of that then. All I knew was that we had failed. I had been leading our group and we had failed. I'd lost all of my possessions. I was exhausted and soaking and hungry. Europe was still a world away across the sea.

The Turkish coastguards were kind to us, giving us sandwiches and water. We were taken to a police station, where they took our fingerprints and asked us some questions before putting us back on a bus to Izmir. It was all very casual and routine – I think it happened a lot.

We hadn't slept and were exhausted. We literally lay on the pavement in Izmir utterly drained. My black shorts had encrusted salt tidemarks on them but there was nothing else that I could change into. Nobody in our group blamed me. They were really sweet about what had happened, telling me that it was Allah's choice. Many of them were like my parents and deeply comforted by their religion.

Before returning to Izmir, we saw the pregnant woman who had been on our dinghy being taken away with her husband in an ambulance. We later found out that the trauma of what had happened had triggered a miscarriage. Although she had looked quite heavily pregnant, the baby didn't survive. It was devastating. A life, a baby in a mother's womb. Gone before it had even properly begun. That was the enormity of the unfairness. Around us people enjoyed their holidays, while a pregnant woman lost her child because she had been desperately trying to improve their circumstances.

I still had a bumbag with all of our group's remaining money in it (4,000 euros) and I used some to buy a cheap mobile phone to share with Aghiad and Alaa. I rang Dania to tell her that we hadn't made it.

'Please don't be sad,' she said. 'Just thank Allah you are safe.' I made her promise not to tell our mother about my failed attempt.

The smuggling system was organized enough that there were some safeguards. Because our crossing hadn't been successful, I was at least able to return to the office, where I made the initial deposit, to get all of our money back. People smuggling was an economy in itself and some elements of it were crucial. If it hadn't been possible to recoup the money after a failed mission, the system would have failed.

Somehow, Aghiad, Alaa and I then found a hotel room and showered, before getting something to eat. We were still laid out in our new room when Aghiad got a call from his cousin, telling us that another smuggler was organizing a crossing for that very night. The price was 1,200 US dollars per person, exactly the same amount we had just got back for our failed crossing. I rang the other members of our group of nine, who were staying in different hotels, about whether they wanted to try again after everything we had already been through. They said that despite the levels of exhaustion they did. We were all so keen to make it happen. It was so late that all the other people who were going to try on that dinghy had already deposited their money, but we were told that our group could join anyway, with Aghiad's cousin assuring the smuggler we would all pay the full amount once we got to Greece.

We napped for around two hours, setting an alarm so we could meet the others at the main square. There was a rumour going around about fake life jackets, stuffed with foam that made you sink rather than float, so I quickly went to one of the tourist shops on the strip and bought some blow-up rings in case our life jackets were some of the dud ones. Purchasing inflatables designed for having fun, for quite a different – sadder – purpose.

We had a bite to eat, then the nine of us caught taxis out of Izmir to the spot by the side of the motorway where we'd been told to meet. A truck arrived shortly afterwards, huge, with a leather covering stretched across the top. It was a vehicle for transporting rocks or sand, not people, but they loaded us on anyway, along with many others who had also arrived. There were around eighty people, standing in the dark. You could hear children crying, their parents desperately trying to shush them. I thought of my pupils. Those boys in Deraa.

That journey was horrific. We went on the motorway and it was incredibly loud. I hated that truck. It smelled of vomit and piss, the physical evidence of sheer terror. It was almost worse than the dinghy. The leather cover moved up and down, letting in slices of orange streetlight, in which I could make out Aghiad, one hand splayed across his forehead, with an expression of despair on his face. He was muttering to himself, possibly praying.

After travelling for around six hours, we arrived at the edge of another forest and were told to descend another slope in the dark. When we reached the bottom, it was apparent that things were different this time. Aghiad's cousin had assured us it was an organized operation and that they would distribute people fairly among the dinghies, so there wouldn't be more than forty to forty-five people on each. Thankfully, this turned out to be the truth.

On ours, Aghiad and I took charge, telling people where to sit, to best distribute the weight. After the earlier crossing, we knew what we were doing and we wanted to give ourselves the best possible chance. The smugglers just left us to it.

When we were all sitting on board, our boat set off. It was a clear night. The moon shone above us. The sea was flat. After a while, I started to make out the Greek coast in the distance. Everyone was chatting quietly to one another as the boat moved forward. I dared to feel hopeful.

That feeling wasn't to last long.

PUSHBACK

They came seemingly from nowhere, erupting into the peaceful night, shattering our hopes of an uneventful crossing. Three men on board a military-style dinghy, larger than ours, with its fierce lights trained on our smaller vessel as it approached fast, ramming us at right angles. The men were dressed head to toe in black with their faces covered. One wore a terrifying skeleton mask, like something out of a horror film.

We had no idea who they were, but our first thought was the Mafia. Why else were they covering their faces?

'Police! Police!' we called. Hoping that somebody might come and help us. Our shouts rang out unheard across the oblivious sea. Some of us threw the rubber rings I'd bought, in the direction of our attackers. It was farcical, admittedly, but they were the only missiles we had.

In contrast, the masked men were armed with guns but also sticks, which they started beating us with, focusing their efforts on the man who had been placed by the smugglers in charge of our engine. In response, the passenger sitting next to him – a big guy – started throwing punches at them from our dinghy. It was chaos.

Suddenly, as quickly as they had appeared, our assailants zoomed off into the darkness, disappearing. We were just collecting ourselves when we heard their engine noise and they were back, this time nudging the tip of their boat over ours and deliberately landing blows on our dinghy's engine. Then one of them reached out and lifted away our petrol tank, killing our engine. He grunted with satisfaction and they left, leaving us adrift in the sea. We were all shaken and distraught.

Luckily, however, the tide was in our favour and despite no longer having an engine, the waves were moving us slowly but inexorably in the direction of Greece.

We still weren't sure if the men had been pirates or Mafia, but later concluded it was likely that they were actually Greek marine forces. Once we got nearer to the Greek coast, I observed the boat that had attacked us going to and from a vast battleship. It seemed clear to me that whatever was happening was being ordered from high up. This struck me as profoundly uncivilized. It was not what I expected but that was our welcome to Europe. As the sun rose, we saw their boat doing the same thing to other boats of refugees that were trying to cross the line into Greek waters. At the time of writing, such 'pushbacks' are still happening in the same area. There are numerous stories from other refugees who have made the crossing, about men dressed in black driving them violently back into Turkish waters. To date, the Greek authorities haven't accepted responsibility.

Back in our dinghy, the waves had picked up and, along with some other men, I'd jumped in the water to try and push the boat towards the shore. We were getting closer but the masked attackers redoubled their efforts. This time, they extended a rope and some people on our dinghy grabbed it, thinking that despite what had just happened, perhaps they were about to help us. Instead they towed us back to Turkish waters and then set us adrift again.

Those of us in the water started pushing our dinghy back towards Greece and the men came at us again, with the rope. By this point, we were starting to run out of drinking water, we'd had hardly any sleep for forty-eight hours and we were getting desperate. Someone grabbed the rope again and the men dragged us back to Turkish water for a second time. At this point I turned into something like a monster.

'We are going to push our dinghy for a third time,' I shouted. 'And if anyone dares to touch that rope again I swear that I'll throw you into the water personally.' I also asked people to volunteer to jump in the water and swim in different directions when they came back, as a decoy.

The men came back again and that's what we did. Exasperated, one of them pulled out his gun and pointed it in my direction. I climbed back on our boat, hauling myself out of the water and banged myself on the centre of my chest. I was absolutely crazed by that point. Overtired and running on pure adrenaline.

'Go on then, big man,' I shouted. 'If you think you have the authority to shoot asylum seekers then be my guest. Start with me!' By then, I knew he wasn't part of the Mafia, he was carrying out official orders to push back refugees, in direct contravention of EU and international law.

He looked at me wearily and then spoke into his radio before they turned their boat around and left. Shortly afterwards a civilian coastguard boat, different to the battleship he had been going to, came and picked us up.

This time everyone asked what flag it was on the boat and we saw it was Greek. We had made ourselves annoying enough that they had eventually given in.

The coastguard boat picked us up and then we were transferred to the battleship that I had spotted the initial military dinghy coming from. We were told to sit on the deck. Nobody offered us water and we sat in the intense heat with people who had been picked up from other boats. Eventually, the men who had been beating us turned up on deck as well. They didn't have their masks on anymore, but it was obvious who they were from their body shapes, the way they moved. They found the guy who had thrown punches from our dinghy and one of them gave him an enormous slap. I could see them studying everyone's faces, looking for me. I looked down and fortunately they didn't recognize me. I think I would have really been in for it if they had, which is totally crazy, if you think about it. It wasn't justice being meted out, but rather the petty revenge of a group of thugs.

We were relieved to have made it onto a Greek boat, but some of our group still worried they might take us back to Turkey. I reassured them that it wasn't possible. I had done my research and I knew that once we were admitted into Greek waters that was against international human rights law, according to the principle of non-refoulement, which guarantees that no one should be returned to a country where they would face torture, cruel, inhuman or degrading treatment or punishment or other irreparable harm. Nonetheless, I didn't relax fully either until we were taken to the port at Lesbos and disembarked from the boat. We had made it to Europe. It was 10 July 2015. The first time my feet had ever touched European soil.

It was just the first step. There was still longer than we could have comprehended to go. But we were so happy. I rang my mother and told her I'd made it on a boat crossing. I didn't mention our agonizing wait in Izmir, the first failed crossing in a dinghy that was slowly sinking, or the precise nature of the second attempt with its violent pushbacks.

'But, Hassan, you told me you weren't going to do that,' she admonished, happy and fearful at the same time. .

'Sorry, Mum,' I replied. 'It was the only way.'

On the island of Lesbos, we had to queue outside a booth to register. We gave our details and they gave us a slip of paper in return, we'd have to wait for the *carta*, the piece of paper that would enable us to go to the mainland. My passport was at the bottom of the Aegean, but I had a photograph of the details.

That afternoon, with nowhere to sleep, I went to the nearest supermarket hoping to buy a tent. I hung around outside, not sure what to do. I wasn't sure if Greek shops would let a refugee purchase a tent, so eventually I stopped a couple of women around my age who were heading inside.

'If I give you the money for it, please could you buy me a tent?' I asked them, hoping they understood English.

'What for?' asked one of them, but her expression was friendly.

'My friends and I just arrived, and we need somewhere to sleep,' I said, deciding it was best to be honest. The women agreed and I gave them some money. Ten minutes later they came out again, one carrying a wrapped-up tent. It was one of those pop-up ones that could be erected without guy ropes.

'Here you go,' said one of them, passing me the tent. 'We bought it for you actually, so here's your money back,' she added.

'You didn't have to do that,' I said, suffused with gratitude.

'We wanted to,' she said. 'Take care. Good luck. Look after yourself.' I couldn't believe it. The kindness and warmth of the gesture eased the disappointment of our first encounter with Europe – the terrifying pushback by the masked men in the dinghy. It dissolved some of the pain, reminding me that many people actually want to help. It was one of those points in my life where I was brought back from disillusionment by an act of simple generosity. Choosing to be kind can have such an impact on the world around us. We all hold that power within ourselves.

After leaving the shop, the adrenaline started to wear off. The three of us hadn't slept a wink in two days. With no other options open to us, I popped our new tent on the ground at the port in Lesbos, crawling inside and passing out.

It was boiling hot and we couldn't sleep for more than a few hours. I woke to find the imprint of gravel marks on my cheek. I realized there was no way we could get proper rest like that, so I went to a hotel and asked for a hotel room in fluent English. The concierge asked for my passport and I pretended to have left it in Athens. I must have been convincing enough because they let me book it. Our group of nine then took turns sneaking in to rest in a proper bed.

The next day, I borrowed some money from Alaa to buy a new GoPro from a shop. My earlier GoPro had been fatally waterlogged on the first failed dinghy crossing and I was keen to document the rest of our life-changing journey.

There were thousands of displaced people on Lesbos. From Afghanistan, Iraq, every city in Syria. The mood was mostly very positive. All of these people had risked a lot and fled unbelievable hardship, but they were safe and hopeful of better lives. As Syrians, we were fast-tracked and I struggled with that. Our suffering was deemed worse than theirs, but who is to decide a hierarchy of hardship?

On the fourth day of waiting, our group was given the documents we needed to catch a vast ferry to Piraeus, the port of

Athens on the mainland. None of us had ever been on a boat that large, a world away from the vulnerability of the dinghy we had crossed on. We took photographs of ourselves, like tourists. We slept on the deck and could even take showers on board.

Athens reminded me of Damascus. I loved it. People shouting in the street, old men on street corners, the heady waft of pollution and a similar, low-rise style of architecture. It felt comfortingly familiar.

We arrived and went to a bus station to get tickets to head north. We had time to kill and sat by a wall on the pavement outside a supermarket. I was shocked when someone handed me five euros. I hadn't even been begging, but obviously we looked quite desperate. I didn't know whether to laugh or cry. I was grateful for the money, but it shocked me how far I'd fallen that people considered me homeless. I mean I was, technically. And yet.

That evening I fell asleep on the bus as we drove through Greece. But then disaster struck. When we stopped, I blearily got off, forgetting that I had left my 'murse' (male purse) containing all my money, in the compartment above my seat. I panicked. There was no way that I would be able to continue the journey without it. I told Aghiad and Alaa, practically hyperventilating from panic. It wasn't the sort of mistake I would ever normally make but I was so wrung out from everything that had happened.

They calmed me down, and together we prevailed on a Greek woman who managed to call the bus company and get hold of the driver. He was heading back to Athens but he pulled over and gave the murse to another driver heading north. We waited and that driver arrived, asked me a few questions and handed it back over. I could hardly believe it. There were close to 6,000 euros inside; the money could so easily have been stolen. Along with the women who bought the tent, it restored some faith in basic decency.

We got on another bus which took us all the way to Idomeni and the border with Macedonia. There was a stampede crossing the border because people were so desperate to pass. It was so chaotic that Aghiad, Alaa and I, as well as Aghiad's friend and his mother, got separated from the others. Once in Macedonia, the five of us bought tickets and were put on a train which took us directly through from the south to the north of the country. Even at stations, we weren't allowed to disembark. We had to hand our plastic bottles out of the window and people on the platform would refill them with water for us and bring them back. The whole thing was very dehumanizing. Your self-esteem plummets through experiences like that. You have no agency at all. We were like cattle.

At last, we were allowed to get off the train. There were policemen pointing in the direction of Serbia and the crowd was ushered along. They wanted us out of Macedonia as efficiently as possible. We started to walk. And we walked. For hours and hours and hours. There was a pregnant woman near me with a toddler, so I put him on my shoulders and carried him.

We were progressing along a train track and I was scared about vigilantes or criminals. We just wanted to get somewhere safe, where we could rest. By this point, an older woman in our group couldn't walk properly and was being supported on either side. Aghiad's feet were also in a terrible state, swollen with what we later found out was uric acid, and he had to be helped along as well. Our progress was faltering but we kept moving. We didn't have a choice.

Eventually, after what must have been about ten hours of walking, we saw a familiar crescent moon shape against the inky sky. A mosque. It was 3 a.m., but other refugees had arrived before us and the imam had opened up the grounds to allow them to sleep outside. A place of refuge.

I remember going to the water fountain and drinking endlessly. The water tasted so good. We camped there, in the tent we had been given on Lesbos.

The next morning, we discovered that we needed to go to a nearby village to catch a bus to Belgrade. Once there, I took a taxi to the local pharmacy. Our group desperately needed medication. Among us, someone was nauseous, Aghiad's feet were swollen and another man's skin had been almost entirely scraped off his heels. The taxi driver took me there and waited outside while I went inside the pharmacy, where I was greeted by a friendly bearded man in a white jacket.

'Do you speak English?' I asked, hopefully.

'Yes,' he said. 'A little.' I went on to describe our various ailments. He started putting medications into a bag. Then he began adding extra items. Band-aids. Anti-bacterial gel. Wipes. He assembled a veritable goodie bag.

'How much?' I said, once he had finished but he just shook his head and waved his hand.

'You don't pay,' he said, in faltering English. I could hardly believe it as I left, clutching the bag. To be treated so empathetically after everything we had just been through, almost made me cry. And when we got back to the others, the taxi driver also told me I didn't have to pay his fare either. Once again, I was overwhelmed by the gesture. Another pivotal act of generosity that has stuck with me. At our darkest hour, the goodness of those two men shone a light in such unfamiliar surroundings, buoying my spirits for the struggle that lay ahead.

I liked Belgrade. It was the first place in a while where I felt human again. I had rung a friend who was already in Sweden and he found the five remaining members of our group an Airbnb to rent in the city. It was surprisingly luxurious, with a flat-screen television, a bathtub and nice furniture. On that first night, we got gigantic pizzas and massive burgers to eat, our first proper meal in days.

The city itself also impressed me. Cigarettes were cheap. A film in the Transformers franchise had just been released and there were huge Transformer statues erected in the main square. I remember taking lots of pictures with my phone camera. I felt almost like a tourist. A day after we got to Belgrade, the remaining four members of our original group of nine also arrived and stayed in a hotel near our rented apartment.

It felt like we had accomplished something huge but I knew that one of the most difficult phases of our journey to Europe was facing us. After the boat crossing and Calais, travelling through Hungary is one of the riskiest stages. The right-wing administration is very opposed to refugees and is known to have committed human rights violations. They also actively tried to capture people so that they couldn't progress any further. They treated people very badly, even detaining some in containers. If we were to get through Hungary without detection, we needed help.

I contacted my friend in Sweden again, and he told me about a guy called Marco. 'He's in the Serbian Mafia, but he works in people smuggling on the side,' he said – a phrase to strike fear into anyone's heart. But once again, our only route was to turn to criminals. I rang Marco and arranged to meet him. He told me the address. I turned up where he'd said but he wasn't there so I rang him again and he then gave me another address.

Finally, there he was, an enormous hulk of a man with a smaller sidekick. A fly and a bear. I told Marco there were nine of us in our group. He told me it would cost 1,250 euros each.

'Is there any way of doing it cheaper?' I asked.

'No,' he said, flatly, regarding me. I paused. That would take up a huge portion of our remaining money. 'You want it?' he asked, sounding unbothered.

'Yes. I do,' I said.

'Okay. I'll call you,' he replied. I went back to our group. That night we checked out of the apartment and stayed in a hotel for what we hoped was our last night in Belgrade.

The next evening, we met Marco in a local park. The others stayed to one side, while I went to hand over the money on my own as instructed.

I was absolutely terrified. He could easily have just robbed me, I had no way of knowing if what he had promised was legitimate. But what choice did I have?

KEEPING MOVING

'Okay, give me the money,' said Marco. I hesitated. 'Don't worry,' he said, clapping me on the back. His huge hand hit me like a mallet and yet there was something in the human touch that really affected me. He was a people smuggler, undoubtedly an extremely dangerous man, but there was a brief moment of connection and it was enough to convince me that he was going to do what he'd promised. I handed over our cash and went back to our group. After around ten minutes, Marco rang my mobile and told us to get ready. Three cars pulled over beside the park. Two Mercedes and a BMW, all estate cars with tinted windows. I relaxed. At least Marco hadn't ripped us off. I got in one of the vehicles with Aghiad and Alaa. The driver screeched away. He drove like a maniac, going at least a hundred miles an hour. But at least we were moving.

I checked my phone. Google Maps. It was my saviour during so much of my journey to Britain. I saw the blue dot heading north, as we were supposed to be doing. I relaxed and shut my eyes. Despite the reckless speed that we were moving at, I found myself drifting off to sleep.

'Wake up,' said the driver. 'We are nearly at the border. I'm going to slow down, and you are going to need to jump.'

'What do you mean?' I said. Surely, he couldn't be serious?

'I slow down. You jump,' he repeated, as if talking to someone very stupid. He slowed the car to a crawl and we opened the doors and rolled out, down into the ditch beside the road. Commando rolls into the earth. We got up, luckily unscathed.

Marco's sidekick turned up by the side of the road and told us to follow him. He instructed us to go behind him and do what he did. So, when he ducked, we ducked. And when he ran, we ran. I had switched on my new GoPro by this point and you can see this footage of me following that man in *Exodus*.

Eventually, we got to a clearing beside a forest. There were around sixty people there and men with AK47s. They weren't shouting, these men, but we were scared of them. They were the Serbian Mafia, after all. When they told us to be quiet, we didn't hesitate. We waited for two hours, until the sun started to rise. Then the Mafia formed us into a queue with the marksmen on each side, watching us closely. We were right at the back but I could see cars pulling over and people getting into them. Most were being forced to throw their bags away as they got inside.

Eventually around twenty-five of us at the back of the queue were put into a van. If I'd hoped this leg was to be a little easier, I was soon rudely jolted out of it.

Our driver was visibly drunk, swigging more alcohol as he sped along. Apparently, this was a deliberate strategy by the smugglers, so that if he was caught he could claim that he had no knowledge of how we had come to be in his van. I was absolutely terrified that we were going to be pulled over by the police. Perhaps worse, the back door of the van broke during the journey and we had to desperately pull it in with our hands, to prevent ourselves from spilling out onto the road.

I kept pulling my phone out of my pocket to check the pulsing blue dot. It was my salvation.

The journey lasted around nine hours, but it could have been years of my life, cramped in that space. We had already decided that when we reached Vienna, our group of nine would go its separate ways. Aghiad, Alaa and I were planning on trying to make it to Britain, but the others planned to stay on in Continental Europe. So, we said our goodbyes during that journey.

Eventually, we pulled up in a residential area on the outskirts of Vienna.

'Go! Go! Go!' shouted the driver and we exploded out of the van, skittering into the calm streets. None of us wanted to be detected. We had reached central Europe finally, but we weren't ready for our journey to end there. In the van I'd had a feeling that it might be a chaotic exit, so I'd told Aghiad and Alaa that if we were separated, to meet me at a particular hotel I'd heard about, which was run by a friendly Iraqi. It turned out to have been the right thing to do because, as predicted, I lost them in the confusion of tumbling out of the vehicle.

I found myself alone, in Vienna. The streets were almost too perfect to comprehend, like a painting. Everywhere, an air of elegance and reserve. It made me uneasy to be honest. So far from the hustle of Damascus, or even of Athens. Like nowhere I had ever been before. I was so thirsty that I went to a shop and bought a bottle of water. I hadn't realized it was fizzy – I'd never had fizzy water before and when I tasted it, I was so repulsed that I ended up spitting out the mouthful, onto the pavement.

Eventually I found the hotel. The staff recognized me as a traveller who needed support and let me sit in the lobby, bringing me lots of water, which I drank and drank. The tap water in Vienna is amazing; incredibly cold and sweet. After a couple of hours Aghiad and Alaa showed up. They had been stopped by the police but had managed to pass themselves off as a couple of Kuwaitis who had left their passports at their hotel. We were incredibly pleased to see one another. The hotel was fully booked but the owner told us about another one that we could stay at.

The next day we booked a train ticket to Frankfurt. Our money was evaporating. We were so petrified of being detected on that train. If we were caught and fingerprinted, our dream of a life in the UK would have been over. According to the Dublin Treaty, you have to stay in the European country where you are first fingerprinted. So, we tried to act as cool as we could.

By then, I was good at pretending. With my tan, my shorts, my mirrored sunglasses, I gave a good impression of a tourist on a relaxing holiday, not a man fleeing torture and oppression.

But when the ticket inspector came, I managed to misplace my ticket. I spent five dreadful minutes of looking for it, panic rising in my throat. If I couldn't find it, I was convinced he would start asking questions and then call the police. Eventually I discovered it, in the top pocket of my T-shirt. I had totally forgotten putting it there. The relief was intense, but it also brought home to me how every interaction was so much more freighted than it would have been for most other travellers. How far I really was from that relaxed tourist that I was desperately impersonating.

We had been following various Facebook groups and we knew that if a police check happened on the train, we should try and lock ourselves in the toilets to avoid detection. With every station we stopped at, we'd hold our collective breath, waiting to see if men in uniform boarded. I would disembark to puff on a cigarette, scanning the platform as I exhaled. But we were lucky. Nobody got on and we reached Frankfurt without incident.

From there, we booked a bus to Cologne, where Redwan was living. By that time, I hadn't seen my best friend for three years. I was so full of anticipation. He was already living a life in Europe, that step ahead of the rest of us.

He met us at the bus station and we hugged, for a long time. I pulled back to examine him. He already looked different. Altered. He wore a really nice outfit and had a female friend, who was German, with him. Redwan is a charismatic man and he makes friends easily. He took us back to his flat and there were other people there, drinking beer. It was high summer, the windows open. From a distance it would have looked like a party but if you listened to our conversation, you would have heard us sharing stories of our frightening boat crossings. Not the typical tales of most twentysomethings. Not so long ago we had been in Damascus talking about the everyday, but now we were talking about difficult journeys, of putting our lives on our backs and risking everything.

We stayed with Redwan for three days. He took us to the cathedral in Cologne and we took photographs. He also implored us to stay with him in Germany. Every time we saw a police car he would joke that he would get their attention, so that they would fingerprint us and we'd be forced to remain in Cologne, with him. 'Over here!' he would call, when they were at a safe distance, so they couldn't quite hear him. We'd laugh and furiously tell him to shut up.

It was only Redwan's second year there and despite having made friends, it wasn't easy for him. He was still learning the language and was lonely much of the time. Nowadays, he is much more settled in Cologne. He has two jobs, a girlfriend and speaks German fluently. He has built a life. But back then he still hoped that his dearest friends might keep him company. But Aghiad, Alaa and I were adamant. We were heading to the UK. However difficult it might prove to be. Despite my deep affection for Redwan, I remained convinced that the best option for me was Britain. It was the place where I'd be able to contribute most effectively and be an active part of civil society, just as I'd always dreamed.

Back in 2014 when I was living in Dubai, I'd gone to Nepal for a holiday. While I was there I'd met a German man who lived in Cologne; I'll call him Dieter. We'd got on well and Dieter had told me to look him up, if I ever found myself in the city. So, I did just that and we met up. When Dieter found out that we planned to go to Calais, he offered to drive us there. He was kind-hearted and genuinely just wanted to help us. Another person in my journey whose surprising generosity truly helped to alter the course of my life. We went out for dinner with Redwan. It was a painful goodbye.

Then we set off. Dieter had bought snacks and bottles of water for the journey and even offered to pay for petrol, although we insisted he shouldn't. Technically he was people smuggling us through Belgium and France, but he couldn't have been more different from someone like Marco. When we arrived at Calais he good-naturedly offered to buy a ticket so we could all get on the ferry. We had to explain that we didn't have passports that would allow us to do that. I didn't even have any kind of passport at all. I knew who I was on the inside – my skills, the languages I spoke, my religion – but I didn't have anything other than my ID card in Arabic to prove my identity.

We asked him to drop us in the centre of town. We were going to have to make our own way. We thanked him and gave him money for petrol. It was eleven o'clock at night. We found ourselves waiting in the car park outside a nightclub. We could hear drunk people laughing, the sound of music pumping. I was desperate to use the toilet, so I asked the doorman, using my English, and he let me through. Once again, I was struck by the sense of parallel lives. The people in the bar were on a night out, getting wasted, having fun. In contrast, we didn't know where we were going to sleep for the night.

I went back outside. We ended up going to a park nearby, unfurling our sleeping bags and lying on the grass, the noise of the revellers floating towards us through the night. There were also rustling noises around us. We weren't the only ones using the park. In the days to come we were to discover that it was popular with local drug dealers, many with young, French girlfriends that they brought to the park for sex.

We didn't know that then. Besides, there was nowhere else to go.

ALLEZ

To say Calais isn't the most alluring of places is an understatement. To my eyes, it's ugly and forbidding. Within days of arriving, I had started to refer to it as 'the graveyard of hope'. We soon met so many people who had got stuck there for months, in a few cases even years. Some gave up in the end and decided to settle elsewhere in Europe.

Nonetheless, on that first morning, woken by light drizzle at around 5 a.m., we were still hopeful. We were on the final leg of our long and demanding journey. The UK was so close. We had so nearly made it.

We kept each other's spirits up. We still managed to laugh at things, looking for humour to try and keep a sense of normality. No longer able to afford cigarettes in cartons, we took to buying tobacco and Rizla rolling papers. But none of us really knew how to use them properly. Alaa learnt first and would roll them for me and Aghiad.

But our first week soon taught us how rough life on the streets of Calais would be. There were kiosks outside the park selling huge portions of chips for two euros. At first this seemed like an incredible bargain, but we soon got sick of those frites – and the buttery croissants we bought at the local Carrefour. We were longing for real food. Hummus. Fresh vegetables. Salads of chickpeas and parsley. Food cooked in a kitchen and eaten on a plate, rather than out of a greasy paper bag.

It was in that park that I also discovered how mean and aggressive seagulls are. They dive-bombed us constantly for our chips. Even now, I shudder if I hear their distinctive cawing sound. It reminds me of being homeless, cowering in a French park trying to protect my dinner from an angry bird.

On the second day, we went to the train station in the town and were stopped by a Syrian man called Mohammed. He was from a middle-class family in Deraa, the place where the Syrian uprising had first begun. He was well dressed with a nice watch and smart shoes. And he spoke beautifully, the Arabic of a scholar. He told us that he was meeting an Egyptian smuggler who had promised that he could walk him into the port in Calais. We said that we'd like to come and try as well.

Around the same time, we met another older man called Abu Mohammed. He was from the Syrian city of Raqqa, in his mid-fifties, the white of his moustache tinged yellow from the constant cigarettes he smoked. He joined our group but, from the start, I found him extremely annoying. He was illiterate and uninformed, but he loved to share his opinions and would always cut over other people when they were talking.

The smuggler was in his twenties, with long, greasy hair. The fingernails on his little fingers were curiously long and sharp. I couldn't help staring at them. I often find myself judging people by their fingernails and I decided he was sleazy, which was born out in his manner when he started talking. By this point in my life, I'd had some experience of people smugglers and I refused point blank to have anything to do with him.

On the second day we saw a couple of Sudanese men who said they were going to jump on the trains at the entry point to the tunnel. We followed them and discovered that there were literally hundreds of people walking towards the tunnel. Along with Mohammed, we spent a night sleeping nearer the station and then climbed over the barbed wire fence where we'd been shown to go. We put our sleeping bags on the top strand of wire as a buffer, so that we wouldn't get ripped to shreds. It was relatively easy. On the other side were freight trains. We found trains and hid inside them. I was with Alaa at that point but we'd lost Aghiad. It was chaos, with so many Syrians, Sudanese, Eritreans and Iraqis all trying to find hiding spaces. It was like the most chaotic game of hide-and-seek you could ever imagine.

We lay there in the darkness, but it wasn't long before a policeman approached with a torch.

'*Allez*,' he said. That was the first time, but that word was to be said to me so many times in the weeks to come. *Allez. Allez. Allez.* If I hear it now it brings back the disappointment. We were led away and reunited with Aghiad shortly afterwards.

During our first two weeks in Calais we tried the train almost every day. This was a time when lots of people were still making it onto the train. We got a routine going. We would walk towards the station at around 6 p.m. and then build a fire in a field to sit around for a couple of hours. Then, once darkness fell, we'd head to the station to try our luck. But every single time, we got caught.

One night, I asked a group of people waiting near the fence for a cigarette. They obviously weren't refugees. I could tell they were British and thought that perhaps they were journalists. I asked what they were doing.

They told me that they were filmmakers making a documentary series for a production company called Keo Films about the refugee crisis, explaining that they'd travelled to Afghanistan, sub-Saharan Africa and Turkey, to give people smartphones so they could film their journeys.

'I've already done that myself,' I said, proudly showing them the film of the boat crossing, which I had by then transferred to my phone. They were profoundly shocked. It was obvious from their faces that they felt as if they'd hit the jackpot. They didn't have any footage of boat crossings at that time and obviously the boat crossing was one of the pivotal parts of the refugee journey. They asked if we could exchange details.

The next day we had lunch in Calais. They asked if they could film me and watch my footage. I agreed but said that I wanted something legal in place saying that they couldn't use the footage without my consent. They drew something up and I signed it.

They watched my footage and were blown away by it. I told them I was happy to work with them but I wanted to be properly paid and credited. Over the next few weeks they filmed me once in a while in Calais, and told me to get in touch if I got to the UK and they would film me again.

That was feeling increasingly unlikely. After nine days, not having showered and growing increasingly desperate, we decided to head to the Jungle, the notorious refugee camp outside Calais. We had our own tent, but there was nowhere to pitch it on the site. We were told by the charity workers on site that we could sleep in one of the big tents they had erected, but they had puddles of mud inside them and cockroaches on the floor. This was before the death of the Syrian boy Alan Kurdi and the Jungle was very makeshift and chaotic. I said there was no way that I could sleep there, so we queued for some food and then left.

Things changed after the tragic death of three-year-old Alan, who was found washed up on a Turkish beach. The image of his discovery shifted the entire debate about refugees. When I later went back to the Jungle it was entirely different, with a much more established infrastructure. But this was before all of that.

Soon afterwards, we met another Syrian, Ahmad, who hadn't been able to make it to Britain and rented two cheap flats in Calais. He lived in one and he sub-let the other. For a few euros a night, we could have a spot on the floor, crowded in with other men. The flat was bad, but it was better than sleeping in the park. We could cook food and we didn't get rained on, but the toilet was thick with encrusted shit and there was nowhere you could go to be alone.

Every night at this point, another Egyptian smuggler would take us to where the lorries were parked by the port. He would open a lorry using a knife he always carried, and we would hide inside. We took water bottles to urinate in, biscuits and dates to eat. The lorries would go through various checks, including being weighed to see if there was anyone on board. The first time that we were inside one, being loaded on the ramp to be weighed, we were so pleased because we thought we were being loaded onto a boat. But it was the scales and we were discovered shortly afterwards.

It happened again and again. *Allez. Allez. Allez.* Calais brought us right down. Aghiad, Alaa, Mohammed, Abu Mohammed and I had formed another group. We heard there was a camp at Dunkirk and we decided to try it instead, buying train tickets to take us to Dunkirk. The camp was mostly Kurdish, but it was better organized than the Jungle. There was a residential area with space for tents and a separate area with two taps for water. It was getting dark when we got there and we huddled around a camp fire. We were so desperate for a hot drink and Abu Mohammed insisted he could make tea, by putting tea bags in a plastic water bottle and placing it near to the fire to warm up. Needless to say, his strategy didn't work. We sat staring at the bottle for nearly two hours but it ended up being totally undrinkable. He was getting on my nerves, he was so obnoxious. But we couldn't tell him off because he was almost the same age as my dad.

It was too dark to pitch our tent, so instead, we huddled around the fire and tried to sleep. All of this was horrible, but we managed to support each other as best as we could. I was in a bad state at this time. I'd been so sure that I would make it, but the hope was leeching out of me each day. I was under a lot of pressure from my family. I tried to sound positive when I spoke to them, not to let on just how desperate I was starting to feel or how dangerous it all was. We were stuck. To this day, I hate the feeling of being stuck, almost more than anything else.

The next morning, we pitched our tent. Behind us were three young Egyptian guys who were smoking weed for breakfast. In contrast, I wanted to keep my head completely clear. I didn't want to get distracted.

There were Kurdish smugglers at the camp, who said they could try and get us into the UK. It was a sophisticated operation. They drove around in cars with British number plates, and also had guns. I was so shocked to see that, in France. I had expected all of northern Europe to feel so civilized and safe, but our experience wasn't like that at all. Many Brits explore the vineyards of Champagne and enjoy the scenic south, but our experience of France was not particularly pleasant. The price quoted was 1,500 pounds and we needed to deposit it through an office, as I had in Izmir. We didn't actually have the money on us, but my brother Bassel in Iraq agreed to transfer it to Aghiad, who still had a valid passport. Alaa's cousin was already in Britain and we wired him money for me and Aghiad. He put in the money for Alaa and then deposited the total in the smugglers' bank account on our behalf. Mohammed and Abu Mohammed also paid the smugglers.

For three days we didn't even try. We were waiting for our turn and Alaa had a bad cold, which made him shiver constantly. Every morning a van of volunteers would park in the middle of the camp to dish out boiled eggs, bread and tea. I really needed the breakfast, but I hated queueing for food like that. It got to me. It was a reminder of how far my life had spiralled out of my control.

A group of medics also came every day. One morning, I helped them translate for an Arabic-speaking guy. This drew the attention of a Belgian charity worker in her twenties called Julie. I noticed her looking at me and afterwards asked if I could bum a cigarette. She was very beautiful and there was a spark, right away, but it didn't feel like something I could act upon. There was too much else going on and the gulf between us felt too great.

On the third night, our smuggler came for us. A Kurdish man in his late twenties nicknamed 'The Bucket' who wore saggy jeans and a bandana. He was constantly stoned and punctuated all his sentences with the word 'innit' – to the extent that I thought it was a Kurdish expression until I arrived in the UK. They stuffed all five of us in a van, but there wasn't quite enough room so they pulled Mohammed and Abu Mohammed out of it at the last minute, but we were left inside. We later found out this angered them so much that the two of them left to return to Calais. The smugglers drove us to a lorry park off a motorway in Belgium. They didn't use the cars with British number plates to actually smuggle anyone. Rather, their system was to remove the side of a lorry by its hinges so that refugees could climb inside. This was done incredibly quietly because the drivers were sleeping in the cabins.

On that evening, we were smuggled, with the stoner Egyptian boys, onto a lorry containing sweets. Our clouds of breath were lit by a tiny interior light as we huddled together like penguins for warmth, surrounded by boxes of candy. There were twelve of us inside. I felt so claustrophobic. Aghiad, Alaa and I had vowed to always be respectful of wherever we found ourselves. There were stories of men pissing in lorries, or messing about, but we felt strongly that what was happening to us wasn't the lorry drivers' fault and we should respect their cargo, so we were always very careful.

Nonetheless, after five hours in that lorry, we broke into a packet of soft marshmallows because we were so hungry. Fleeting sweet comfort in the moving dark.

After several hours on the road, we got to Calais. We passed through the sniffing dogs but then our lorry was placed on the scales. Predictably, with twelve stowaways on board, the weight showed a discrepancy and we were discovered and thrown outside. *Allez.*

We walked for about two hours and then got a bus back to the camp at Dunkirk. We had failed again. The second night we tried again but the Kurdish smugglers opened up a truck only to discover that it was refrigerated, so they couldn't put us inside. Instead, they stole all the fish from within. The next morning the air at the camp was thick with the smell of barbecued fish. That was common, apparently. If the smugglers couldn't get people on to a lorry, they would steal the contents and pass it around.

The morning after our second failed attempt, I ran into Julie again. This was our fifth day at the camp and I smelled pretty dreadful. She asked if I'd like to have a shower at her flat. I hesitated – I didn't want to get her into trouble – but the thought of a warm shower was so compelling that I agreed. She lived in a really nice place with a balcony overlooking a narrow street in central Dunkirk. There was a power shower and I'm not sure I had ever enjoyed getting clean so much. When I got out, Julie offered to get some food. She came back with a bottle of wine as well. We ended up chatting and laughing as we ate supper together. I felt more normal than I had done in weeks so I didn't hesitate when she offered me the chance to sleep on her sofa bed.

In the middle of the night, she emerged from her room wearing only her underwear. We ended up sleeping together and, to be honest, it was really beautiful. It was my first sense of normality in so long. Sometimes people ask me what I did for sex in the months of my journey across Europe. That was my only encounter, but it really helped to make me feel better, just at a time when I was starting to give up hope. Another moment on my path where someone showed me warmth and affection at the time that I most needed it. That filament of warmth and connection that has run throughout even my most difficult periods.

I stayed with her for two nights before returning to the camp. I didn't have a phone on me to let my friends know where I was as our shared one had been left with Aghiad and Alaa.

'Hassan!' said my friends. 'Where have you been?' They thought I'd somehow managed to cross to the UK without them. But no, after my brief interlude I was back, in exactly the same position as before.

A NEW IDENTITY

It was Alaa's cousin, already in the UK, who first suggested the idea of trying to enter the country on a fake passport.

After eight days we had given up on Dunkirk and the Kurdish smugglers. Their route on the lorries hadn't worked for us and we decided to go back to Calais. We re-joined Mohammed and he introduced us to a friend of his – Wassim – who had been the head of an entire unit in the Free Syrian Army. Wassim was an incredibly athletic, tough-as-nails guy, and from his first day there he approached Calais with absolute vigour, jumping fences with ease, looking for routes that we might have missed.

We'd head to the trains with our sleeping bags so we could find somewhere to sleep for a couple of hours and then try to board cargo trains. But every night, we would get arrested and thrown out. I was starting to get seriously depressed. Throughout the journey we had passed through cities, but in Calais, we were in limbo.

The physical effort involved in scaling fences every night, running, hiding, waiting for hours, was absolutely exhausting.

Our only place to sleep was back at Ahmad's flat crowded with other refugees. It was horrendous.

So, when Alaa's cousin in the UK told us that he had found someone who could provide fake passports, we were eager to find out more. He suggested that one of us try first and if it was successful, the rest of us could attempt it. The cost was 4,000 euros. I had some of my savings left and I asked my brother to send me another thousand, but that was the end of my money. It was agreed that I would try first, because I had the best English.

The smuggler responsible for the fake passport was based in Athens. He asked me to send him two head shots on WhatsApp. He needed an address to send the forged document to and I gave him the Paris address of a friend of mine, Hamade, from Beirut who had married a French woman called Lea. Hamade and Lea were away, so I stayed in their flat to wait for the passport. Paris is a big deal for some Syrians, because of the French occupation of Syria, so I was very excited to go to the city but it was under such weird circumstances that I couldn't enjoy myself at all.

The day after I got to Paris, the passport arrived. It was Czech. My new name was Feredo Nistorova. It was so weird to see it. It was my face, but it wasn't me. At this point I had no other form of ID. I was suddenly this new person.

Along with my passport there was another fake document, a Greek ID card. I rang the smuggler and he told me that it was for another Syrian who was also staying in Paris. He asked if I would drop it to him and passed on his number. I rang this man – Imad – and arranged to drop it to him at the hotel he was staying at if we split the taxi fare.

I pulled up and saw the man pictured on the ID sitting outside. He was wearing exactly the same loud shirt that he was also wearing in the picture on the ID card and had a very welcoming, warm face. We sat and chatted, starting a friendship that endures to this day. He is also from Damascus and had done the same journey as I had but he had been sleeping on mattresses on the steps of a church in Calais. I told him that he probably shouldn't wear the same shirt when he tried to use the ID card, because it might be a giveaway.

His flight was from Charles de Gaulle the following morning, and I had booked one at 3:30 p.m. We parted for the night, wishing each other luck.

The next morning, I woke up excited and absolutely terrified. I put on my shorts and my Nike T-shirt and headed to the airport. As I arrived, I rang the Greek smuggler to ask him how Imad had got on with his own fake document.

'He got to London,' he replied. 'He crossed.' It was just what I wanted to hear. Heading inside the airport terminal, I felt so encouraged and when I got to border control I looked so convincing that the border control officer merely glanced at my passport and handed it back to me. I was thrilled. That had been the part that I was dreading the most. I'd got to the gate and I was sitting there waiting when suddenly I heard my fake name on the intercom. I couldn't understand the French, but it was undoubtedly my new name.

'Feredo Nistorova. Feredo Nistorova.'

For me to leave the gate, I had to pass back through border control. This time a different official checked my passport. He immediately suspected that there was something dodgy about it so he starting asking me questions, looking at me intently.

'Where are you from?'

'The Czech Republic,' I replied. I had memorized the name and other details on the passport by heart. I had been prepared for such an interrogation but it was extremely hard to accept that it was happening after I'd just been sitting at the gate and felt so close. And meanwhile my new friend Imad was in London already.

The border official looked at me and frowned. He got out a magnifier and started looking at the passport in more detail. He asked me more and then he got his colleague who looked at it again. They were suspicious, but because I was so convincing and played my part well, they still weren't sure. They then called a third person over, an older man who was an expert in forged documents. He looked at it and said it was definitely fake. By then, three police officers had arrived. They told me just to say where I was from. I kept on talking in English, saying that I was going to London to see my girlfriend, fabricating wildly to try and convince them.

'Look, we know this is fake. This is one hundred per cent fake. This is going to be easier for you if you just say where you're from,' said one of the officers.

'Okay. I'm from Syria,' I finally confessed. The officers were very sympathetic. They said they were very sorry, but there was absolutely no way I could travel on a fake document. They took it away and walked me outside. Everyone was looking at me and it felt awful. They put me in a car and took me to a police building at the airport where I was put straight into a cell with glass doors, with a couple of other men. It was the first time I'd been in a cell since Damascus. In a storm of emotions, I struggled for breath. The past and the present swirled around in my head. I just felt so disappointed. I had felt so close to making it, I'd genuinely thought I would.

I was kept in the cell for twenty-four hours. They brought us food wrapped in plastic and, despite how upset I was, I managed to sleep a little. They then interrogated me, and told me they had found me out because the stupid smuggler had booked my ticket on a traceable credit card. He had booked so many smuggled people on the same card that it had alerted the authorities.

They asked for my real name and I gave it. Then they said they would have to take my biometrics.

'What do you mean?' I asked.

'Your fingerprints,' they said.

'Listen,' I replied. 'There is no way I'm giving you my fingerprints. I don't care if you detain me forever.' I knew that if they got them, it might end my dreams of building a life in Britain forever. I had made it this far! An Algerian translator interpreted between me and the officer. He promised me in Arabic that the fingerprints were just for French internal affairs and that they wouldn't be logged in the system. But I still refused.

A couple of hours later, they tried again. They told me it was compulsory: as I'd tried to fly from France to Britain on a fake passport, they had to take my fingerprints. I gave in. They took my fingerprints, three-dimensional photographs of my head, and they weighed and measured me. Then, I was made to sign a document saying that I wouldn't do it again. I was released and dropped on a motorway. It was pouring with rain and I was soaked to the skin within minutes. It took two hours, but eventually a Romanian guy picked me up and drove me back into Paris.

We came into Paris and by some huge coincidence I saw the hotel where I met Imad. I got out and went to the hotel reception to ask if Imad had left any clothes or anything else. The receptionist informed me that he was actually upstairs. The smuggler had lied and Imad had also been caught at the airport. His fake ID card had been picked up by the airline staff and they let him know that he had five minutes before the police turned up in which to leave. So he left, swerving a night in detention.

I was drenched and very upset. Imad comforted me and lent me a pair of his jeans, although because he is much larger than I am, they kept almost falling down. As we ate in a nearby Moroccan restaurant, I felt extremely dejected. My own failure had been compounded by the fact that I'd just discovered that, in my absence and against all the odds, Aghiad and Alaa had managed to cross over from Calais.

I'd tried calling them, but they hadn't picked up so I'd rung Alaa's cousin.

'Where are they?' I asked him.

'They both crossed,' he said. 'I'm sorry.' I exploded. It was the worst feeling ever.

It happened that Wassim had found a route that was so efficient that he, Alaa and Aghiad all managed to cross in the space of two days. They'd swum across the marina at Calais and then got in to the port, up some unsecured stairs. The lorries there had already been checked so they managed to avoid the pitfall of being weighed and detected.

But the route hadn't been without risks. Aghiad had tried a method nicknamed *dangara*, which involved resting your back along the wheel shaft of the middle wheels and holding on to the lorry above. His lorry boarded the ferry. The advice on the Facebook groups is to go to the passenger lounge on board the ship once on board, but Aghiad was so worried about detection that he stayed clinging on to the lorry, planning to emerge when they stopped at Dover. But the lorry driver didn't stop at Dover. Instead, he pulled off the ferry and drove directly to Nottingham with Aghiad hanging on in the pouring rain, praying not to slip. Eventually the lorry stopped to refuel on the outskirts of Nottingham and Aghiad got off. He was so covered in splashed mud that he looked entirely brown. The lorry driver gaped at him and then called the police.

I was genuinely happy that my friends had made it, but there was this awful feeling that I was on my own again. It brought back how I felt in the cell during my detention, when I would be pleased on someone's behalf that they were released, but also devastated that it wasn't my turn. We had been so united in our quest to get to Britain together. From the start of our journey to Europe we had looked out for each other at every step of the way. For them to have succeeded without me was heartbreaking. We had been a team, for so long.

In a real state, I went back to Calais. I wandered around all the places where I had been with my friends, but they were no longer there. They had made it while I was still no closer. My only route was to go back to trying on lorries. But I could hardly bear the thought of it. When you do that, you become the cargo. You are reduced to being an object. A news report at the time told of a group of refugees who had died in a refrigerated lorry on the side of an Austrian motorway. There had been seventy-one refugees inside, including eight women and four children, who all suffocated to death. It affected me deeply. Those people had only been trying to do the same thing as me.

I spent a whole day reflecting on whether what I was doing was worth it. Okay, I thought, I want to get to Britain because I can speak English, but is it worth the risk? I felt broken. Aghiad and Alaa were gone. I had led a group, and they were now all at their destinations apart from me. And the French police had fingerprinted me which could ruin my hopes if I ever got to the UK.

I went to the Jungle because I couldn't bear to stay in that awful flat again. I was shocked by the change. It was 3 September 2015, the day after Alan Kurdi had died, and the camp was overrun with caravans and British cars. People were there handing out clothes, building toilets, creating an infrastructure. Sadly, it had taken the death of an innocent three-year-old to mobilize the world, although after this brief moment of mobilization conditions in the Jungle deteriorated again and it was officially cleared in October 2016. Similar camps have inevitably re-formed nearby.

I had almost entirely run out of money. I was more reliant on food hand-outs and started buying cheap cigarettes from the Jungle, which really messed up my lungs. I spoke to Julie on the phone; she asked a lawyer she knew about the finger-prints and the lawyer said they might mean that I would be deported if I got to Britain. My whole future seemed hopeless. I couldn't stop crying.

My mother was ringing me every day during this time, trying to convince me to give up and go to Belgium. I remember sobbing on the phone to my dad, properly breaking down.

And yet, despite everything, I still felt convinced that the best future lay for me in the UK. Alaa and Aghiad had been released from detention in the UK by this point. Alaa was in Manchester and Aghiad in Birmingham. They had changed their profile pictures on WhatsApp to photographs they had taken in their respective cities. They looked so happy. I wanted what they had.

'Please keep trying,' they would both tell me when I rang. 'You can do it. Don't give up.'

THE JUMPER

This new phase in Calais lasted for almost a month. It was one of the worst times of my life. I was so tired and desperate, but still fixated on crossing. Along with others, I tried almost every night.

Once, I was with Abu Mohammed and we managed to get onto a lorry together. The lorry driver got to the port and he realized that we were there. He was in his mid-thirties, slim and clean-shaven. Not your average lorry driver.

'You're going to have to get out,' he called back. But he sounded almost apologetic rather than angry.

'Couldn't you just pretend you, um, haven't spotted us?' I asked him, in my good English.

'I wish I could,' he said, making eye contact with me in his rearview mirror. 'Listen, man – I'd really love to, but I can't.'

'Please.'

'Sorry.' He looked at me again. 'Where are you from?'

'We're from Syria,' I said.

'I'm so sorry you are in this position,' he said, sounding as if he really meant it. 'But I would probably be severely fined or put in prison. I just can't risk it.'

We got out. His humanity, his sympathy stayed with me as we went back to Calais. That night I slept on the steps of the church. I tried to avoid returning to Ahmad's wretched flat as much as I could. The next morning, I was cold to the bone and really wanted something warmer to wear. There was a van handing jumpers out. It had a long queue and once upon a time that would have ruled it out for me. But I'd had to swallow my earlier pride; by then I'd lost so much that a queue was the least of my worries. I waited for ages. It started to rain and get dark, but still I stood there, occasionally jiggling on the spot to try and stop myself getting too cold.

A man from Liverpool was in the van. When my turn came, he said, 'I'm so sorry, I have run out of jumpers.' It was as if the universe was conspiring against me.

'Shit,' I said. At that moment it felt like things couldn't get any worse. The clothes I was wearing were soaked through. 'Are you sure? There must be something.' The man saw the disappointment in my eyes.

'It's all right – take mine.' He lifted his own jumper off over his head and handed it to me. It carried his body heat.

'Seriously?'

'Of course,' he said, smiling. I pulled on the warm garment in relief. His amazing gesture stood out brightly against the bleakness of the moment. Over and over again, I have been pulled out of despair by acts of real humanity like this. Incidents of kindness which inspired me to keep on going, reminding me of my firm belief that goodness predominates in most people. I wouldn't have been able to continue without them.

The next night Abu Mohammed and I wanted to try from the

port but the police caught us almost immediately. I started speaking English. But that day my fluency was to put me in trouble. They thought I was a journalist and they took pictures of me on their phone and put me in their car for half an hour, handcuffed. They looked for me online but couldn't find me. But before they released me they radioed for another car, promising to release me in five minutes. The French police officer who got out of the car looked exactly like me. He was literally my absolute spit. The French police fell about laughing.

I began to question everything I'd done to date. Was any of it worth it? Had I been right to go and protest against the regime back in Syria? I had been so certain that I was acting on the side of good but my current circumstances in Calais were so dehumanizing, it made me doubt every decision I had made in the previous five or six years.

I started having suicidal thoughts as I had in solitary confinement. I was spiralling into negativity. Everything looked bleak.

My last attempt from Calais was in a lorry which was transporting batteries. I followed the blue dot of my location on Google maps and realized we were heading south rather than towards the port itself. I banged on the back door of the lorry for hours before the driver eventually let me out. He asked me if I was trying to go to Spain, but I told him that I wanted to go to Britain.

After that, I rang the Greek smuggler who had provided the fake passport. I told him that I wanted to try again, but not from Paris because of what had happened. He said he would post a new one to the same address but that I should make the booking myself this time. Hamade and Lea were at home this time and it was so good to see them. I spent a couple of days with them and the passport arrived. This time I was Bulgarian. I was from Sofia in Bulgaria and my name was Traycho Anatoliev Trayanov. That certainly took some time to memorize.

I didn't try immediately, but instead went back to Dunkirk and stayed with Julie again for a day. I didn't want to take advantage of her because I could sense that she was developing feelings for me. She kept asking me to stay with her, but I didn't want to join her life in Belgium, I wanted to make my own in Britain. We stayed together for a final night and the next day she drove me to Brussels Airport, parked her car and waited for me outside.

I walked in alone, deliberating with myself about the best way of not getting caught. I decided to book a ticket through British Airways, reasoning that going for a higher-end airline would be safer. I would look more credible. There was a flight two hours later.

'I'd like to book that flight this afternoon, please, and return in – um – four days.' Just a tourist on a mini-break, looking to explore London like all the other holidaymakers. Walk along the South Bank. Go on the London Eye. Wander through Hyde Park.

'That's fine,' said the woman on the desk. 'That will be 400 euros.' I had only 200 euros in my pocket. It was the last money I had left in the world.

'I'll book a plane there and catch the train back,' I said, changing tack.

'That's fine,' she said. 'Passport please.' I handed it over. It was completely freshly printed, each page totally clean and without a single stamp in it. She went through it and I could tell that she was a little suspicious but she didn't say anything.

'Okay, here's your boarding pass,' she said to me. 'Go and check in on the other desk.' I went back outside to the car park to chat with Julie. I was so nervous. We spoke for a while and then I worked up the courage to go to the check-in desk. The next woman that I encountered was more overtly suspicious.

'When did you get this passport?' she asked.

'Oh, it's new,' I said. 'My old one expired.' She frowned but I kept talking. She could tell there was something wrong with the document, but she pointed at border control anyway. 'You'll need to go through there.' I got the distinct impression that she couldn't be bothered to deal with me any longer herself and she assumed I'd be stopped.

I looked at border control. There were booths with queues stretching in front of each one. At the first, there were two old men. Then a woman in the next and then a man. The two older men were looking at each passport with a magnifying glass. I knew there was no way I could get past them. I went back and found Julie.

'I don't think I should do this,' I said to her. 'They are scrutinizing each one. Why would I do it? I don't want to get arrested again.'

'Okay,' she said. 'Don't do it. That's fine.' She didn't sound too distraught. If anything, she sounded a little pleased.

'But maybe I should at least try?' I said. I had got that far. I was so tantalizingly close. I knew that while Julie was keen for me to stay, even to begin to build a tentative life near her in Belgium, I didn't want that for myself. I had always been honest with her about my ambition to get to the UK. 'I'm going to give it a go,' I said, finally. I decided to queue where the woman was, thinking that perhaps I could try and charm her. But as I queued up, someone pushed in in front of me and I got shunted into the queue for the younger man on his own.

I made a split-second decision to try anyway. It was a noisy airport, but I was in my own bubble. I could hardly hear what was going on around me, just the drum of my heart in my chest. With every speck of my existence I was trying to control my breath. I had to give it a shot. Each step took me closer. I felt as if my heart was about to explode in my chest.

The official signalled for me to approach him and I stepped forward with my passport out. It was in his hand and he opened the first page, but then – a stroke of luck. The woman next to him said something and he became distracted. He handed it back to me without opening it properly and turning to the back pages.

'Thank you very much,' I said. I walked in and went straight to the first toilet I found. I was crying and splashed water on my face, looking at myself in the mirror. I'd got through. I got out my mobile and called Julie.

'I'm through,' I said. 'I can't believe it.'

'That's great,' she said. 'Well done.' I knew she didn't want me to go, but she was trying to be supportive. I hung up. I had made it this far before and knew that I wasn't yet out of the woods. Last time I'd got through border control and to the gate before I'd heard my name on the intercom.

Still on high alert, I went to my gate. I know that members of staff check passports again at the gate, so I went to one of them and started having a chat with her. I asked her about work, told her that I was going to London to visit my girlfriend, everything I could think of to make myself sound as credible and normal as possible. Trying to establish a human connection.

I queued when they opened the gate; they were checking every passport again. But I waited in my new friend's queue and when I got to her, she barely glanced at my passport, checking it quickly and letting me through with a smile. I got on the flight and sat down next to a couple.

A pair of airport maintenance workers with high-vis jackets

got on and I thought they were coming to get me. I was still so paranoid. I was trying not to look suspicious but I'm sure I did. I was desperately trying not to catch the flight attendants' eyes. When they announced that the flight was about to set off and the wheels started rolling, I was in disbelief. It was 27 September 2015 and I had been travelling across Europe for eighty-nine days. Finally, it was happening: after everything I had been through, I was about to cross the Channel.

As soon as the seatbelt light went off, I headed to the toilet to destroy my fake passport. I had read somewhere that you shouldn't land with a fake passport on your person. I went into the cubicle and started ripping it up. I tore the pages into small pieces and flushed them. The plastic covering was more difficult. Using brute force, I broke it into small pieces, then bandaged it in loo roll and put it in the bin.

I went back to my seat. Tears were leaking out of the corner of my eyes. The man sitting next to me looked at me. 'You all right, mate?' he asked.

'Yeah,' I said.

'Why are you crying?' he asked.

'Um. I just said goodbye to my mum,' I said.

'How old are you?' he asked, looking at me curiously. I felt like telling him to shut the fuck up but I just politely asked him if we could stop talking. I kept my eyes fixed forwards, looking at the screen where they show you the course of the flight. Once again willing a dot to progress, to take me from one place to another. Despite the evidence in front of my eyes, I genuinely doubted if I'd got on the right flight. Perhaps I'd accidentally got on one to Oslo or Rome?

There are some happy moments that really stand out in my life. When my father told me that he was proud of me for standing up for my beliefs. The first time I taught a class of children and realised I was good at it. But right up there is the moment on that flight when the pilot said, 'Ladies and gentlemen, welcome to Heathrow.'

Apparently, there are signs immediately where you disembark for people wanting to claim asylum, but I didn't see them when we disembarked and kept moving in the same direction as everyone else. Wearing the T-shirt, shorts and running shoes that I'd left Turkey in, I queued with the other passengers in arrivals. It was a long line but, as I said, I'd got used to queuing by that point. I had been humbled, shuffled around like cargo, systematically stripped of all my basic rights. Waiting was nothing.

I was happy and disorientated. Heathrow looked fine. To my mind, it's a good-looking airport.

When I was in Calais, I had posted on a Facebook group, Solidarity with Calais. A woman called Cassy Chamberlain asked me if she could get me anything. I'd requested a coat because the one I had was red and I kept getting spotted by the French police. She showed up with her boyfriend, Joe, and they handed out lots of donations. I told her I was planning to swim to the port as my friend Aghiad had. She was so paranoid and worried about me. She ended up giving me her phone number and telling me that if I ever got to England, I should give her a call and she would put me up. Soon after our encounter, she posted my picture on Facebook, recounting the conversation we'd had and urging everyone to be more compassionate to refugees.

Eventually, it was my turn. I approached the officer. He was a kind-faced man in his late thirties. I walked up and cleared my throat. Technically that was the moment when I needed to explain my circumstances, but I found that the words wouldn't come out of my mouth. I froze, rooted to the spot, my mouth slightly open.

Still, they wouldn't come. It was another experience, like getting on that dinghy, when I was struck by the reality of what was happening to me. How much my life had altered beyond anything I could recognize. Technically when I claimed asylum, I would become an asylum seeker for the first time in my life. Words matter. For me, language is deeply important. And that sentence, 'I would like to claim asylum.' It's a sentence I never thought I would say. I looked at him and the words just wouldn't come.

'Your passport?' he said.

'I don't have a passport,' I said.

'Your ID?'

'I don't have an ID.'

'What do you have?'

'Nothing,' I said. I had nothing but what was inside my head. My memories, preferences, hopes for a better future. No possessions, aside from my mobile phone, a few T-shirts in a rucksack that Julie had bought for me and my Syrian ID, which was useless because all the details were in Arabic. No home waiting for me, anywhere in the world. Not one that I could go to.

'Okay,' he said patiently. 'What is your story?'

'I'm Syrian and flew from Brussels on a fake Bulgarian passport which I destroyed on the plane and *I would like to claim asylum.*' Finally, the words presented themselves. Asylum. I was an asylum seeker. At last.

THE KINDNESS OF STRANGERS

After disappearing for a moment, the man came back with a form. He ticked a box that said 'detaining for immigration purposes'. Then he led me to the back of the queue where there was a row of seats and told me to wait.

I took a selfie while I was sitting there and, with the last of my phone credit, sent it to Dania, my older sister. 'I'm in Heathrow!'

'Hassan! You made it!' She was so happy for me.

After a while, a man in a suit turned up with the original border control officer. I was taken to a side room. They asked if I needed anything to eat, medical assistance or an interpreter. I was fine on all fronts, but it felt so good to be offered – civilized and welcoming, the very antithesis of my first encounter with Europe when those masked men attacked us on the boat. They told me they would like to do some checks and that they needed to confirm my identity.

'Have you been fingerprinted before?' said the border control officer.

'Yes . . . In Turkey, Dubai and Syria,' I said.

'Anywhere else in Europe?' I thought of that police interrogation room at Charles de Gaulle and those fingerprints I had so desperately not wanted to give.

'No,' I said, emphatically, praying that they hadn't been entered into a wider database. They then fingerprinted me and took photographs of my face, before entering my details into their computer. I saw the page loading and held my breath. If the French fingerprints were registered, I would have almost certainly been deported back to France.

Then the wonderful words 'No match' appeared on the screen. The Eurodac is the European database of asylum seekers' fingerprints. According to it, I hadn't been registered yet. I was free to claim asylum in the UK. My shoulders sagged with relief and I broke into a smile.

The men didn't understand the cause of my relief. They were desperate to find out my identity and whether I was who I'd claimed to be. We went around in circles for a bit. Then I remembered that I had previously applied for a tourist visa to Britain but had been rejected. I told them this and they found me and my documents. They were so relieved to be able to place me. After that they checked my rucksack. They looked in all of the side pockets, took everything out. Eventually they said they had finished and I said, 'But you forgot somewhere!' showing them a compartment at the bottom that had been missed. They smiled. I think it helped to establish trust.

I was then taken to a detention room. Of all the places I have been detained, it was the least horrible. It was a bizarre but unthreatening room. There was a vending machine in the corner selling snacks. A Bible on a side table. A prayer mat on the floor. A water dispenser. Seats arranged around a television that was playing one of those talk show programmes where people shout at each other and sometimes fight. Jeremy Kyle or Jerry Springer. I had never seen anything like it before and was agog at the screen. As I watched, the contestants broke into a brawl.

There were other people in there too. A Pakistani man who had been caught entering with too many cigarettes. It was the third time he had been caught doing it and in the end his student visa was cancelled and he was deported.

There was a map of London on the wall. I went and stood in front of it, trying to work out where I was. I was fascinated by how large the city was. All those streets, the fragments of green that denoted parks.

'Where are we on this?' I asked the Pakistani man and he showed me Heathrow on the map. I hadn't realized we were so far from the middle of the city.

A man and a woman were in charge of the detention room and they were really nice to me. Again, I think my good English meant they warmed to me. At the time it felt good, but in the years since, I have felt guilty about this. A kind of survivor's guilt. It's easier for me to navigate things in Britain because I speak the language and look 'unthreatening'. But it prompts a sense of injustice in me, as most other refugees don't have the advantages that I do and are thus dismissed and discriminated against. This guilt was actually one of the factors that led to a deterioration of my mental health later on. But at the time, it was just an advantage. I asked the people in charge to buy me a phone card and they did. I rang the rest of my family and told them where I was. They started crying on the phone, which set me off too. We talked for ten minutes and they told me they had prayed for me all along the way. I was then called for my screening. They wanted to interrogate me so I was taken back to the small room with the same border control officer and his colleague.

'Are you sure you don't want an interpreter?'

'Don't worry, I'm fine,' I said. And they started. It took at least four hours. A proper grilling. Every last question you could think of. Why did you leave? I told them the story of my protesting and resultant detention.

They asked whether I'd joined the Free Syrian Army and I said I hadn't, that I didn't want to. I didn't think it was my place to fight and that's why I left. Then I told them the details of my journey. How I'd gone to Lebanon, Egypt and Dubai where I'd started to try and build a life but suffered repeated visa issues. With my passport about to expire, I'd decided to go to Turkey. They asked where my passport was and I told them most likely the bottom of the Aegean Sea.

They asked which countries I had been to and asked if I'd been to North America. They thought I must have had some connection with America because of my accent.

They asked me if I wanted asylum accommodation and I told them that I had somewhere to stay, passing on the details of Cassy, the woman I had met in Calais who offered to help. I didn't want to take the government-sponsored shelter, I was determined to do it on my own. They told me that they couldn't release me that night because they needed to check with the American and Canadian embassies that they hadn't heard of me. They didn't spell it out, but I knew that I didn't conform to the stereotype of what an asylum seeker looks like. I spoke too well in my Nike T-shirt – I confounded their expectations.

'How come your English is so good?' they kept asking. I told them that I had taught it for five years and that I'd studied English Literature at university but they were still unconvinced that someone who had never been to Britain or America could speak so well. How to explain all those hours of listening to

Eminem and memorizing lyrics. Of longing to go to Britain and imagining it in my mind? Some people in the West hold misconceptions about what refugees are capable of; much ignorance and prejudice persists. So many people who weren't born in Britain speak good English.

That night, I tried to sleep as best as I could, laid out on chairs in the detention room, but I was so excited that I hardly got a wink.

The next morning Cassy came to meet me. She turned up with her boyfriend Joe, who was younger than her. They made for an odd couple, coming towards me. Cassy is a character. She is unconventional and wonderful, usually dressed flamboyantly. The kindness she showed me, without any expectation of reward, was instinctive. She's someone who understands that all people are equal, deserving of love. Without her support, I would have had quite a different start in Britain. As it was, I was released and we went outside and got in her car.

'Do you mind if I smoke?' I asked.

'That's fine, darling,' said Cassy. I smoked three cigarettes in quick succession out of the car window, still parked at Heathrow. Afterwards, we drove to Hitchin in Hertfordshire, where Cassy lives. I was disappointed that we didn't pass through London. I was so keen to see the city that I had heard so much about. Red Routemaster buses. The Houses of Parliament. Trafalgar Square. I had all these images in my mind and I wanted to see the reality.

I also found it very disconcerting that everyone was driving on the other side of the road. I kept asking about things, like a little child, pointing at buildings, gaping at all the Victorian houses.

We arrived at Cassy's house. She had a daughter from a

previous relationship, Molly, who was thirteen at the time. Cassy showed me where I would be sleeping, on the living room sofa. She had a sweet little house and was so welcoming, but everything was disorientating.

In those first few days, I struggled with the food. Cassy made me toast from sliced bread, which I'd never tried before. I put on way too much butter. She also made me a cup of tea with milk, which was also totally unfamiliar. In Syria we drink it black with lots of sugar. Again, I didn't like it. Everything was so different from what I was used to. On the third morning I found a jar of Marmite in the cupboard in the kitchen. I sniffed it and it didn't seem to smell of much, so I decided to try spreading it on my toast like I'd seen Cassy doing, to see if it improved it. I took a bite and had to spit it out, immediately. It's no exaggeration to say that it was the most disgusting thing I'd ever put in my mouth.

Joe then decided to take me for a kebab. He told me it was going to be amazing and really hyped it up. The closest thing to what you call kebab here is *shawarma*. It's a national dish, our beans on toast. I was excited. Finally, a taste of home. But I found the British version stomach-turning, although I pretended I liked it. It was a poor imitation of my favourite food.

I struggled to understand food labels, with no idea what 'organic' or 'free-range' meant. Back home everything was organic and free-range but nobody bragged about it. And I was stunned at all the different types of milk in the local shop. Almond. Oat. Soya. At home, we only had dairy milk.

The only meal that I really liked was when we went for fish and chips. I'd heard about it before and it was properly delicious.

I liked Hitchin. It was different from anywhere I'd ever stayed at in my life. A proper English market town. I kept video calling my parents to show them my new surroundings. They really liked it too. I went for long walks on my own, just looking around me.

Cassy had told her friends that I was coming to stay. They knew that I'd arrived with nothing and many of them gave me shoes and other items of clothing. Their goodwill was so touching. It helped me appreciate once again just what a difference seemingly incidental acts of generosity can have on someone's life. Later, working in the hospital, I tried to pass it on. I knew by then just how profoundly important the kindness of strangers can be.

Her Sikh friend Bob even drove me to the nearest shopping centre in Stevenage in his Porsche. He drove there fast, and it was like being with a friend in Damascus. Once inside, he bought me three-hundred-and-fifty pounds worth of clothing. A coat, a pair of jeans, several good-quality jumpers. After so long relying on hand-outs, I could hardly believe it. Clothes have always been quite important to me, it helped restore a piece of my self-esteem and dignity. Later on, I was offered tickets to an Arsenal and Bayern-Munich match. I took Bob, to pay back some of the generosity he had shown me when I first arrived. To attempt to close the circle.

After a few days I went into an Oxfam charity shop in Hitchin and asked if I could volunteer there. The lady who was running it was really kind. When you are an asylum seeker you are banned from working, but I knew that I couldn't sit still. I needed to be doing something. I started volunteering there three days a week, classifying the clothes and using a steamer to iron them.

On my first two or three days in the shop, people kept asking, 'Are you all right?' when they came in. I didn't realize it was just a normal greeting, I thought it must mean that there was something wrong with how I looked. I would go into the toilet and look at my face, trying to work out if I looked ill. I thought I spoke English fluently but there were so many idioms I hadn't heard of, nuances I missed. And the pronunciation was so very different from what I was used to. I would listen to people and only understand about forty per cent of what they were saying.

Despite my best efforts, I was still walking in a world of triggers from the past. On Bonfire Night, Cassy took me out to the celebrations in Hitchin. I hated it. The massive bonfire, the sound of fireworks being let off. The whine as they ascended and the bang of an explosion. It was just all too reminiscent of being in Damascus during the time of the bombing. I couldn't imagine why people were doing this for fun.

Once every two weeks, I had to check in at a Home Office Centre at London Bridge. The first time I went with Cassy and we caught the train into Kings Cross St Pancras station. I was amazed to emerge and see such a stunning, Gothic-looking train station.

When I got to the centre, I had to go through security checks as if I was in an airport. Such meetings are purely to prove you are still around. They don't really ask you anything but you just have to show up every two weeks, to register yourself.

That first time I went to check in, I met up with Aghiad and Alaa afterwards. We met in a little park near Victoria station. It was good to see some familiar faces. In Damascus I could bump into twenty people I knew just walking down the street, but in Hitchin I didn't know anyone.

Later, I went to meet my uncle Hani, my mum's brother. He didn't know that I was making the journey. I hadn't wanted to share it with anyone really, aside from my parents and siblings. He has two sons and two daughters, my cousins. I rang one of them to say that I was in London and asked if I could come to see them. He told me to come that day and I turned up at their flat, totally surprising my uncle. It was such a touching moment but staying with Hani and his family wasn't an option. They had fled Syria before me and were in the process of rebuilding their lives in Britain, living in a small flat with no space for me.

I lived with Cassy in Hitchin for three months. After that, it was time to move on. She really looked after me well and I am forever grateful to her, but it got to the point where I couldn't keep occupying her sofa any longer.

Luckily, I was able to move in with a friend of mine from Damascus, Farouk, who was living in a flat in Kilburn with three other people. He had a sofa bed in his bedroom and he offered to let me stay. We spent a lot of time playing FIFA and Call of Duty. It was excellent. We were just two young guys, hanging out, in a new city instead of our old one.

Around this time, I was asked to go to Croydon to the Home Office, for an interview to prove that I was Syrian. It was a new thing they had started because people were arriving without documents and lying about which country they had come from. Many were claiming to be Syrian knowing that the conflict increased their chances of gaining refugee status in the UK.

I arrived to find a female Home Office employee in uniform and an interpreter.

'I don't need an interpreter,' I said.

'You have to have one,' they told me. Then the phone rang and it was a third-party company. They told me that someone was going to call to ask me about living in Syria, to ascertain if I knew the country. Minutes later there was a call from a Syrian man. I don't know where he was based, whether he was still in Syria or in the UK.

He started asking me questions, asking me about Damascus.

'Where do you live?' 'Where did you go to university?' 'Which bus would you take?' And then, 'What is the ritual in Eid?' I answered each one with precise details that I knew you could only know if you were from Damascus, but at that last question, I really went to town.

'We go to the graveyard and lay a plant by the graves and then we would go and visit relatives,' I said. 'Then my dad takes us to the butcher and we would watch him slaughter a goat. Then the meat was divided, half for the poor and half for our relatives.' In truth, I had only gone to this event once and found it far too gory to go back.

'What famous meals do you have in Damascus?' asked the man. I decided to go full-on *Shami*, which means someone from the city of Damascus. I am known for having a really *Shami* accent in Arabic among my Syrian friends, which means you really elongate your words when you talk.

'Oh, there are plenty,' I said. 'Cow tongue salad. Stuffed intestines. Sheep legs with yoghurt and tahini. Sheep's head.' He giggled. I could easily have said falafel and hummus, but I really laid it on thick. He tried to stop me but I carried on reciting Syrian dishes. 'Stuffed vine leaves. Yabra'a . . .'

'Okay, you are fine,' he said. As he hung up, I could hear him saying, 'He's definitely from Damascus.' I laughed. I had really enjoyed myself.

Even at my first screening at the airport I hadn't been frightened. My story was genuine. When you know that, you aren't worried about being found out.

Later that same week, I was asked to a 'substantive' interview about my application for asylum. I was asked to go to an office in South London. There, I was seated in a small room on my own, in front of a computer. My case worker was in Liverpool, so we spoke over web cam. The idea was to check if I was giving the same answers.

'What were your political views in Syria?' she asked. Now this is a question that required a careful approach. It could determine the outcome of my asylum claim and I had thought in advance about my response.

'My view is similar to that of the British Government,' I said. The woman on the screen smiled fractionally. It was a smart answer. 'I am completely against Assad and I'm on the opposition side but I do not condone extremist groups. However, I understand why the rebels are taking up arms against the regime. Because of the barrel bombs. The chemical weapons. The torture . . .'

'What are your immediate reasons for leaving?'

'I got detained and tortured. I was sacked and couldn't work in my profession anymore.'

'Do you have any scars?' she asked me.

'Yes. I do.' I started to show her my scars over the web cam, which was an unsettling experience, to put it mildly. Those marks on my arms that will always signify what happened to me when I was taken to the *mukhabarat* headquarters.

A month later I was granted asylum. My legal aid solicitor rang me to tell me and I received a letter of confirmation shortly afterwards.

'You have been granted asylum in the United Kingdom. Your claim was decided on 12/03/2016. You have been granted asylum for five years. Your leave ends on 22/03/2021.'

I felt so relieved and thankful. Five years of not having to worry about being safe. The letter also explained that I would need to enrol for a 'Biometric Residence Permit'. I also became eligible to apply for a travel document which is like a refugee passport. It's enabled me to travel all over Europe in those five years.

It has been incredible how quickly those five years have sped by. At the time of writing this, my asylum is shortly due to come to an end. I'll have to apply for indefinite leave to remain. Logically I know I should get it, but there is still a needling fear that I might be denied.

CONTRIBUTING

My life as an asylum seeker was characterized by both disappointment and kindness. Both carried an equal weight in my first year in Britain.

As an asylum seeker, you are eligible to claim five pounds per day in the UK. You are given an ID called an ARC card that you take to the Post Office to collect the money. I had the card but despite that, the money never came through. I sent two letters, but never got a reply. So aside from the 250 pounds Legal Aid for the solicitor who applied for my Leave to Remain, I haven't actually claimed a single penny since I arrived in Britain. I'm not saying it's right, but I have never personally wanted to. There is rhetoric that refugees come to drain benefits. That they are bankrupting Britain. They really aren't. All sorts of things might be bringing this country to economic ruin, but it definitely isn't the fault of the most vulnerable people in society. And all I have ever wanted to do is to make a contribution and to work.

Until I had my Leave to Remain, I wasn't allowed to work officially and could only volunteer. Once I moved to London, I started going to an office on Hoxton Square to translate documents for a charity that helps reunite unaccompanied minors with their families in the UK. I also started occupying myself by giving talks about my experience. Around this time, the refugee crisis was being discussed all the time on social media and in the news. Alan Kurdi's death had sparked a change. Many people wanted to understand it better and to work out how they could help. After around four months in the UK, I realized that I really wanted to contribute to the discussion that was going on. The journey might be over for me, but I really needed to help others still facing it. The best way that I could do that was to raise awareness.

I knew that I had certain privileges that not all refugees have and an instinctive understanding for how to deliver and articulate my story. My friends moved here and got on with their lives, which is a brilliant thing and completely right for them, but I felt that I wanted to do something different. I needed to use my advantages to help advocate for other refugees who might not have them.

I was still active on Facebook, looking at groups discussing the refugee crisis. An academic living in Stroud called Leah Wild got in touch with me on the site, asking if I would come and give a talk to her local community, which has done incredible things raising money for refugees and volunteering in camps. I decided to do it and went to Stroud, a town I immediately loved. Leah's house was cosy and atmospheric: full of things she had bought from eBay. She is a modern-day Orientalist but not in an annoying way, with a real interest in the Arab world. She goes to Morocco a lot and she had amazing artefacts in her house. She even had a picture on her wall of the same verse from the Quran that my parents had up in our apartment, and an Arabic squat toilet.

I stayed for two nights and gave a talk in an old pub called the

Prince Albert. It was the first time that I had shared my story and it was very odd to be doing it in an old English building, in a place I could never have imagined being just six months earlier. At first, I sat down with the audience and nobody realized that I was the person who was going to be talking. They were surprised when Leah turned to me and said, 'Hassan is going to talk to us tonight.' I stood up, unsure of how it was going to go and then I began to talk.

I was so emotional and I struggled with some parts of the story, but it was very cathartic to share it. Stories are so powerful, they can change things. We shape our societies through the stories we tell about ourselves. They connect us; melding our anxieties, hopes, memories and preoccupations. Conversely, untold stories are painful and divisive. They sit inside us and ache. Not being able to speak your truth, to be shut out of the human narrative, is nothing short of dehumanizing. I understood that by articulating what had happened to me, offering up my version of events, I was shaping my own, often brutal and apparently arbitrary, experiences into something cohesive and meaningful. Moreover, I was speaking on behalf of so many others who had been through similar experiences and weren't in a position to do the same. And I was moving towards a greater connection, the best human impulse there is. I could see, by the faces of the people watching me, that it was bringing home the refugee crisis in a way that no amount of reading articles could ever do. At the same time, I felt like I was really exposing myself. It takes a lot to say such things to strangers. I told them about Syria and why I left. The protests. Our boat crossing. How we were rescued by the Greek coastguard. Flying to the UK on a fake passport.

There were so many tears in that pub. It was probably the first time that everyone sitting there had met a refugee. It was so strange for me. I'd gone from being an English teacher telling the stories of others, to sharing my own. It took me a while to realize that this was a new phase in my life. It was wonderful on the one hand, but also hard to process on the other.

After that, I started giving talks all around the country. At universities and colleges and local community action groups. I went to Cambridge, to Cornwall, Brighton, High Wycombe, Warrington – all over the place. From pubs to auditoriums to village halls. It was a crash course in getting to know the UK. I found it worthwhile, but I can't deny that it was exhausting to keep reliving the experience. I also found it hard when everyone told me how amazing I was. It made me feel so guilty. As I've said before, I don't consider myself a hero. I carry survivor's guilt with me. I think to myself, 'Who am I, to share these things?' I carry the sense of the other people with me, the ones that didn't make it to freedom.

After a month of staying with Farouk, I had begun to feel as if I was imposing on him, so I spent a few weeks sofa-surfing with other friends. Then through someone I knew, I found a family who were looking to support refugees by hosting them in their home. Rachel worked in the City and her partner Chris worked for the NHS. They lived with their toddler son Joseph in a lovely house in Brixton, near Brockwell Park. From the start they made me feel incredibly welcome. They host refugees to this day, their kindness changing the lives of so many. They gave me my own room and really helped me. I stayed with them for a whole year. They were so supportive. They didn't ask me to do anything. The room was beautiful. It had a fireplace and shelves on both sides. I began to take out my things and put them on the shelves. I felt settled for the first time in so long. I could exhale.

I spent my first Christmas in Britain with them. I'd never really celebrated it before. They made me a stocking, full of little presents. I bought Chris a scarf and Rachel a necklace. I felt wrapped in their love and security.

But I was still adapting to life in London. I found it so competitive, fast paced – and expensive. Back home you could get a delicious two-course lunch and a drink for a single pound. And I was struck by the drinking culture here. People love to drink alcohol, back home it would be tea.

My romantic life was erratic. While I was living with Farouk, my Belgian friend Julie came to see me in London. We stayed in a hotel room for a night, but it was clear there wasn't going to be a future between us: she couldn't come to live in London, and I wanted to stay. We couldn't be together in the long term. After that, I started briefly seeing a charity worker who I met at a talk. Libby was also a set designer and lived in Hackney. She was covered in tattoos and piercings and was very cool, even organizing for me to jump out of an aeroplane for my birthday. She introduced me to my first British house party, which was quite a culture shock. We saw each other for five months, but at that point I still didn't want a long-term relationship and we eventually parted ways. Everything was so new for me and I was still processing a lot. I found that some of the women I met fetishized me, as a refugee. One even wanted me to talk about my boat crossing when we were being intimate. As if it would help her to fulfil a fantasy. It was so demeaning and it made me feel sick. While I wanted to tell the world about us and what happened to us, I have never wanted anybody's pity. I am not just someone who has claimed asylum. I am so much more than the things that have happened to me.

This was also the problem with all the talks that I was doing.

I was proud of it, but it forced me to relive my experiences over and over again. I felt stuck in them, in the past. I needed to move forwards, to start building something new.

As a Syrian, my asylum application had been fast tracked and only taken six months. There is a hierarchy of refugees and Syrians were at the top. We were the sexy refugees. The most acceptable ones, seen as the most deserving. Everyone knew about the brutality that had happened in our country. It had been all over the news. Britain was also less complicit in Syria than in some of the other countries from which many people were fleeing, like Iraq and Afghanistan. Hence, we were put to the top of the list.

I was grateful but although I had suffered badly under the Syrian regime, this advantage still bothered me deeply. I felt again that guilt that still follows me around, to this day. What about all the others left behind? Or those who had made it to the UK in perilous circumstances but then were left in limbo without Leave to Remain? Unable to work or contribute or make tentative steps towards building a new life? I couldn't help thinking about them.

I came to Britain in the build-up to the Brexit referendum. It was something that I didn't want to see happening in a country I was trying to make my new home. In Syria one of the reasons that society had collapsed was because of how polarized it had become. Having fled such a divided society, I didn't want to see my new country, somewhere I had long idealized for its tolerance, split into two sides: Leave and Remain. Most of the referendum was centred around immigration. The Leave camp spoke of Turkey joining the EU and how that would mean millions of people would pour in from Syria. Then-leader of the UK Independence Party Nigel Farage stood in front of billboards with the phrase 'Breaking Point' printed over pictures of people who took the exact same route I had recently been on. I could have been on that poster. I was deeply disappointed by the rhetoric.

I was at Glastonbury when the results of the referendum came out. I'd gone with some of the new friends I had made in London and had the most wonderful time. I ended up accidentally getting stoned after I fell over and had to get my knee stitched up at a first aid centre. A couple camping next to me offered me a large cookie to cheer me up. I ate it all, not realizing that it was a space cookie and ended up getting pretty high!

The highlight was going to watch Coldplay headline the festival. I've always liked them, although I've discovered that everyone in Britain thinks they are cheesy. But it was a truly wonderful performance. Everyone was given wristbands and halfway through the set the bands all lit up, so it was like dancing in a crowd while surrounded by stars.

Despite how much fun I was having, one thing really disturbed me over the weekend. I walked past so many people who were saying 'I wish I'd voted.' I was so shocked that they hadn't. People don't realize the privilege they have here. You can vote and your vote counts. Your privilege is on the ballot. I have never voted in my life. I would love to vote and for my vote to matter.

It has been extremely saddening to see the country deteriorate in front of my eyes. The twenty-two countries of the Arab world share the same official language, have similar cultures and predominantly follow the same religion, but if I wanted to go from east to west, I would need about ten visas. There are so many differences in Europe and yet it had managed to unify. Britain already had a brilliant deal. It wasn't part of the euro and the Schengen Area. Its citizens could work, study and retire in any European country as if it were their own. I could not understand why some people were willing to vote to reduce such freedom.

It was inspirational to me and profoundly depressing to see it thrown away. And having witnessed extreme nationalism in Syria, it was disappointing to see the rise of nationalism here, with consequences like Brexit.

Before I came here, I had an idea of what democracy was. But I felt profoundly let down by the reality. Yes, Brexit was a democratic process but people made their choices based on lies, which was so upsetting to witness. And all the corruption I've seen under this current government isn't something that I thought would ever exist here. Inequality transcends borders. Having come so far and arrived here illegally, I had no idea that I'd find food banks and children struggling to get benefits.

Despite my growing political disenchantment, there was so much I was happy about. I loved being in London. I adore the tube. We don't have an underground in Damascus. I took pride in learning all the stops so that I didn't need to look at the map to navigate my way around. I spent a good chunk of my first days here living like a tourist. I went to all the museums, the food markets, wandered along the South Bank.

As part of my work to raise awareness about refugees I appeared on Victoria Derbyshire's TV programme and I met fellow-guest Josie. We went on to become friends and I started working with her charity Choose Love, which does a lot of work fundraising for refugees. It started with a hashtag on Twitter and has grown to be one of the most influential grassroots movements in the world, spreading a message of humanity towards those who are displaced. Through them, I did a shoot with a photographer called Greg Williams based in Mayfair. He asked me about what I'd done back home. I told him about taking pictures and how I'd filmed my journey.

'You should get back into that,' he said. Then he went into the cupboard in which he stored all his equipment and took out a Canon 5D camera, much like my beloved one I'd had at home. 'Take this,' he said. 'Start again.'

This gesture stuck with me. People don't want sympathy, they want opportunity. Refugees don't want people to pity them. They want internships, job opportunities, concrete offers. He helped me get back into photography by doing that. I began going onto the streets of London to take photographs much like I had in Damascus. Greg Williams didn't treat me as a victim and that meant so much to me.

THE FACE OF A CRISIS

Throughout this time I was in touch with Keo Films, the production company that I'd encountered in Calais. Their filmmakers had come to film me while I was living in Hitchin. I'd also gone to their offices on Old Street to meet the team. It was a thrilling experience for someone who wanted to be a filmmaker. I knew they were planning to use my footage in the documentary series they had been working on, about the journey of refugees to Europe. The prospect was very exciting.

The programme was called *Exodus: Our Journey to Europe* and was to be shown on BBC2 in the UK, Canal+ in France and PBS in America. I had sacrificed a lot to film my journey, from shoving a memory card up my bottom to spending money on camera equipment in the direst of circumstances. I had managed to keep the camera rolling even when I was afraid for my life: scrambling after a human trafficker crossing the Hungarian border, on a dinghy that was letting in water, in a van with a broken door being driven by a drunk man. It had been an absolute compulsion for me, to be honest. And I had always wanted people to see the reality. So they knew the truth. Now it was really going to happen.

A few days before *Exodus* aired on television, the production company showed it to me in the edit room. It was an odd feeling, sitting there in the darkness, seeing my journey – those things I'd lived through – played out on the screen. It made me emotional, but also really proud. My footage was going to raise awareness in just the way that I'd always intended.

Indeed, as soon as it was shown, *Exodus* created a buzz. People were so engaged. Overnight, people started recognizing me in the street. The day after the first episode went out, I took the tube from Brixton and a man opposite stared at me.

'All right, mate, aren't you the bloke from the boat?' he said.

'Yes, I am,' I said, incredulous.

'Well done, mate,' he said. 'Good on you.'

Soon it was happening almost everywhere I went. I was pleased that people had connected with the story but it was also strange, to be such a visible face of the refugee crisis. I became known as the guy from the boat. My looks and clothes have always meant that people don't necessarily think I'm from somewhere else. I am 'white passing', which has been another one of those advantages that can make me feel guilty at times. Yet suddenly, I was this extremely visible refugee.

I started doing even more talks, all over the world. I became the poster boy of the refugee crisis. The mayor of Porto asked me to speak there and I also went to Amsterdam, Madrid, Paris, New York. I enjoyed the travelling side of it. My story took me to many places and helped me to connect with people, and people to connect with the subject. I always managed to end with a call to action, and I knew I was influencing my audience. But every talk took it out of me. I was reliving my experience and, furthermore,

I constantly questioned if I deserved to earn money in that way. Increasingly the opportunities I was being presented with compounded my guilt and trauma.

The series started to win awards. Then it was nominated for a BAFTA award. We didn't necessarily have high expectations of winning but the prospect of attending the awards ceremony was so exciting. I bought myself a cheap black-tie outfit for seventy pounds. My hosts Rachel and Chris were really pleased for me and a little bit shocked, I think. I was too. The BAFTAs was the sort of awards ceremony that I used to watch back in Syria. I had never expected to be there myself, nominated for a film I'd made, walking the red carpet.

As we sat down in the audience, the series director James leant over.

'Hassan, if we win, we should both get up and say something,' he said. I wished I could have known earlier, to prepare something.

When they announced *Exodus*, I couldn't believe my ears. As usual, I was filming myself, and you can see the joy erupt across my face. I had only started documenting myself twenty months earlier with the view of recording a milestone in my life, but also countering the anti-migrant rhetoric that I was reading online. I had never expected to win a BAFTA for it.

I stood up and made a speech, off the cuff, about my intentions in making the film. It didn't actually get shown by the BBC – I think they thought it was too political. But I was proud of what I said, especially without having had time to prepare. It was a moment to get up on that stage, in front of the world.

I ended with this. 'Since we made that film, many people have died trying to claim asylum in Europe. The story is still ongoing. This award goes to the untold stories. While I've had the opportunity to tell my story, so many didn't.'

It was a great night. There were lots of celebrities milling around. I even went outside and smoked a spliff with a famous actor, which was absolutely surreal. I stayed up until four in the morning celebrating with the production team.

My parents were absolutely amazed. They couldn't believe it. They shared the news with everyone and my siblings kept texting me to congratulate me. Nobody in my family could quite believe that I'd managed to achieve this huge thing in Britain, so soon after arriving. I wasn't just a Syrian refugee now, I was a BAFTA-award-winning filmmaker.

Pouf. Just like that, my life changed again. I was suddenly asked to even more events. Things escalated. Sophie Dahl contacted Choose Love. She had suggested a feature idea to *Vogue* and wanted to interview a refugee. They put her in touch with me. We got along so well that she asked me out to lunch afterwards. It wasn't until I looked her up afterwards that I realized she was well known in Britain. From the start, she was incredibly kind, seeming to like me for myself rather than my story. The interview was beside the point – we became true friends. She asked me over to her house in a village outside London. I met Jamie her husband and have spent several Christmases with them. They have become like family to me. They never made me feel like the token refugee. They just took me as I was.

My speaking career had ratcheted up so much by this point that I was invited to talk at a large summit in Italy in August 2017. It was a high-status event based in a five-star hotel, with people parking their yachts nearby.

It was insane. Stuffed with A-list celebrities, the super-rich, CEOs of multinational companies and newspaper editors. I felt as if I had stumbled into a parallel universe. You could see the Italian police circling the whole area keeping the press out.

It was surreal. I felt as if the people in that hotel could literally eradicate global poverty if they felt like it. I had been on a sinking dinghy just over two years earlier and now I was milling around the fanciest of hotels. It was such a paradox. I talk about injustice a lot but I had found myself in a situation that most people never get to experience. To be honest, it didn't make me entirely comfortable but I wanted to experience it nonetheless.

I sat down for dinner on the first night.

'What do you do, then?' I asked the man sitting next to me. I didn't recognize him. Maybe he wasn't that rich or famous.

'Oh, I'm one of the co-founders of Twitter,' he said, casually.

'Cool,' I said, inwardly gobsmacked.

The next day I was in the lobby of the hotel when the actress Emma Watson approached me with her PA. We chatted briefly and I couldn't quite believe it. I have always been a fan of her activism and how she uses her platform to make the world a better place. Later in the day, I gave a talk which went down well. Emma gave the speech after mine and I listened with interest. In a Q&A afterwards, the female interviewer kept returning to the supposed controversy surrounding Emma's recent photoshoot with *Vanity Fair* magazine, in which the side of her cleavage was just visible. It had generated fierce debate online with some calling Emma 'anti-feminist' for the pose. Emma seemed visibly frustrated by the focus of the interview, trying to move the conversation on to another subject but the interviewer seemed unable – or unwilling – to do so. It gave me a sense of the unique pressures that a woman in Emma's position must face, where every move she makes is picked apart and analysed.

When the speeches were over, many of the people in the audience – including Emma – approached me to ask more questions. I was visibly shaken up, as I usually am when I recount my story, and Emma asked if I was getting any therapy, adding that she would be happy to arrange for me to get some. It was such an instinctively kind offer that when she asked for my feedback on her speech, I didn't do the usual celebrity-worshipping thing. I told her what I liked but also, crucially, what I didn't. I think she found my honesty refreshing. She even welled up a bit.

Because she was upset, I suggested that we borrow one of the Maseratis that were being loaned to guests and go for a drive. We were ushered into a convertible and I drove us around for an hour, as we listened to music. There I was, driving a car with Emma Watson through stunning countryside. I kept saying how surreal the whole experience was and so Emma started filming me on her mobile phone. We went back and that night we danced together at the hotel. It was so much fun.

The next day, a member of the Royal Family (I'll leave you to guess which one!) asked if we wanted to go to a yacht party. We went on this dinghy to get to it – me, him and Emma. As we were moving through the water, he got out his key chain.

'I'm going to puncture this dinghy. You'll know what to do won't you?' he said, laughing uproariously.

'That's a really dumb joke,' I said, with a poker-straight face.

'Sorry. I'm so sorry,' he said.

'Don't worry. I'm playing you,' I said, breaking into laughter. It honestly didn't bother me. I could tell he was trying his best to put me at ease with his teasing and I liked the fact he hadn't tiptoed around my past. Perhaps it wasn't a great joke, but I teased him back and warmed to him. We're still in touch now and we occasionally exchange emails.

The yacht party was really glitzy and we didn't stay for that long. None of us was comfortable with it so we made a decision to go back. Wealth inequality is everything that is wrong with the world and while it was an experience to have a glimpse of that kind of lavish lifestyle, it didn't sit entirely well with me.

Back in the UK, my friendship with Emma grew. We went to a music festival together and she introduced me to her friends. We have a shared passion for photography and films. I made her hummus one day and she loved it. We would usually spend time at her house because she didn't want to go out and be recognized. One time, I'd been to a wedding in Nottingham and she picked me up from the train station when I got back into London. We decided to go for a walk on Hampstead Heath.

'Do you think people will mob me?' she said, as we drove. 'I'll wear my sunglasses and hopefully it will be okay.' I had seen how bad it was when people crowded around her, but I reassured her that it would be fine.

We got to the Heath and three people stopped us. But the hilarious thing was that they had recognized me, not her.

'Hassan, we saw you in your film.' None of them clocked Emma at my side. We both laughed about that.

I felt so comfortable in her company. I told her about my life back home, the shoebox that I'd left behind forever in my bedroom, full of all my most treasured mementoes. Shortly afterwards, she sent me a shoebox in the post, containing a jasmine-scented candle, books, an elegant pen and a beautiful, heartfelt letter. It was such a sweet gesture. She went above and beyond to be supportive.

Although I found forming friendships easy enough, I struggled with dating in London. I had suddenly become recognized, but for being on a sinking boat. It really played with my head. I never knew what people wanted from me. I was defined by being a refugee, but that had only been eighty-seven days in the course of my entire life. It didn't define me. I also had no idea how to deal with British women. I would google questions about how to approach girls in this country. In Damascus you would invite someone to dinner and be upfront, but here the terms of engagement were so unclear. Girls would say they wanted to 'hang out' and I didn't understand what that meant.

Although it looked to the outside as if I'd been having a lot of fun, I started to struggle with my mental health. The gap between the glamorous things I had experienced and my difficult journey was disorientating. And running behind my day-to-day life was a thread of desperate homesickness. Sometimes I would ring the number of our flat in Damascus. The phone was in our sitting room and for a second or two I could picture it, I'd be transported there. It would comfort me briefly. Yet a deep sadness lay behind everything that I was doing.

I also had specific symptoms. Repetitive nightmares. Flashbacks to the torture. I was constantly triggered – a loud noise or a man in uniform could make me freeze in a state of absolute anxiety. One day, the series producer of *Exodus*, a woman called Jane, noticed this and sent me a link about the symptoms of PTSD.

'Hassan, I think you should read that,' she said. I read the article and it was like a light bulb going on my brain. I had every symptom that was outlined. I finally had a name for what I was going through. It was a moment of sheer reprieve. Knowing that PTSD is a recognized phenomenon, shared by so many, cast my symptoms in a totally new light. I felt so relieved but I wondered if I would ever be able to beat it.

In 2018, I went to see my family in Georgia. After three years of not seeing them since I'd arrived in Britain, I couldn't bear it any more. I started looking up the logistics of how I could arrange to see them again. While my British refugee travel document gave me good options, at the time, their Syrian passports meant that only four countries were on the cards – Sudan, the Bahamas, Georgia and Malaysia. Sudan didn't really hold much appeal, while the Bahamas and Malaysia were really expensive. I was paying for my parents so such destinations weren't really possible. Georgia seemed the best option. It's affordable and in between us geographically, so not a long flight for anyone. I was really excited. After we made the reservations, I started counting down the days. We booked a flat in downtown Tbilisi. I looked for one with a nice balcony, to remind us of home. We ended up spending a lot of time on that balcony, just as we had on the one from our apartment. The view over the streets of Tbilisi was rather different than that over Damascus, but it brought back some of the same feelings.

I arrived a couple of hours before everyone else. Our reunion at the airport was deeply emotional. Everyone was crying and hugging. My youngest sister and brother couldn't come so it wasn't a full reunion. The last time we were actually all together was 2012. But it was so wonderful to be able to embrace my family members. To hear their voices and see their beloved faces.

We had the best time in Tbilisi. We went for walks and hired a car. My nephew, Zaid, and niece, Maria, had never seen snow before. Watching them run around, scooping it into snowballs, with an expression of absolute wonder on their faces was really special.

I had so much to talk about with my family. So much had happened since the last time I saw them. The hardest bit was saying goodbye at the airport. Zaid would not let go of me. They literally had to prise him out of my arms in the airport hall. It broke my heart. It was so nice, but it was too short. It brought up all the things I miss about living as part of a large and happy family.

That was the only time in the last five years that I've seen them. And despite how wonderful it was, it also made me realize how much I've changed during that period. I'm much more liberal politically than my family now. I've travelled, lectured, attended talks, listened to podcasts, watched documentaries, seen a therapist – had all these experiences, which have shifted my view of the world.

Growing up in Syria, I didn't have a lexicon to describe things like mental health or homosexuality. And, in many ways, my parents still don't. I tried to tell them that I had PTSD once, via WhatsApp of course because that's how so many of our interactions happen. The diagnosis was deeply significant for me and it helped to explain much of what I was going through. Sadly, my parents just couldn't understand it. They told me I should turn to Allah. I tried to explain that PTSD is an illness, like having the flu. But they still didn't get it. And then I gave up because I realized that our perceptions are fundamentally based on our experiences. It wasn't fair to demand that they see things as I do.

OWNING MY OWN NARRATIVE

After *Exodus* aired, Keo Films offered me a job as a researcher working on the second series of the programme. At the time, I was really pleased. This was my break. I threw myself into it, learning everything I could from researching to casting and contacting contributors, as well as data analysis, determined to do the very best job that I could. It meant going back out to Calais and Greece, the places I had been to on my own journey, to find new contributors willing to share their stories and document how the situation had changed.

I relished the opportunity to travel knowing that I had a document now which meant I wasn't stuck anymore. A piece of paper had changed my life forever.

And I knew the story wasn't over. I felt a responsibility. There were still so many people fleeing trauma, sleeping on the steps of that church in Calais, cutting their fingers on barbed wire, queueing for clothes and food. If anything, things had only become more difficult as Europe had shut and militarized its borders. Revisiting those places, I saw that they were much more static than they had been. People couldn't move through as quickly. There were people in limbo on a Greek island for years rather than weeks. Living in squats in Serbia because they couldn't get any further.

Since I'd arrived in Britain, Turkey had signed a deal with the EU which meant that people could technically be returned from Greece to Turkey. This pivotal agreement has had profound repercussions. Essentially, the EU paid Turkey six billion euros to stop people from crossing the Aegean Sea, and afterwards pointed the finger at Turkey, as if Europe itself wasn't completely complicit in the securitization of its borders and the consequent deaths that occurred daily during the crossings. That March 2016 deal had changed everything. I was there when they demolished the Jungle in Calais in October 2016, which was profoundly triggering because I witnessed people fleeing with their rucksacks on their backs. Afterwards they were forced to live in squalid makeshift camps in the woods. By then my friend's Choose Love charity had warehouses in Calais and Greece. There was a new infrastructure in place to help people, but politically speaking things had become so much more difficult.

I even saw people in Calais who were still around from my own time there, stuck in the holding pattern of desperately trying to get to the UK and failing.

Despite all the efforts I'd made, unfortunately not one of my contributors from Calais and Greece made the final cut of the second series of *Exodus* and nobody really explained why. Although I'd been honoured to do the work, I don't think anyone at management level at the production company quite realized how devastating it was to go back to those places. Of course, there were lots of individual freelancers from my experience working on *Exodus* that I really liked and remain in touch with, but I was very disappointed not to get clear answers.

The experience underscored a growing sense of disappointment with how the company saw me. Even though the team meant well generally, I felt I was used as a mere token by them. They couldn't take me seriously as a filmmaker – despite using all my footage. They didn't pay me, or even give me a proper credit. I was given an 'extra footage' mention when my work was integral to the film and I should have been credited as a co-director. It is frustrating that, despite their best intentions, I was pigeonholed as a refugee – confined to be the subject of a film rather than a filmmaker or co-creator. Most people in exile are highly educated, resilient and ambitious. We aspire to professional success as much as anyone. The notion that we should be grateful to work for free is insulting.

But it's important to remember that claiming asylum shouldn't be dependent on how much someone goes on to contribute to their new community. Asylum is a fundamental human right, and the willingness to offer it speaks volumes about a society's values.

My personal sense of discomfort began when I was interviewed for the programme. At the time, I said quite clearly that I didn't want to talk too much about Syria, or to end up crying. I felt that the footage spoke for itself. I didn't want to just be the victim. Despite how emphatic I was, they showed me a clip of my boat crossing before I started talking and of course I ended up crying, which is what I had really hoped to avoid. I felt manipulated.

I've since discovered that they did the same thing with at least one other person featured in *Exodus*. They re-traumatized someone, in order to get the exact reaction that they wanted for the film. I think their intentions to raise awareness were sincere but their methods in hindsight seem cynical. The stories were enough in their own right. I had almost died making the footage and I desperately wanted to make the film successful to challenge people's perceptions, but that didn't mean that I wanted to lose all control over how I was portrayed. I felt that somehow they wanted to reduce my role to that of a mere participant even though my footage was crucial to the film's award-winning content. I felt that I had unwittingly been stripped of my authorship.

After my work on the second series of *Exodus* was finished, Keo Films gave me a list of other production companies I could apply to for work experience. Even though I had an incredible start, it was impossible for me to get a foot in the door. I must have sent thousands of CVs, literally, yet I struggled to find work.

I had been a photographer for so long and I knew I had a knack for storytelling. And I wanted to use my skills to make other films, about important issues. Subjects that matter. This is still my ultimate ambition now. I didn't want to be forever stereotyped as simply a refugee. I knew I had more to offer. Not being able to progress and the rejection from all the production companies compounded the mental health problems I was already experiencing, triggering a period of depression that is still hard for me to revisit.

During this period, I was doing some work as a consultant on a comedy programme about a refugee called *Home* that Channel Four were making. I was also working on more shoots, as well as helping my friend Imad, the friend I'd made in Paris, with his pop-up kitchen to raise money for refugees. I was manning the fryer, organizing volunteers, and helping him with social media. I got to be an expert at stuffing falafel boxes, spraying tahini and chilli. I could practically do it in my sleep. It was really successful, raising almost 200,000 pounds for refugees, but it wasn't my life's ambition.

I moved out of the house in Brixton with Rachel and Chris after a year, hoping to give another refugee the opportunity to use the room. And after a brief stint in Shepherd's Bush, I moved into a flat-share in East London, paying £900 a month for a tiny room. I'd wanted to feel independent, to make my own way, but I hated that place. I didn't get on that well with my new flatmates and I spent much of the time feeling lonely.

I was lost. I didn't know what to do in my life. I sank deeper into depression and even became suicidal again, with feelings of hopelessness and dread consuming my waking hours. I would call the Samaritans and someone would pick up, but I then found I couldn't say anything. I found it so hard to articulate what I was going through. England wasn't the place I'd thought it was going to be. Although I'd made some wonderful friends, I'd found it hard to connect with people day to day. I didn't have my family around. Ninety per cent of the people in my life at that point were only interested in me because of my dramatic story. I couldn't escape this because there was a documentary being shared around the world that repeated my escape story again and again. What's more, I felt compelled to keep sharing it because of the guilt that dogged me, and the sense that I owed it to other refugees to keep bearing witness to their predicament.

These feelings led to a kind of collapse. I'd had some therapy when I was working on the second series of *Exodus*, when I'd realized I had PTSD, but it hadn't been that effective. I even reached the point of searching online for 'What is the easiest way to kill yourself?' I had got to the place where I was safe, physically, but I felt deeply uncomfortable within myself and hopeless.

We have a WhatsApp group for our family, called the 'Akkadians'. Even though we chat every day, I couldn't tell them how bad I felt. Eventually, I told my sister Dania individually and she then told everyone else. She contacted Redwan, who started calling me every day from Cologne to check that I was okay. Despite this visible display of love and support from those closest to me, I still felt terrible. Looking back, I believe that the loss of control I felt in my dealings with the production company really triggered my PTSD.

I'm a big believer in karma though. Later, after my work in the pandemic and a video message to Boris Johnson in support of the hospital cleaners and porters went viral and my life changed overnight, I had plenty of production companies contacting me, including Keo Films. I turned them down. One of the things that I really want to demonstrate is that people have the right to tell their own stories. To own their own narratives. Western film-makers have to be careful not to exploit their contributors. It's so important to maintain high standards of ethics.

AL-MAWADDA

I'm lucky with my friendships. From Redwan spurring me on to get my university degree in Damascus despite everything, to the support of Aghiad and Alaa on our long journey across Europe, my close friends have lifted me up repeatedly in the most difficult of times.

Ultimately, when I had my mental health crisis, it was friendship again that saved me – but this time the support of some of the incredible people I've met since coming to Britain really made the difference. In Arabic, we use the word *al-mawadda* to describe friendship and intimacy, which is exactly what they gave me.

I've been shown so much kindness and support by Josie, whose wonderful charity Choose Love promotes empathy and helps people to better understand the plight of refugees. And through Josie, I met two of my other closest friends – Gabriel and Heydon. I have significant trust issues because of what has happened to me, but my connection with all three of them has always felt very natural.

Heydon is a comedian and Gabriel an art dealer. They are both extremely well-educated and undeniably privileged, but also incredibly sweet. They share a sarcastic sense of humour and never walk on eggshells around me, but I prefer that and I've learnt a lot from them. It's no exaggeration to say that they've helped me to navigate British culture. Remember, I arrived without a clue of how normal life works in this country. My lack of knowledge used to make me so anxious about getting things wrong; when you claim asylum you aren't handed a leaflet telling you how to pay taxes, or to use the post office or the self-service checkout tills at the supermarket. I remember asking Heydon what I should do if I get stopped by a police officer, a scenario that played on my mind because of how frequently it happened in Damascus. He told me that I had the right to ask why I was being stopped, which would have never occurred to me. He and Gabriel gave me a crash course in British life and helped me to understand the system. I'm so grateful to them for that.

And when I began to struggle with my mental health, they both realised that something was wrong. Heydon suggested that we go to stay at Gabriel's parents' house in Switzerland for a holiday. I didn't know exactly what to expect but it turned out to be the most wonderful trip and helped me begin to get better. We didn't have mobile phone reception for most of the time and so we were able to really disconnect, digitally. I always feel better when I'm in nature. We were in the Alps and every day we went on amazing hikes in pine forests and skinny-dipping in crystal-clear ponds. We walked bare-foot, the grass warm under the soles of our feet. It was like heaven, the heaven my parents described to me when I was a small child.

I found myself opening up to both of them about how hard it had been, to reconcile my survivor's guilt, my PTSD, the discrepancy between the difficulties I had endured and the occasionally glamorous existence I now found myself living, a life which – for all its successes – was still one of exile.

Heydon asked me if I thought I might be depressed. I had to ask him what he meant. At that point, I still didn't have much of a mental health lexicon. He explained and helped me to connect the dots. Both he and Gabriel reminded me of what I had already accomplished and promised me that, with time, things would definitely improve.

The pleasure of being in such an amazing place, with such good friends, had already reminded me of how it felt to be happy. For the first time in a long time, I felt hopeful about the future.

The improvement in my mood even gave me the courage to get in touch with a woman I liked through Instagram. I'd been following her for a while and she seemed beautiful and intelligent, so I messaged her while I was away and asked if she would like to meet up.

We had our first date when I got back from Switzerland and, from the start, I knew the relationship with her was going to be important to me. We became friends and – over time – it developed into a love affair. I am not identifying her in this book because – sadly and despite our best efforts – our relationship has now ended. But I didn't want to erase this chapter in my story entirely because it was so significant.

You see, after everything that happened to me – the torture and abuse, my perilous journey and separation from my family – I wasn't entirely convinced that I would be able to truly fall in love. I never had before, despite meeting many women that I really liked. So, it was just the most wonderful feeling to tumble headfirst into romantic love for the first time in my life and to understand that I was capable of it, despite all the hardships I'd endured. As our relationship developed, I could feel my perception of myself shifting and my survivor's guilt lifting.

For the first time since coming to Britain, I had someone to see on a daily basis. My partner soon became the security that I had lost. Home gives you love and protection; she was all of that for me. After dating for a while, we moved in together. I really enjoyed building a home with her and cooking meals, trying out a more domestic life for the first time since I'd been forced to pack up my things from the apartment in Maysat Square. It was an intensely happy time of my life and I will always remember it with the greatest fondness and gratitude. Finding that love made me whole again.

Just as I enjoy having friends with different political opinions and alternative perspectives, I also want to have friends from different communities because it's a way of understanding and learning. While I love my British friends and the window into the culture they afford me, I also have got lots of Syrian friends in the UK.

I see Imad, Aghiad and Alaa, of course, but since coming here I also met a man called Ayman who lives nearer me in London. He came from the Syrian city of Aleppo and was smuggled into Britain in a suitcase. Ayman is five years younger than me, but we have grown incredibly close. He is also a self-taught filmmaker and started working in shisha bars back home to earn enough money to buy a camera. He is doing really well, making content for different organisations, but during the pandemic work was slow and so he earned money as a Deliveroo driver. That's what I love about him – he's a hustler and he doesn't give up. We often go to the gym together and we talk on a daily basis. If one of us is having a dip, he is encouraged by the other. Unsurprisingly after his traumatic journey here, Ayman also has PTSD and his life has been transformed by the recognition of this and the therapy he has had for the last two years. He means so much to me. We understand the nuances of Syrian culture and it's a relief to be close to someone who knows how it feels to be so far away from our families.

I feel lucky to have such strong bonds with my friends. All of them contributed to my recovery. They've become nothing less than my replacement family and, just like a loving family, they picked me up when I needed it most.

THE PRICE OF EXILE

As my mental health recovered, I reflected on the reasons it deteriorated so much in the first place. The honest truth is that I miss being embedded in my own culture. I really like it here but I can never feel totally at ease. When you live in exile, everything is heightened. If you feel bad, it spirals quickly. If you worry about your family, you start to imagine you might never see them again. Then you ask yourself the question – was it worth it? I came here so that any future children I have won't have to go through what I went through. So that I could pursue a career that I am passionate about in a language I was already familiar with. But you have to weigh such freedoms against living away from family and never having complete normality again. I'm safe and able to be the active member of society that I always wanted to be but couldn't in Syria because of the regime. Yet the price has been incredibly high.

The most difficult part about living in exile is the impossibility of ever rebuilding the life you lost in its entirety somewhere else. This was really brought home to me when my brother and one of my sisters got married. Weddings are so important in our culture. You are bringing two families under one roof. For the ceremony itself, about four hundred people are invited, there is a feast and so many customs. It's such a remarkable thing. The women join together for a henna night. On the wedding day, they dance and sing alongside the large drums, while men chant loudly to celebrate the union of the bride and groom in something called an *arada*. I'm good at it if I do say so myself, and I always imagined that I would be leading the *arada* with my father at my brother's wedding. But when Bassel got married in Iraq I couldn't even get a visa to go. Instead of a grand Syrian wedding, he had a low-key reception in a restaurant with around forty people. I couldn't attend when Ghalia, my youngest sister, got married either. I was so upset. I was on the phone all day, just waiting for my family to send me videos. We had hoped to connect over Zoom, but we couldn't pin the right time to do it because of the time difference.

I felt so sad to be missing these key days in my siblings' lives. It was hard but this is our reality. This is what it's like to be a refugee, to live in exile. We won't ever get these family moments again and they are all so different from how I'd always imagined they'd be. When my sister gave birth to my nephew there were twenty people ready to step in and help out at any point, but if I have children now I will never have that experience. It still hurts a lot, but I have learnt more about recognising and processing the pain.

When coronavirus hit, it made life for people in Britain something similar to what it is always like for people who have been displaced. I started thinking about this when people described the pandemic as the 'greatest equalizer'. I don't agree with that sentiment at all. Rather, this crisis has exposed the inequalities that exist in our society. Covid will go, but these injustices won't. The virus will be dealt with eventually, but refugees will carry on living separated from their loved ones because of the documents they have or the ones they don't have.

The world is divided into people who can move freely and those who can't. The immigration system is what pushes people into taking dangerous routes into Europe. Sometimes this has the very worst of consequences.

On the morning of 23 October 2019, news broke that a lorry containing thirty-nine dead people had been found at Waterglade Industrial Park in Grays, Essex. Politicians quickly began referring to the incident as a case of 'people trafficking'. But this terminology, often used for people who have tried to get into the UK, is deeply problematic to me. None of those involved was actually charged with trafficking offences in the end. For that, certain criteria need to be met and they weren't.

The choice of language was deeply political. It encourages the public to lay the blame at the feet of traffickers, who are undoubtedly criminals, rather than blaming harmful migration policies, which force people to take unnecessary risks. Those people who died in the van had made rational decisions to try and improve their lives and those of their families. They had agency. They took a risk but it might well have paid off. If there had been a safe and legal route open to them, they would obviously have taken it. Bandying about the word 'trafficking' and describing them merely as victims of it is a cynical way of legitimizing – and distracting – from policies that trap so many in intolerable circumstances.

During the pandemic, many people had a taste of what it's like to have their travel possibilities restricted. To yearn to see loved ones but remain unable to do so. To long for a holiday but have to stay put. But just imagine if being unable to move around the world freely was your everyday reality? That's how it is for so many people.

Attending weddings and funerals on Zoom was our normal long before coronavirus arrived. All of this familial separation is why when the virus came to the UK, I perhaps found it easier than many to understand the implications and how our lives would change. In contrast, my close friends in London were so shocked that they couldn't go where they wanted, couldn't see their families. For them, it was a new feeling, but for me it was achingly familiar.

Every Christmas my British friends complain about going to see their family for three days and I find it really difficult to understand their attitude. They don't know how lucky they are. There is such a different approach towards family in this country. Of course, I argued with my siblings and parents when I was growing up, but I really enjoy my family's company and can't think of anything better than seeing them. In Syria there is no welfare state and every Syrian I know sends money home. Parents have multiple children as a safety net for the future because they won't be able to claim benefits. This was one of the reasons that I really felt pressure to sort myself out after arriving in Britain. I wasn't only responsible for myself, I also needed to look after my parents. I miss them every day.

A NEW CRISIS

As soon as news emerged of a mysterious illness in Wuhan, my anxiety levels rose. My emotions were like a rollercoaster. I read every article about it and watched every news report. There was footage of people collapsing in the street and I couldn't help but think that something extremely serious was coming our way. That danger radar I mentioned earlier was activated.

Everyone around me was taking it lightly. People were posting jokey memes and saying that it wasn't going to be worse than something like SARS. They seemed to feel that it was such a long way away, a different continent, it could never reach us here in Britain. But I couldn't muster the same sense of steadfast security. I had previously been in a situation where the unimaginable happened. Where all previous certainties had fallen apart, the life I thought I'd looked forward to taken away without warning. I knew that such things were, in fact, eminently possible.

Among my growing fears was a certain disappointment, too. I felt as if I'd escaped danger after fleeing Syria. Put simply, I'd been mortally afraid and now I no longer was. When I came to England

I reasoned to myself: what's the worst that could happen? There was no war. It was a democracy. What could possibly put my life at risk? But this virus had the capacity to change all of that. And so it did. A new, airborne enemy. Not able to break my bones, like Assad's men, but potentially just as lethal.

I was still doing some filming. Every time I went to work, people would be talking about the virus. I went to a shoot and read that there had been a case in Canary Wharf. I sat outside in my car listening to LBC radio. Knowing that this virus was out in London was incredibly frightening. I knew that it was only a matter of time before it became a full-on crisis. I was certain. There were all these people coming back from skiing trips in Italy and France, obviously bringing it with them. They were arriving at the airport without being stopped, going back to their families and towns and workplaces as if nothing was happening.

I began losing my mind. My thoughts really began to spiral and I decided that I needed to prepare myself for disaster. At this point, in mid-March, nobody knew what was coming next but I decided that I should leave London and try to go somewhere safe. I was so scared of being back in the place of fearing for my life, that I resolved to take action.

As you probably know by now, one of the things I hate most is a lack of agency. If something is happening outside my control then it really freaks me out. The pandemic did exactly that. Even joining the anti-Assad protests or on my journey to Europe, I had felt I was in control. Yes, there were risks, but I was able to make decisions and be in charge of myself. This was impossible against coronavirus. And not only could I not control my immediate circumstances but I had no way of ensuring my family, spread across the world, was safe, either. They all seemed far too relaxed about the threat for my liking. I constantly sent my siblings articles about coronavirus and video called my parents to tell them to be careful. That this thing was real, that it could affect them. They told me they would be fine. They would pray. I was exasperated but eventually I gave up. I was only increasing their anxiety levels.

I decided to leave London for the countryside. I had already given up one city almost overnight. Leaving this new one would be comparatively easy. London was so crowded, I knew that it would be only a matter of time before there was an immense strain on hospital beds. At that stage it was what everyone was most worried about. If the NHS ran out of intensive care beds – or ventilators – then decisions would have to be made about who received treatment.

By that point, we had seen footage of people trapped in their houses in Italy. The idea of being confined to the small one-bedroom flat in Leytonstone that I'd moved into by then, was deeply troubling. I knew that there was no way I could do it.

I decided to visit my friend Juliette who lived in Canterbury. Juliette was a friend that I had met in the Jungle in Calais. We had become close and I had been to visit her in Canterbury before and liked it there. When she had seen how stressed I was becoming, Juliette had offered me the opportunity to stay for a while.

I drove to Canterbury. I had bought a car in 2017 because I often need to drive for work outside of London. There wasn't a plan. I didn't know how long I was going for. What I would do when I got there. I had just been struck by an overwhelming urge to be somewhere else. The countryside. I was chasing an illusion of safety. The idea that there was anywhere you could go and hide.

Juliette's mother had made up a spare bedroom for me. A clean duvet cover, flowers in a vase. I was so touched by the effort. But after only about half an hour, I felt deeply uncomfortable. Everyone knew by then that the virus was riskier for older people and I felt worried about the potential risk this posed to Juliette's parents. So I awkwardly made my apologies and said I felt as if I had made the wrong decision. I left soon afterwards, not even staying for one night.

The drive back into London was surreal. Spring was in touching distance and the day was drawing out. But the city already was oddly quiet. Altered somehow. Nobody knew what the immediate future held. I felt a simmering panic about what was to come next. About being stuck within my tiny living space indefinitely, with no way of distracting myself. Since what happened to me in Syria, I always need to keep myself busy. It's become my way of coping.

That's when I remembered that taking action and helping other people always makes me feel better about difficult events. It was a lesson I'd learnt from my teaching days in Damascus, when I changed from being a bit of a thug to a committed teacher. One that I'd applied to the injustice I had seen under the Syrian regime and then later, in leading a group of people looking for better lives in Europe. Having purpose and moral accountability changes everything. It makes for a better, more meaningful life. Deep down, I knew that fleeing and trying to secure my own personal safety was the wrong thing to do. For my community but ultimately also for myself.

After that, I applied myself to how I could best help in my local area. In the few months since moving there I had grown to love Leytonstone. It was somewhere that I felt comfortable. There is a modest but charming high street, exemplifying London's wonderful diversity. The Halal butcher where I go to get my meat, not for religious reasons but simply because it tastes better. The Indian grocer with the bowls full of fruit and vegetables ranged on a table outside. The cafe run by an Algerian, where I go for coffee and a chat. At that time, I was freelancing and I had plenty of time on my hands. I went on Twitter and tweeted, 'I'm in Leytonstone with a car. If anyone needs anything – just let me know.' I didn't get much of a response and a friend suggested an app, where you could deliver food and medications for people who were self-isolating. I downloaded it and started doing some of the jobs. The people were generally elderly, but there were also pregnant women, those with chronic health problems. From voices on intercoms, glances through windows, I could tell how anxious everyone was.

It was hardly surprising. The disaster was unfolding all around us without anyone taking charge. The politicians clearly had no idea what they were doing. Some shops were shutting and people were queueing outside others. Many shelves were bare. I would go to a large Asda late at night, when I knew it would be quiet, and be struck by the devastation. From plenty to scarcity in a heartbeat. Things can change so quickly. My life has shown me this time and time again.

I wasn't immune to the urge to hoard. I had even done my own version of a panic shop, driving to an Arabic store in West London to buy lots of hummus, fava beans, dried figs, a massive twenty-kilogram bag of basmati rice – and lots of dates. As a Syrian, I adore dates. I had taken many with me on my journey to Europe and so I thought they would be a good thing to have around to help face this fresh uncertainty.

After lockdown was announced, I stayed at home but kept on doing the delivery jobs for people in the area. In helping them, I was helping myself because it meant I could leave the flat. And yet, I could feel my mental health – which had started to recover in the eighteen months since my trip to Switzerland – begin to fray. I'd truly felt safe in London and was building a life to be proud of, building friendships and working on my career. But deep fear was back in my life, both devastating and intensely familiar. The trauma response kicked in quickly thanks to the scars of PTSD. I wasn't sleeping. I would lie in the darkness and shut my eyes, willing it to happen, but then I'd think about my parents in Sharjah in the UAE. My brother in Erbil. Or my grand-mother still in Damascus. I was confident that if coronavirus hit Syria, the results would be a disaster. It would spell complete economic ruin and the collapse of whatever fragments of normal society remained. Medical facilities had been bombed by the Assad regime and the Russians in all the rebel-held areas. If Londoners were worrying about a shortage of hospital beds, it was nothing compared to Damascus.

I resolved to do more. I couldn't help my family. But I could help others, just as I'd want someone to help those I love in my absence. The deliveries were something, but they weren't enough. I needed to go a step further.

That's how I found myself searching online for ways to help the NHS. I found the job listing looking for cleaners and porters and decided to ring the agency number. The female voice on the phone told me cleaning was in high demand. It was essential work and they were looking for people to start straight away. I asked about portering and she told me that meant moving dead bodies around the hospital, so I decided to stick with cleaning. Yes, I wanted to help, but I wasn't sure that I could face trans-porting corpses. I expressed my concerns about PPE since by this time in March 2020, many clinical staff had already died. But the call handler reassured me that I would definitely be provided with it.

I was still unsure if I was going to go ahead. But then she

mentioned the extreme need at Whipps Cross, somewhere I walked by every day during my allotted daily exercise. It was just ten minutes' walk from my house. It seemed clear to me that this was the way I could contribute directly to my neighbours. In the weeks since the pandemic had started, the sense of local community had swelled, with people clapping on their doorsteps for the NHS. This was the way in which I could do my bit.

The wage offered was eight pounds and forty pence an hour: two pounds below London minimum wage to risk your life in a Covid-19 ward. I still don't know how they are able to offer that. For me, it was something I wanted to do to help, out of a sense of personal responsibility, but for so many others, it was a way of buying food for their children, paying their bills, surviving. This inequity in a society simply doesn't make sense. Coronavirus showed just how essential so many low-paid jobs are, from wheeling away bodies, to delivering groceries, and cleaning toilets. We have got something gravely wrong if we don't value the very people helping to maintain the infrastructure of our society. It was also clear to me that cleaning was at the very heart of the crisis. So much was still unknown but decontaminating surfaces seemed like such a direct way of combating the spread of the disease.

I've been asked several times if I felt that taking on the cleaning role was my way of 'paying back' my adopted community. The answer is both no and yes. The right to seek asylum and freedom from torture is innate and inalienable. My refugee status is also my right under international humanitarian law. Refugees like me shouldn't have to 'earn' protection twice. I volunteered to work at the hospital and if I hadn't made that decision, I would still be just as entitled to my asylum status.

However, as a proud Londoner, I did feel it was my duty to support my community. If we come together in kindness and love, wherever we're from and whatever we look like, we can fundamentally reshape this world.

FINDING COURAGE

Despite walking past it so many times, I had never been into the maze of Whipps Cross, with its forbidding Victorian buildings in their dark-red brick. I kept away from hospitals. As a young man, I hadn't had much need for them in my life before. Apart from that one time in Damascus. And on that occasion, the abuse I had received had completely destroyed my trust.

I still can't lift my left wrist properly. The range of movement will be impaired for the rest of my life. Sometimes, when I'm tired, it starts to ache. I can imagine the day will come when I'm an older man that it causes me more trouble. Instead of observing a doctor's duty of care, the man in the military hospital that I was taken to left me a lifetime reminder of his absolute contempt.

With my PTSD as a legacy, you can understand, then, my abject terror on that first morning that I arrived at Whipps Cross. It was two days after I made the initial call to the agency on the phone. I had been told to turn up for an interview. I stood outside the reception, steeling myself for a good ten minutes before I went inside. I knew that I wanted to help, to contribute, to do something practical. My reasons were well intentioned and compelling. But nonetheless, fear coiled in my gut.

Historic fear from what had happened to me in Syria combined with fresh fear about coronavirus, making it quite a heady cocktail in my bloodstream. Everyone in Britain knew how dire the situation was. That was the point when infections were starting to run out of control but doctors still had very little knowledge about how to treat serious cases. We had all seen the news footage of doctors in intensive care wards talking about the techniques they were trying, people in the background lying on their stomachs to boost blood oxygen levels, hooked up to all sorts of monitors.

Eventually, after reminding myself again why I was there, I managed to walk inside. I was greeted by a scene of total mayhem. It was chaos. There were people everywhere. The chairs were all full and a queue for reception ran around the corner of the room. The temperature was semi-tropical and the terror almost tangible. I felt like walking out again immediately. I yearned to get back to my cosy flat with its comforting cooking smells and carefully chosen posters on the walls.

I stayed. Eventually I spoke to a receptionist and she sent me to an office on the ground floor from where a company called Serco hired cleaners and porters, telling me to speak to the trainer. He was the man who was to give us an induction and he was one of the meanest people I have ever met in my life. In his defence, everyone was frightened at that point but he definitely didn't make things easier or inject any humanity into the situation.

I was supposed to be interviewed – that was what I'd been told on the phone – but instead was just taken directly to an induction with a group of ten others. Some people wanted to help the NHS, some needed the money, some both – our motives were mixed.

There were two teachers, an out-of-work actress, someone who had worked in HR. The trainer walked us through a ward and then sat us down. He gave everyone a booklet about the situation.

Then he started talking. An aggressive monologue that appeared to demonstrate only deep contempt for all of us. Phrases like, 'This is a very stressful time, so if a doctor or nurse yells at you, don't be offended. Just go to the toilet to cry.' 'You can't speak to one another in your native tongue.' 'If you can't follow the rules, I will walk you out of the hospital myself.' 'This is a serious job.' 'Three people quit just yesterday.'

Yet there was much that he didn't say. He didn't tell us about PPE. Or that we would see people on oxygen gasping for breath. Or witness people dying every day. That the job we were doing was vital to keep the hospital running. That there was still so much that the doctors didn't know themselves.

We moved on to a ward that was being prepared for new patients. It was a new area they were prepping and we were to clean the entire room as a trial. The trainer told us to disinfect every inch of the bed and all the hot spots – light switches, sinks, door handles, every touchable inch. Then he watched us doing it, occasionally interjecting with a comment. We all tried hard, but he didn't seem pleased with what any of us were doing.

The induction session lasted four hours and we had a break in the middle. I got chatting to a girl in her twenties who was one of the teachers. She told me she felt as if she were going mad at home, that she just wanted to do something to help. But she didn't like the way in which the trainer was speaking to us. Two or three people at the induction never came back. There was also a Polish guy who shrugged his shoulders and walked away, never to be seen again. I could understand why. It seemed as if the hospital had no idea what was going on. The trainer was rude. There was no sense that we would be protected or that what we were doing would be valued.

After the induction was finished, I went to the office to be assigned my shifts. I was given 7 a.m. to 3:30 p.m. every day. Then I went to reception again and had my picture taken. Afterwards, I was handed my NHS badge on a lanyard with my new job title: 'domestic assistant'. It made me so proud to be part, in however humble a manner, of such an amazing institution. I left the hospital and sent a selfie of me and my badge to my friend Heydon. He was frankly amazed. When I'd told him that I was going to get a cleaning job, he hadn't believed me. I also sent one to Josie. 'Hassan, I'm so proud of you,' she texted back.

The next day was my first official shift. I rose early and arrived at the office on the ground floor. The woman in there looked at her list.

'You're going to be working with Albert on Birch Ward, a Covid ward,' she said.

That's when I knew things were getting real. I was to be spending the day up close and personal with the virus.

A supervisor was called to take me to meet Albert. I followed him through the corridors inside. We mostly stayed silent. Everywhere was busy, with that barely suppressed sense of panic.

Eventually, we got to a bridge linking two buildings. I wasn't to know then that it would later become a place I would hang out for breathers, occasionally to have a good cry. It had yellow rubbish bins on it. It wasn't sealed, but a tarpaulin was stretched over scaffolding along the sides, giving it a provisional feel and letting the wind whistle in. Sometimes I would go out there just to gulp the outside air, to remind myself that there was another world out there still, beyond the ward. That first morning, the man leading me there paused to put on a mask. I felt scared. If he needed a mask, then why didn't I? But I followed him over until we got to the other side of the bridge. The man tapped his pass on the door to let us in. There was a hall with a series of doors leading off it. One was for the pharmacy, another for a kitchen, a toilet, the staff room, a doctor's office. And then there was a door with a sign saying 'Red Zone' on it and that ominous print of a red circle, behind which the patients lay.

The man who had taken me tapped on this door, gesturing to a man behind it who was mopping the floor.

'Albert, come,' said my helper. I saw Albert lift his head up. He was wearing full PPE, so it was hard to see his face, but beneath the layers, the visor, mask, gloves and plastic apron, his body looked spry. I was later surprised to discover that Albert is fifty-one. He doesn't have a scrap of body fat on him, I had assumed from that first glimpse that he was a much younger man.

Albert exited from the red zone and commenced what was clearly a well-rehearsed routine. He removed the gloves and aprons and binned them. Next he washed his hands at the sink, rubbing them hard on the back and at the base of his fingers. Then he did something which has stayed with me. As he took off his mask, he gave a tiny jump, as if for joy. As if he could finally breathe. The relief of getting a bit of fresh air was obvious. It was very strange to me then, but later I came to understand exactly what it felt like to take off your mask after hours of wearing it. The relief of release.

'Hassan will be working with you, so show him the ropes,' said the man who had taken me up there.

'Welcome bro,' said Albert, sweetly, in his distinctive Ghanaian via East London lilt.

'Thanks Boss,' I said. To this day I call Albert, 'Boss'. He always tells me not to but it seems appropriate somehow. He has worked as a hospital cleaner for fifteen years, after moving to the UK in the 1990s. He was the one who showed me what to do. There were two cleaners assigned to every ward, so he had to train me up.

Albert is very particular. He likes things his way and he was a tough taskmaster for me at the beginning. Rather than the trainer, he was the one who told me about wearing PPE and washing my hands carefully. He doesn't know many words in English, but he got his message across forcefully, repeating the same mantra. 'Wear PPE. Wash your hands all the time. You have to protect yourself and your family.' It was frankly very useful to be told. You might think that I would have received some training on how to take these lifesaving measures, but it came down to Albert to show me how to remove the gloves, peeling them off carefully so that you don't spread infection around.

He showed me how to put the PPE on. Every day when I arrived on the ward, I would take all my clothes off and put them in a plastic bag in the staff room. Then I would put my scrubs on before heading to the counter outside the patients' bays to layer on my protection. I would start with the gloves, then the mask, a plastic apron (similar to those worn by people making sand-wiches in cafes) and then the visor. When I finished my shift, my scrubs would go into the laundry box and all the contaminated PPE would be binned, aside from the visor.

For the first couple of days that I was there, the hospital didn't have the more protective FFP3 masks available so we had to use surgical masks. I chose to wear two because I was so terrified about contracting coronavirus. I didn't know what I was doing, but they seemed so flimsy that I reasoned it would be a good idea.

After I was kitted out, I followed Albert inside. The ward was full. I had never seen anything like it in my life before. Everyone had oxygen masks on. There was a mixture of ages, from the forties up and all the patients looked extremely unwell. It was very sobering. Some were really panting for air. Birch Ward was for cases who weren't deemed bad enough to need ventilators – yet. Many were later moved to the ICU. Later I was allowed to take photographs of the staff in the ICU and was struck by the contrast. All the patients were in an induced coma and it was eerily calm compared to Birch, without any coughs, screams or shouts.

But I knew none of this on my first shift. All I knew was that I had to shadow Albert and watch closely what he was doing. People's lives depended on it. He took me to the cleaners' room and showed me how to organize the trolley of equipment. To mix chlorine tablets with water and attach disposable mop heads. After half an hour, I was starting to realize why Albert had been so happy when he took his mask off. It was really hard to breathe. It was difficult for me, triggering memories of being in that cell, gasping for a breath of air.

There was no time to let the past intrude, however. Albert moved quickly. He was very scared and it was blooming into anger. Albert has a wife and two daughters. He knew just how risky his job had suddenly become with the arrival of this new virus. He was risking his life and he didn't have a choice because he had to earn enough money to eat. It was as simple as that. It wasn't a joke, or a game, or a choice. He was very strict with me. When I mopped a patch of floor, trying to copy his movements, he immediately told me I'd done it wrong.

We cleaned a toilet together. He told me to start from the outside and then move inside. The outside is not contaminated but the inside is. We did every inch of the shower, taking it very seriously; it felt like such a huge responsibility. Then we went to the bay where the patients were. Albert was on it. He did the bed frame and then underneath the bed, then the mini cabinet next to the beds, the side table and the chair. Not a scrap was missed. I stood watching him, but I couldn't make eye contact with any of the patients. I was too frightened to look them in the eyes.

'You do the next one,' said Albert, after I had watched him do a few. I moved towards the chair next to the patient's bed. I was barely inches from a coughing coronavirus patient but I couldn't look at them. I was so worried about breathing in the virus, but equally I didn't want to reveal just how nervous I was. To transmit my own terror. There were so many things going through my head.

I held my breath and cleaned.

THE WORLD IN A WARD

Within days, Whipps Cross started to remind me of the Titanic. A vast ship, with the upper classes – the doctors and nurses – on the top floors and the lower classes – cleaners like me, porters, ward hosts, the Serco staff – on the ground floor. The class divisions were clear and yet it was swiftly obvious how deeply reliant everyone in the building was on those who worked on the lower deck.

Such an obvious separation wasn't what I anticipated when I'd come to England. But then I hadn't expected that there would be people dying because of PPE shortages. Or that a disproportionate number of ethnic minority workers would die of coronavirus. It was striking how the doctors and management team at the hospital team were predominantly white, while my new colleagues weren't. They came from a vast array of different places. The mix of nationalities reminded me of being in an airport terminal. I didn't meet a single white British cleaner or porter or healthcare assistant during my time at the hospital. They were predominantly African and Caribbean, but there were also Spaniards, Palestinians,

South Americans and many others. As a snapshot of mankind, it could hardly have been more diverse. Straight away, I felt like I belonged. I had spent the last four years advocating for the contribution of migrants to this country and Birch Ward was literally being held up by it.

Since I'd arrived in the UK, most of my friends had been middle-class white people. I was in a bubble. Sadly, it took getting a job on Birch Ward for me to actually sit down and eat lunch with people on minimum wage, with a totally different perspective on life. They opened my eyes, giving me an insight into what life is really like for people living on the poverty line in this country.

Our ward host was Gimba, who had originally come from Nigeria. I adore Gimba. She is the most amazing woman with a smile like sunshine. To see her is to want to hug her. She made me porridge every morning before I started my shift and within days she was calling me her son. We got into a routine where I would take her pass to go and collect her lunch from the canteen. She and Albert became like my proxy parents. In the sixty-five days that I was there, they looked after me so well – and I looked after them. I felt as if I had so much in common with them. They had made England home and hadn't been born there. We were doing the same kind of job. But while I knew my stay would only be temporary, they are doing those jobs because their chances of getting other ones weren't high. In the eyes of society, they are accorded scant recognition or reward. Yet one was preparing food for patients and the other cleaning, both completely essential work.

They had a really beautiful friendship. Gimba would call Albert her 'hospital boyfriend'. Her actual husband worked as a cleaner in a different London hospital. When he rang up, she would put him on the phone to Albert so that they could catch up. Gimba commuted from south-east London to Whipps Cross, ninety minutes each way. She spent three hours travelling every day, for a job on minimum wage. But like so many of the other staff I met there, she approached it with absolute dedication and warmth.

Underneath, it was obvious that they were scared. Everyone was. Albert isn't able to read or write, but he listened to the news extensively. They both knew how risky the virus is. They had families at home that they worried about infecting and, both in their fifties, they appreciated how dangerous it might be for them if they contracted it. Apparently when Gimba had first heard about it she had started crying and crying. She knew that she couldn't work at home, that she wasn't going to have a choice about whether she was on the frontline or not. Albert comforted her and managed to cheer her up. They both did that for each other, in the most difficult of circumstances.

Anyone who questions the value that refugees and migrants bring to Britain or how hard they work should walk in the shoes of Gimba or Albert – or any of the other amazingly dedicated and compassionate people I met on Birch Ward.

Sister Pilar from northern Spain was the ward manager and the boss. She has worked as a nurse for the last twelve years and I saw her doing everything in her power to protect her patients and staff. On my first morning, she called us all into a meeting in her office to explain that nobody should be stepping onto the ward without full PPE. When the FFP3 masks had finally arrived three days after I started, someone from the infectious team told us we would be fine with just surgical masks; Pilar overrode his decision, saying 'I'll decide what's best for my ward, don't listen to other people.' She simultaneously led us and held us together with her care, professionalism and compassion.

There was the healthcare assistant Vittorio from Turin, in

northern Italy. He was an avid chess player and bookworm, with two sons who are both guitarists. His mother was isolating in northern Italy and he was extremely worried about her, but obviously unable to visit her and check she was okay. Everyone was so worried about their families in other countries. I was so far from being the only one.

There was Catharine, another healthcare assistant, who everyone referred to as 'Mama' because she was the oldest and wisest. She had moved to London from Trinidad twenty-six years previously. She was so full of grace and kindness, literally standing for hours next to patients to keep a watchful eye on them. A single mother to one daughter, Catharine had worked for years to afford to send her daughter to Cambridge University, where she is studying to become a lawyer.

Cherelle was a twenty-four-year-old British Caribbean who loved reggae and R&B. After her shift she carried on caring, looking after her father who had been fighting prostate cancer and leukaemia for more than twenty years. Her father – and the nurses' dedication to him – was why she had decided to become a nursing assistant herself.

These stories are just a small selection of the amazing staff. People sacrificing so much for those they loved and those they didn't even know. It was humbling to witness.

I loved the multiculturalism. It was so positive and enriching. Until the age of twenty-three I had hardly mixed with people who weren't Syrian, and during my childhood my family had mostly socialized with other Sunni Muslims. This wasn't a deliberate policy, it was just how things were. My parents would repeat the saying, 'If they are similar to us, they can come to us'. But working on Birch Ward showed me just how wonderful it is to see multiculturalism in action. And how what unites us as humans is so much more significant that what divides us. It taught me so much, opening my mind to how a society should be.

At first, I struggled to win Albert's approval. He continued to be very tough with me and I would grumble about him to my friends, that I didn't seem able to do anything right. But after four or five days, I was able to mop and clean in a way that he was happy with. When I got to that point, he said we could alternate.

The work was intense. We would do around the beds, the floors, the toilets. We had to disinfect the bins, which were full of adult nappies because most of the patients weren't able to get to the bathroom. Anywhere that had high traffic had to be repeatedly cleaned – like taps, light switches, door handles. We didn't stop moving from the minute our shifts began until our brief break. Meanwhile, so much was happening around us. One morning, a patient collapsed and they closed the curtains around her. There was blood in catheters. Staff everywhere. Each bay had a nurse and four healthcare assistants assigned to it. The nurses would prescribe and assign medication, but the healthcare assistants did so much of the actual caring. They spoon-fed patients, administered medication, changed their nappies, held their hands.

Two of our patients on Birch were actually medical staff from other hospitals – a nurse and a doctor both in their late thirties or early forties. That was extremely anxiety-provoking because they had obviously been exposed where they worked, which was somewhere just like where we were working. The worry about PPE was a constant rumble, like a thunderstorm. It was chaotic and the recommendations were never entirely clear. The rules kept changing; we worried constantly that one morning we would turn up and be told there wasn't any PPE available. That we'd have to make a choice about whether to do our shift without it or not to work.

I offered to take over the patient bays and let Albert do the offices. The bays were by far the tougher part and it seemed fair. The work was absolutely gruelling and he was almost twenty years older than me. I would come off a shift and my phone would show that I'd walked 20,000 steps, and every muscle in my body ached. I cannot imagine what it would be like to keep that job up, day in and day out, for as long as he had.

Despite how slim and wiry he was, Albert's body was showing the strain. While I was there his shoulder developed an injury and he needed physiotherapy, which he couldn't afford to pay for. The toll on your body is enormous. It didn't take long for my damaged wrist to start playing up, strained by the motion of mopping. Albert would massage it with a special lotion he had from Ghana which really helped.

I didn't tell anyone about my background. On the first day we'd had lunch in the staff room. Albert had asked if I was Algerian and I'd told him I was actually from Syria and had been here five years, but I left it at that. I didn't want to make it about me. I was so proud to be working alongside them. I could see the contribution they were making. The courage required at such a frightening time. At lunch time, in the staff room many people looked at their phones, WhatsApping, scrolling, watching Facebook videos from around the world. Gimba checking what was happening in Nigeria, Albert looking at ones from Ghana. There might be a bit of chatting. Someone would usually be crying because a patient had died or they'd had to tell somebody's loved-one bad news.

When I started, the canteen was putting on free lunches for the staff because of the crisis. Despite how stressed he patently was, one of the cleaners confided in me one day that he didn't mind the pandemic because it meant he didn't have to pay for lunch –

leaving him more money to buy food outside of work and help his daughters. It absolutely broke my heart to hear him say that. The level of poverty that so many people in this country are enduring with forbearance and dignity – but little hope of escape.

The pervasive sense of death has really stuck with me. Even now, if I shut my eyes, I can see those patients on Birch Ward. During the peak of the first wave, at least one person every day lost their life. Despite coming close to death, in that Syrian prison, I had never witnessed dying on such a scale. The first time that the blue curtains were drawn around a bed, I asked Albert if I should go over to help.

'No, don't,' he told me, shaking his head furiously. I learnt that they closed the curtains when people died and they needed to deal with the bodies.

The ward was always full. We never had an empty bed. So many of the patients' faces will stay with me forever. People I only knew for a short time, many at the end of their lives, but who I'll carry in my heart until the end of mine. One of those faces belongs to a Turkish man on oxygen. He was an extreme case, in a bad way. But every time I came near him he would remove the oxygen mask to talk. He wanted to talk about Turkey and Turkish food. *Pide. Mezze. Adana kebab. Baklava.* He knew I'd spent time in his country of birth. He wanted to remember. But as he spoke his chest would heave, his blood oxygen saturation dipping.

The nurses would always scold me, 'Please, Hassan, don't talk to him. He mustn't remove his oxygen mask.' I would tell them that it hadn't been my idea.

In one bay there was a forty-year-old man from Wood Green. Every day he would cry, telling me how much he missed being at home.

In the corner of another was an elderly lady in her seventies. Propped on top of her bedside cabinet was a get-well card, the first line unavoidable as I cleaned. 'Me and dad miss you.'

Another old woman spent the entire fortnight that she was on the ward screaming, 'I'm in charge. I'm in charge.' Over and over again. She was trying to reclaim her autonomy in a situation in which she been entirely stripped of it.

There was an old man who couldn't do anything. He couldn't eat on his own and was always fed by nurses.

There was a Pakistani lady who kept saying something in Urdu, but none of us could understand what she wanted. It sounded as if she were pleading. One day I saw her on a video call with her son. It emerged that he was in another bed in a different hospital, also with Covid.

Initially, I didn't know when someone was dying. I would see someone really out of breath, struggling to breathe, but couldn't tell how bad it was. But after a while on Birch Ward, I started knowing when someone was about to die. There were tell-tale signs. Their skin would change colour and their breathing would really rattle. They could no longer do anything on their own, like contacting their loved ones on the phone, eating or going to the toilet. They would stop moving completely.

When a patient died, I had to do something called a 'terminal clean'. That's when you go to their section of the bay and disinfect every last inch. You take it apart and clean everything. Every patient's name is written on a white board above their bed. And although I was able to clean the whole area after a death, I could never bring myself to wipe away the name. It was triggering. I had worked in a school using white boards and never imagined that I'd be wiping dead people's names off one. Initially I was embarrassed that I wasn't able to do it. Yet I still couldn't bring myself to. Within time, the sisters understood. 'Don't worry, Hassan,' they told me. 'We'll do it.'

So many people passed away. What had been profoundly shocking became, sadly, routine. The curtains around a bed pulled shut. That terrible encasing sound. The porters arriving. Big burly men. And then all the remaining patients' curtains being pulled shut while the body was put in a body bag and wheeled away. Initially, I couldn't look. Then I started looking. It was happening too often; I couldn't pretend it wasn't.

I got really close to one particular patient. She was in bed eighteen. Some patients were a bit rude at times, especially to cleaners, but she was always really friendly. Every day she greeted me and wanted to chat. She had worked as a hairdresser for twenty years. She was a big lady. She would always tell me how bored she was. How she wished she could be doing something else instead of just lying there.

As the days passed, I got to know her. I always made a special effort, cleaning items for her that I wasn't required to – like her phone and glasses. I just wanted to do everything I could to help. As well as coronavirus it turned out that she had terminal cancer.

Three weeks later, the doctors knew she was coming close to death. They rang her daughter and asked her if she wanted to video call her mother, but they didn't tell the patient herself that she was nearing the end. She and her daughter spoke on the screen. I had asked the doctor if I could be present because I had developed that closeness with her and they had agreed it was okay.

'I love you, Mum,' said her daughter, who was visibly trying to hold it together but didn't let herself cry.

'I can't wait to leave this place,' she said. Two hours later, she was dead. It was no kind of life, being that poorly and immobile.

She is resting now. But it broke my heart. The impossibility of her suddenly no longer being there.

This schism, between presence and absence was also really brought home to me on another occasion. I had just got home from my shift at the hospital when I had call from someone there, asking if I could go back with my camera. There was an employee in her fifties who had been working at Whipps Cross for eighteen years. She had terminal cancer and was in the ICU but wanted to fulfil her dying wish of marrying her partner and they wanted me to photograph the ceremony.

It was, without doubt, the hardest thing I'd ever seen or witnessed in my life.

When I got to the ICU her partner, a middle-aged bald man, was sitting outside her room with the registrar. They were signing documents and when I arrived someone said, 'This is Hassan the photographer. He also works here as a cleaner.' He started making jokes, in the way that someone does when they are trying to mask their grief. I didn't know what to say, but I smiled.

Then we went inside. The hospital staff had made a real effort to make the room look celebratory with flowers and balloons. The woman was leaning back on her bed, hooked up to lots of tubes. She had that look about her that I'd come to recognize.

'Thank you, Hassan, I really appreciate you doing this,' she said. 'It's so kind of you.'

'Please – don't worry about it,' I said. I felt such an acute sense of responsibility. I'm not a wedding photographer and I know that's always high-pressured because it's such an important day in people's lives. But this occasion was on a whole new level. I started taking pictures of them together. The ceremony started and he sat next to her. Eight or nine clinical staff were by the door. I was like a fly on the wall thanks to my camera, which has an amazing feature where I can turn off the shutter sound.

Everyone was holding it together but when the registrar asked the woman to say, 'In sickness and health . . .' we all started crying. I remember my tears falling behind my camera. It was so deeply emotional.

After the ceremony there was cake and a non-alcoholic drink. They had managed to make it feel special, despite the circumstances.

Before I left, I held the bride's hand for moment. I didn't know what to say. What do you say to someone who is about to die?

'Congratulations,' I finally managed.

'Thank you,' she kept saying.

'Please don't mention it,' I replied. 'I did nothing.' The husband had offered to pay me but there was no way I was going to take his money. It was an honour to share that moment with them. To document it. This wasn't about putting photographs online to raise awareness. It was for the family, capturing that most intimate and poignant of events.

I remember leaving the hospital and driving home, pulling up on a road near my house instead of directly outside. I sat in the car for two hours without moving. I couldn't say or do anything. I stayed in my driving seat and looked straight ahead. Thinking. About the events of the previous months and the ones that came before that. The fragility of human life – so fleeting, so provisional – but the enduring nature of love. In that hospital room, decorated with so much care, I'd been privy to something that I think we all know, deep inside us. That when it comes down to it, the connections we make with other people are what really count.

Our chief source of true happiness while we're here and our legacy when we leave.

Watching that dying patient marry the man she loved but couldn't stay with had been really tough to witness. I'd felt death again, at my shoulder. But the hospital staff had gone to so much effort to make her dying wish come true, treating her with a kindness that far transcended obligation. That's the essence of humanity, showing up and making a difference to others. Friends, loved ones, even people you have never met before. Frequently, I've seen that when confronted with the worst of things, the hardest of days, humans surpass themselves and come together.

When I went into work the next morning I was told that the patient had died overnight.

I could see how worthwhile what I was doing at Birch Ward was and it afforded me the opportunity to contribute. But at the same time, being there in such fraught circumstances was extremely triggering for me. There were echoes of my time in detention, of my flight from my home.

In Birch Ward, the patients were people separated from their loved ones, just as I had been in Syria. Just as I still was. There was so much suffering and loneliness in plain sight, it was every-where you turned.

Within days, I knew that if I was going to cope, I needed to speak to someone. My friend Josie found me a phone therapist and I'd sit in the car after my shift and talk to her. By that point, I often drove in because I was so exhausted and wanted to sleep a bit more before starting the shift. Sometimes, on bad shifts, I'd have emergency sessions where I just rang her from the hospital in a break, trying to cope with a cresting wave of distress.

The therapist was based in Cornwall, so many miles away. She was very supportive. I told her my background and she said I undoubtedly had complex PTSD. She told me that the hospital was obviously a triggering environment for me to be in, but that if I felt like the work gave me purpose I should continue doing it as long as I kept talking about it. Every time that someone died, I'd ring her up.

I didn't want to talk to my colleagues because I didn't want to be a burden. And I didn't want to tell my other friends about the things I was seeing either. The traumas. I wanted to protect them, I suppose. But it meant I had to close myself off. This kind of work isn't something you can leave behind when you go home. It bleeds into every area of your life.

I hadn't initially told my parents about my plan to go and work at the hospital. I knew it would make them anxious. After a week, I sent them a picture of me in my PPE. Then I immediately panicked – I realized they might think I was a patient myself. So, I rang them to explain.

'I didn't want to tell you and risk you saying I couldn't do it,' I explained to them. 'This is really important to me.'

They were surprised – worried, yes – but ultimately supportive. My parents know me well enough by now. They know how important it is for me to keep moving, keep helping, to be a part of something.

I have seen both the best and worst of humanity in hospital settings. After being tortured in that military hospital in Syria, I had expected to encounter only more horror in Whipps Cross, albeit of a different kind, in the form of the dreadful virus. And yes, it was true that what I witnessed was horrific and traumatic. Yet seeing the pure kindness and dedication that accompanied it on Birch Ward was actually deeply healing for me. To realize that hospitals could indeed be places of refuge and togetherness, where people were looked after with the utmost dedication, restored some of that faith in humanity which had been taken away from me.

#HASSAN

I consider myself a storyteller. I love it and had tried to use this ability since arriving in Britain, to speak up for refugees who might not have been in a position to advocate for themselves.

Since I first picked up a camera, taking photographs has always been one of my deepest loves and I'd felt driven to record my journey to Europe, to share the truth with the world in the face of so much misinformation.

Despite this, it never occurred to me that I would share what I saw inside Whipps Cross. I had taken the job to help the NHS and my community. It wasn't about drawing attention to myself. It was about showing up and doing the work. Finding a way to help during the largest health crisis of modern times.

When I started working at the hospital, I had around 8,000 followers on Twitter, a following that had grown after *Exodus* aired on the BBC. In my first week of cleaning, I was usually too tired to check social media when I got home from my shift. I couldn't believe that people did such gruelling physical work, day-in and day-out. I would get home to our flat, leave my shoes outside the door and shower, despite already having showered at the hospital. I was doing everything I could to stay safe. It seemed obvious to me that I must have been exposed to the virus, despite my PPE. I was so close to people who had it.

But after a week, once I'd got to know some of the amazing people I was working with, I started to wonder about putting something up online after all, in the hope of raising awareness about the people whose stories we don't normally hear about. The hard-working, underpaid strata of British society approaching their difficult lives with love and dedication. The Gimbas and Alberts of this world.

After all, despite spending the previous four years advocating for those who make Britain their home and highlighting how much value they add to their communities, it wasn't until I worked on Birch Ward that I had really spent time with people on the poverty line and witnessed what their lives were like. And if I hadn't fully realized their reality, so many other people wouldn't know either. I've always tried to be generous in sharing my story; believed it crucial for raising awareness and fostering empathy. It occurred to me that perhaps now wasn't the time to stop after all.

So, on April the 7th, on my way to start a shift, I tweeted a picture of me that I'd taken the previous day in a toilet mirror, wearing my full PPE. And a message. *Honoured to join an army of cleaners disinfecting Covid wards in our local hospital after receiving training. London has been my home since leaving Syria, and the least I can do is making sure my neighbours and the amazing NHS staff are safe and sound. #StayHomeSaveLives.*

I wanted to highlight what I was seeing. That army of people doing so much. And I was proud. I felt as if I'd joined the fight. At that point, Boris Johnson had been admitted to hospital. Everything felt extremely dicey, as if the country were on a knife's edge. If I could help encourage people to stay at home to stop the spread of the virus then that would just be an added bonus.

I arrived at the ward, put my phone away in the plastic bag I used to stop it getting contaminated and then tidied it away, forgetting about it. It was only when I went on my lunchbreak that I took it out. Checking Twitter, I was stunned to see 'Hassan' trending. My name. My tweet was blowing up. I had tens of thousands of retweets and messages. It was insane. I didn't expect the scale of it. I felt humbled and dazed. I was just trying to put out a positive message during what was a very tough time. But it had struck a chord. That initial post eventually went on to have more than 94,000 likes, but in that moment it just felt so good to feel supported. I'd taken the job to try and help my community – to have that appreciation reflected back at me was phenomenal.

I was blown away by the response and wanted to try and use it to do something positive. So I took to Twitter again and added a sub-tweet to my initial post. *Thank you for all the love! It would mean a lot to me if you can donate some money to the hospital I clean. They launched a Covid-19 appeal and need a bit of help during this tough time. Link below. Thank you again xxx.* I linked to the coronavirus appeal of Bart's Charity, the dedicated charity for Whipps Cross, and people began to donate. My Twitter app was constantly aglow with notifications as the message was retweeted and shared around the world. Even the United Nations shared it, which seemed appropriate somehow. It was a message about what happens when people from all different places pull together.

Immediately, requests for interviews began to pour in. But I was cautious. I wanted to raise awareness, but I knew that I needed to be careful. I was doing the job temporarily. I didn't want to be the person stealing the show. The temporary cleaner trying to make the situation about himself. I really didn't want to do that.

I rang my friend Juliette and explained the situation. I told her that I was getting all these requests but that I didn't have time to screen them and respond because I was working. I asked if she could help out. She agreed and I put her email address in my bio. A week later, she said she couldn't cope with the scale of it and so another friend, Nathalie, was also enlisted to help.

I wasn't sure how to manage the situation I had found myself in. It felt like being handed a huge opportunity, but I felt the weight of responsibility keenly too. I wanted to push out a positive message about the diversity of the NHS and all the people I was working with, but I was exhausted, still working gruelling shifts every day and witnessing extreme trauma.

I decided to be extremely selective about the interviews that I gave, trying to choose the ones that would provide maximum impact. I was strategic. The very first one I did was with Piers Morgan and Susanna Reid on *Good Morning Britain*. I did it before the start of the shift very early in the morning, when I was sitting in my car in the hospital car park.

It was a very emotional interview for me. I told them that I was worried about my own parents and that if something happened to them I'd want someone to look after them and so I was looking after other people's parents. I added that I felt proud and that I'd love people to donate to the hospital's charity. This helped to raise around 50,000 pounds. It made me feel so good. To have such a tangible impact wasn't something that I had ever dreamed would happen when I had posted that picture.

After that, I did interviews almost every day after finishing my shift. Juliette and Natalie helped me deal with the sheer volume that was coming in. They also supported me with preparing for interviews and discussing what I should say in the op-eds I was being asked to write, refining what I was trying to articulate to the world and the messages that I hoped to spread. Lots of people shared the articles that I wrote and contributed to. I was also getting international attention, including from the Middle East. My parents were so proud. It was especially good to feel that pride coming from my dad. It was a perfect uplifting story in that frightening time. A Syrian refugee BAFTA-award-winning cleaner supporting the NHS by working in a coronavirus ward.

Then I started questioning the positive slant of the narrative. There had been so many government failures in the handling of the pandemic by that point. I had been dismayed by the creeping authoritarianism I'd witnessed in the UK since moving here. How the beautiful democracy that I had always admired from afar was being trashed by an uncaring elite. The people in charge had misled voters over Brexit, and now they were letting them down during the pandemic, too. I didn't want to be part of their propaganda drive. So, I decided to get political. It was a conscious decision. I felt as if it was my responsibility, to be honest. I'd been political back home in Syria, and it had got me into terrible trouble, but I never once regretted standing up for what I thought was right, despite all of the difficulties it brought into my life.

I decided to start sharing some of my colleagues' stories. By then, people knew my story and I had added thousands of followers on social media from that viral tweet. I'm a photographer and a filmmaker. Because I had those skills and I had a platform, I could share the stories of people like Gimba and Albert, who would never normally have had the opportunity to tell the world about their lives. My story had gone viral, but who was I compared to them?

I started with Gimba. By that point, she meant so much to me. Her open-heartedness, humour and generosity had helped me get through some of my darkest hours on Birch Ward. She treated me as tenderly as my own mother would. She was a shining light in my life. I asked if she would mind if I took her picture and she agreed to it. Gimba trusted me from day one, she's like that. Her mum had fallen ill in Nigeria and been rushed to hospital. Gimba had been crying her eyes out but she hadn't taken a day off. She had been so upset but she kept saying she had a job to do. She took so much pride in her job, despite how anxious she was. She didn't realize what a great woman she is. I just felt like the world needed to know about Gimba.

I went and got her lunch and then I took a picture as she was finishing it. Fork in mouth, her face turned towards the light from the window she sits next to. She was wearing her regulation blue hair net and scrubs, sitting in front of the scruffy wall of the staff room and her handbag. But her expression makes it. She radiates warmth and peace. I was so pleased to have captured this essence of her and I shared the photograph on Instagram with a caption about Gimba and the contribution she made to the NHS.

Later, this image was selected by the Duchess of Cambridge to be part of her Hold Still exhibition with the National Portrait Gallery, which is a collective portrait of our nation during lockdown. It was one of just a hundred final portraits chosen from 31,000 entries, which makes me exceedingly proud. That Gimba's beautiful face and spirit will be seen by so many is just wonderful. But I didn't know any of that when I put her picture on Instagram.

The picture got so much traction. It was widely shared and people loved it. Some of the healthcare assistants had seen me interviewed on *Good Morning Britain* and news spread about what I was doing. With every interview I started highlighting the diversity of the ward and the fact we were all united. I felt like the spokesperson of the ward. And people liked what I was communicating. They started warming up to me and thanked me. So, when I asked to take other people's pictures they agreed. It was always done in the staff room. I'd take their picture and ask a few questions.

On Channel Four News Jon Snow said, 'Hassan, you fled a war-torn country and you're here – why would you end up working in a hospital?'

I didn't script my response. I just said the first thing that came out of my mouth. 'Our nationality does not dictate our kindness.' It was off the cuff but it encapsulates my view. Reflecting on my colleagues, we came from something like twenty countries. But our nationalities didn't matter. It was meaningless that I was Syrian and Gimba was Nigerian and Albert came from Ghana. We were all just humans. We all wanted to help. And for many of the staff on Birch Ward they didn't have the privilege of working from home.

I didn't do all the interviews offered to me. I did GMB and Channel Four, CNN and Al Jazeera, sharing stories of my colleagues in the evenings after I finished work. When I had first asked Albert if he would let me take his picture, he said no. But as the response to the posts grew, he changed his mind. He saw the comments on Gimba's post, people saying things like, 'Gimba you're a hero.' He decided to let me do it. He could see that I was talking about us faithfully, the people on Birch Ward. But he was still hesitant. He wasn't warm with me. Arms folded, he looked quizzically at my camera. Like the Boss he is. I like to think that I captured that amazing and hard-working man who I came to admire so deeply.

It made me proud to demonstrate the diversity of the NHS workers responding to the crisis. How they pulled together. I wanted to acknowledge it in a concrete way through the media work that I did. But of course, I remain convinced that what is truly needed is action and policy change.

My friends at Choose Love summarized it perfectly. They said, 'While the hard work and sacrifices many migrant workers are making on the frontline of this crisis should be recognized and remembered, no one should have to risk their lives to be recognized as a human being. A person's "usefulness" should not define their worth. We should recognize and respect our common humanity, regardless of immigration status. Not just in a crisis, but all the time.'

I was reminded once again of my belief in the significance of language. Before the pandemic, as Britain discussed its role leaving the EU, the phrase 'low-skilled' workers was bandied about a lot. Within a matter of weeks, those very same workers were being described as 'key'. The public would come out into their doorsteps every Thursday evening to clap for them. One of the remarkable things about the pandemic was that it made people realize how important such low-paid jobs are – they keep the world moving and they are disproportionately done by immigrant workers. Witnessing that first-hand is an experience that will never leave me.

Often, when it comes to scary things that feel out of our control, we want to turn away. But for some of these key workers, this is their reality, they can't turn away. And we are not powerless to help them. I hope I demonstrated that. While the pandemic showed us some truly terrifying things, it also highlighted how interconnected we are and how willing we all are to change our lives and routines for the good of our community. You only had to look at the mutual aid groups that mushroomed around Britain, people printing 3D-visors in their garages, sewing scrubs for local hospitals, sending out food parcels. The community response was nothing short of incredible, going far to fill the gaps left by an inadequate government.

ONLY CONNECT

When the pandemic first hit, I recorded what I saw around me in Leytonstone – empty shelves, people queuing outside Tesco, discarded rubber gloves on a patch of grass, hastily printed signs in shop windows. My way of processing events is to document them. But when I got to the hospital and saw the reality of what was happening inside the ward, all thoughts of filming left my mind for once. There was no room for them. I had a job to do.

But after my PPE post on Twitter went viral, many production companies got in touch with me. A considerable number of approaches were from ones that hadn't even bothered to reply when I'd previously sent them my CV. The problem was that most of the production companies were similarly asking me to be a contributor on a potential future programme. But I had learned my lesson and valued myself as a skilled filmmaker. I didn't want to create something that I had no control over.

By then, I had become more well known and recognized at the hospital because I'd raised so much money for the hospital's charitable trust. A week after my viral tweet I emailed the hospital administrators, explaining my background and saying that I'd like to film my colleagues, if it was possible, on my breaks but also my work, as I was moving around the ward. They agreed to it. They could see that I was raising awareness and shedding light on the diversity of the NHS. I was a good advocate for the hospital. So, I began recording video as well as taking photographs. It became very intense. I started working fourteen-hour days. I wanted to do justice to my colleagues' stories. I had interviews with various publications. I was writing articles myself. It became surreal. But I felt like I had this responsibility to tell the world about my colleagues on Birch Ward.

On the morning of May the 20th, I checked my phone before starting my shift. I came across an article in the *Independent* about the bereavement scheme. I couldn't believe what I was reading. The scheme guaranteed that the family of every migrant working in a frontline role against coronavirus would get indefinite leave to remain – but it excluded healthcare assistants, porters and cleaners. I felt so angry and upset. Betrayed. The news meant the families of all the people I was working with would get nothing if their loved ones died on the frontline. The loophole was deeply cynical – the government knew how many people in those low-paid roles were migrants. Their contribution was deliberately being ignored. It was so blatant, reminding me of the injustice I had experienced in Syria. I was working with these people on a daily basis. They were family to me now. I had seen how hard their lives were. And they were being hung out to dry.

When I got inside the ward, I could see how shaken everyone was by the news. It wasn't just the practicality of it – it didn't affect everyone, for example Gimba was already a British citizen. It was also the message that was being sent. We don't care about you. You aren't worth anything. You aren't a part of this country.

Everyone was so let down. Working with Gimba and Albert had opened my eyes to the contribution of the working class in our communities and how much they had risked. Then the government essentially said: 'If you die we won't look after your loved ones.'

I couldn't live with it. I felt like I simply had to do something.

I spent the whole of my shift wondering what to do, burning at the sense of injustice. I was cleaning and thinking hard. I knew that I was in a unique position. I had direct experience of one of the excluded roles, but I also had my storytelling ability and my platform on social media. But it wasn't about me. It was the sheer magnitude of the number of people who would be affected by it.

I decided to put a video up. I went to my car to do it. I was super nervous. I had lived for five years in Britain and not felt as if I'd had the right to speak about issues here. I always spoke on subjects affecting those displaced across the world. I didn't consider it my place, as an outsider. I had posted something once about Brexit but that was all. I didn't have the right to vote.

But when that unfair decision happened, I didn't feel like an outsider anymore. I was literally in the trenches of the worst public health crisis in modern Britain and I had the full right to talk about it. It was my protest. Back in Syria I'd gone to that protest at Umayyad Mosque and this sprang from a similar impulse. Walking to my car, to do that video, was my protest. Times had changed – I didn't have to go and shout on a street, I could upload a video.

I fixed my phone and set the record button. The first take, I stumbled on my words. It was so hot that day. I was sweating. I did a second take and also stumbled on my words. I knew expressing my opinion this way wasn't going to get me into any serious danger, but it was still new to me in Britain. When I'd faced injustice in Syria, there had been a long build-up before I made the decision to protest. I had the same feeling. And although I knew I wasn't going to get into serious trouble, I was on a temporary visa, with the risk of being deported always present.

I didn't know what I wanted to say exactly. Every take was different from the last. It wasn't scripted. I was just imagining Boris Johnson sitting in front of me and I was speaking to him. I was so upset, you can hear the tremor of emotion in my voice. I still wasn't completely satisfied with the third take, but I wasn't sure I'd ever be. I hit upload and went back to work. Once again, I didn't look at my phone.

In four hours, the post generated around four million views. The response was like nothing I could ever have imagined. Everyone of every political persuasion shared it. It was a message that transcended politics. I had been very careful. I didn't want to be shouty and aggressive, I wanted to appeal to his humanity. When I'd gone to speak to Assad, that was what I'd tried to do as well. It hadn't worked, but there was the same sense of wanting to connect to the human part of them.

I went back home in disbelief that I'd gone viral again. There was my name, trending once more. It made me so nervous. I hadn't told Juliette and Nathalie that I was going to put the video up. It had been entirely my spontaneous decision. Immediately afterwards, both of their inboxes exploded with media requests. It hadn't just been me talking on this subject. Keir Starmer had raised it in parliament and there had been campaigners from the unions, but I put a face on it. I made it personal.

Then at 5 p.m. an announcement came from Priti Patel's Twitter account that they were extending the scheme to NHS support staff and social care workers. The government was making a full U-turn after my plea for them to do so. In that moment, my story went from a Syrian refugee working as a cleaner to someone who has triggered a government U-turn. Everything completely exploded.

I felt I was in a position to get political. To say it how it was. My protest had worked this time and it really brought my self-esteem back. I had never felt so empowered in my life. I'd failed before, despite being able to discredit Assad and expose what they had done, since arriving in Britain I hadn't been able to create change in Syria. This time I'd actually made a change. I had been sitting in my flat, glued to my phone screen all afternoon and, when I saw the announcement, I leapt up. I began jumping and yelling with joy. It felt like I'd won the lottery. One of the two or three stand-out moments of my life. I could not believe it. This is what I want to do. It's what I've always wanted to do. To help. To campaign. To use my skills to raise awareness. And it worked. It actually worked.

The next day, I was greeted on Birch Ward like some kind of returning hero. Virtual high fives from all my colleagues. My picture was on the front page of the *Metro* along with the head-line 'Shamed by Hospital Cleaner.' My colleagues brought it to the staff room and pinned it on our notice board. They had felt so abandoned by the government; it was an amazing feeling to have made them feel recognized.

But, despite their praise and my own sense of achievement at having successfully driven change, I don't consider myself a hero. I struggle with the term. I have known many heroic people and many of them are dead.

I had gone to the hospital with the best of intentions. I'd wanted to help. But while I worked there, I had realized that the real enemy wasn't just Covid-19. It was injustice. Reports showed how people from BAME communities were disproportionately affected by the virus because so many of them lived in crowded accommodation. All of that became visible to me when I worked at the hospital and it crystallized when the government excluded those people from the bereavement scheme. Yes, England was relatively safe in that I wasn't about to be bombed or tortured, but there were still things to protest about. The pandemic lifted up the rug and exposed the corruption endemic in Britain. On some level, I felt like that kind of misconduct, on a greater scale, was what I'd fled from in Syria. Which is part of the reason I found it so chilling. Nobody in government had apologized properly or taken responsibility. Even Priti Patel's rescinding tweet was not truly apologetic. That was the kind of behaviour you might expect from someone like Assad. Having joined the hospital, I felt like I'd truly joined the country, a nation being held together by its working class who were being so badly let down.

And while I was pleased about the U-turn on a personal level, I do think the number of U-turns that there have been during the pandemic demonstrate just what a mediocre administration this is. A hospital cleaner shouldn't have to make a video begging for the bare minimum for people risking their lives in a pandemic. Captain Tom, a hundred-year-old man shouldn't have needed to walk tirelessly for days to raise money for the NHS. And the footballer Marcus Rashford shouldn't have had to force a reversal on free school meals. This is not a good or just system of governance. It's too arbitrary and largely contingent on the intervention of people who have power.

After the video and the U-turn, my follower numbers soared. My platform grew even larger. With that power comes responsibility. I'm so aware of that. I did a follow-up video for Twitter thanking everyone for all the support. And I promised to use my platform carefully. To call out injustice where I see it. To advocate for those who don't have the same privileges as me.

I was so proud of what I'd done. I'd managed to accomplish a lot of things during my time there. I'd repeatedly disinfected the ward, I'd used my own privileged position to platform my colleagues and talk about the contribution of migrants around the world, as well as helping to reverse a harmful policy. My depression in the past had been related to not being able to accomplish what I hoped to in Syria, but I had been able to do it here and I had made a direct impact. In a very strange way, despite all the traumas I'd experienced at the hospital, my time there helped to mend me. I encountered the best of what humanity has to offer and I was also able to make a difference in helping others. In showing generosity towards others and doing something to help my new community, I found a deeper sense of connection again. The one that I had been missing since I'd left Syria, or that I'd only felt in small, intermittent bursts. It reminded me of what is truly important and of my own capacity to make a difference.

I started to receive even more interview requests. I'd built myself a makeshift studio in my flat because every day I had to do an interview. I set up my laptop on a pile of books. I put a microphone and a light at the side. I wanted to make sure that I was as professional as I could be. And in every interview, I used my own perspective as a springboard to tell the stories of my colleagues. To push a message about diversity, about multicultural Britain, about how we have to step up when governments and people in power fail us. How important it is to hold people in power accountable. The importance of not sharing misinformation. I was broadcasting to the entire world. Japan. South Africa. France. Italy. America. Canada. The same world.

On 16 June 2020, I got a letter from Sadiq Khan, the Mayor of London:

Dear Hassan,

On behalf of Londoners I want to thank you for your valuable contribution during the Covid-19 pandemic. Your decision to join the NHS and help your community in east London in becoming a cleaner at Whipps Cross University Hospital is a selfless contribution to be commended. I have been touched and inspired by the generosity of Londoners in recent months and your care for your community is one such example of the spirit of Londoners during this time. Thank you for telling the untold stories of your NHS colleagues whose everyday heroism symbolises the hard work of so many migrants and refugees who fulfil important roles across the NHS and other key sectors. Many Londoners and indeed those further afield will recall your passionate plea to the government on the extension of the bereavement scheme. I want to thank you for using your voice and your platform for good and for standing up for your fellow Londoners. Nobody should have to suffer the devastating loss of loved ones before they feel safe and secure and like you, I will continue to champion migrant rights and call to the end of the hostile environment.

Wow. From sitting on a dinghy to getting a letter from the mayor of the city I had chosen to make my home.

LEAVING BIRCH BEHIND

On June the 1st, they started rolling out testing for clinical staff at the hospital. I went with Albert and Gimba to help them fill out the forms. The woman who was taking our blood asked me which ward we were working in.

'Birch,' I replied.

'Birch – you had it really tough there,' she said, drawing the blood out of my arm.

'Yes. We did,' I said. It was an understatement. The test was for an active infection not antibodies, and my own came back negative, as did, Albert's. But Gimba was told she had the virus. I was deeply worried about her. She was in the profile of people who were getting it really badly, in her fifties and black. That people from ethnic minorities have disproportionately died from coronavirus says everything you need to know about the pervasive injustice that exists in this country. Luckily, Gimba turned out to have only a mild case. In the end, she was off for two weeks before returning to work.

On June the 4th, Birch Ward was closed as a Covid ward. It

was the second-to-last ward at Whipps Cross to be reassigned to general patients. During this time, I would get asked to go to deep clean wards that were shutting. It was actually quite fun because they gave me this steamer jet and I'd blast everything clean.

But I was sobbing as I did it to Birch Ward on the last day. A chapter of my life was drawing to a close. I knew my time at Whipps Cross had come to an end. The first wave of infections had waned and I'd only ever wanted to do the role to help at a time when it was so crucial. It had been sixty-five days of sheer intensity, unlike anything that I'd ever encountered before. I felt like I'd been in a warzone. I know military metaphors can be a bit of a cliché, but nothing else feels as appropriate. The intensity. The rush. The fast pace. The work. The tears. The laughs. The people I met who were discharged. The people I met who died. Perhaps it's not the most original of metaphors, but it felt like a battle.

I finished cleaning the ward and throughout that last shift I was filming, with my GoPro attached to a chest strap.

Walking out of the hospital after my final shift was such an odd feeling. I had never encountered something like that in my life before. Working with a team of people I hadn't previously met on the front line in such a public health crisis, at the same time as being interviewed constantly and advocating for my colleagues. It had taken every ounce of my energy to navigate it. I'd had no downtime at all. When you run on adrenaline for such a long time, it takes a toll on your health. I felt absolutely drained, physically and mentally.

The knock-on effect on my friendships had also been huge. This is something I want to highlight, because people can't do jobs like that without it having a wider impact on those closest to them, yet this is seldom talked about. I withdrew from many of my closest relationships because of both the intensity of my workload and the difficult sights that I was witnessing on a daily basis. I slept solidly for about a week after finishing. By that point I'd stopped doing interviews. I felt like I'd done my part and needed to recover.

I was taking things easy but nonetheless, two weeks after leaving the cleaning job I was walking down the high street in Leytonstone and I saw a sign for a food bank. I walked in and asked if they needed any volunteers. Later they rang me and asked if I could deliver food to people that were shielding. At the time of writing this, I'm still volunteering there. Once a week. It's much more manageable than being at the hospital but it really helps me to give something back, especially as the pandemic is still unfolding. These aren't simple times.

I can't explain this instinct to keep busy. It's not a constant battle to prove something. I just can't *not* do anything. It's a way of giving back. Five years ago, I was the one standing in a queue in a refugee camp in Dunkirk. I'd found it incredibly difficult to be in that position but I was so grateful for the support. And now I'm the one handing food out. I've come full circle. I've been on the receiving end of humanitarian work, advocacy and fund-raising, so now that I'm able to help others I feel a responsibility to do so. I could go back to that one day. Anything can happen to anyone. My life has taught me this. You are never completely safe. You can hit rock bottom in a second. Even here in Britain.

This is why advocacy on behalf of refugees is so important for me. I had been working with the artist Marc Quinn on some filming just before lockdown. He is known primarily for his sculptures, including a statue of Alison Lapper which was installed for a time on the fourth plinth at Trafalgar Square. When I stopped working at the hospital I started doing shoots again, mostly for charities like Choose Love and Freedom from Torture. Slowly the world was opening up. Marc was working on a new project and he asked for my help.

He had seen a photograph of a woman taken during a Black Lives Matter protest in Bristol. Her name was Jen Reid, and the photo showed her standing on the empty plinth where protestors had removed the statue of the slave trader Edward Colston. Marc decided to make a life-size black resin-and-steel statue of Jen and erect it on the plinth. He wanted me to film the stunt and I agreed.

On July the 15th, the sculpture, entitled *A Surge of Power (Jen Reid)*, was erected shortly before 5 a.m., without the permission of Bristol City Council. I rose early, as dawn was breaking, to document the process throughout. They brought a crane to lift the statue and then bolted it onto the plinth. The whole operation took around ten minutes and I filmed it all. I couldn't miss anything and I really felt the pressure, but I absolutely loved it. This is exactly the kind of work that compels me. Jen is amazing and it felt like a rare thing to be able to do. Erecting a statue of a black woman instead of a slave trader was a huge message. I knew all about that bleak aspect of Bristol's history. When I was at the hospital I was working with many black people who had been seriously let down by the government. So, in a sense, it was an extension of the work I'd already been doing.

The statue was up for twenty-four hours. But it didn't really matter whether it was there for twenty-four hours or a week or a year. What matters is that efforts like that keep the conversation around social justice and equality going. That's what we need to do. It was good to see it go viral. Some people were critical but it became huge, garnering so much attention and publicity. But more importantly, I had witnessed how happy Jen was with what happened. I'd seen lots of people bringing their children to see it that morning. It was a beautiful moment.

TRUTH-TELLING

Activism, like placing Jen's statue on the plinth, always reminds me how crucial it is to bring things out into the open. To speak your truth. I try to do this with mental health issues too, both for my own benefit but as a form of advocacy for others.

I think every single Syrian has PTSD. I'm not exaggerating. The things we've seen and lived through. The barrel bombs. Children dying. Torture. Beloved family homes reduced to piles of rubble. The separation from loved ones.

And yet mental health problems remain stigmatized by many in our culture. You are dismissed as a *majnoon* – a crazy person. I want to encourage everyone, particularly people from back home, to understand that there is no shame if your mental health has been damaged by what you endured. Indeed, it would be strange if it hadn't.

Let me tell you a story about my aunt Lama. She won't mind, I've asked her – besides she appreciates, perhaps better than most, how transformational it can be to tell the truth.

Lama is a legend. In her fifties, she is dynamic, intelligent and fun. She is married to my mother's brother. Back in Damascus, their flat was always so beautiful – immaculately clean, with everything laid out perfectly. Pictures in frames, good china, patterned rugs. Trinkets from their time of living in Saudi. She took real pride in it.

But during the war their area was hit by repeated bombing and she and my uncle had to leave. They returned during a break in the fighting to find their home entirely destroyed. Charred walls with nothing left within.

From that moment onwards, a part of Lama was broken – only she hadn't had a name for it.

She and my uncle had nothing left and knew they had to flee but it was decided that she would make the difficult journey to Europe first, since he isn't in the best physical condition. So that's what she did, setting out with great courage. She ended up in Germany, like Redwan, and applied for family reunification so he could join her.

Despite trying to build a new life, everyone in our family knows that Lama hasn't been her old self since her home was destroyed. A previously cheery and upbeat person, she has been frequently depressed in the intervening years and suffers from flashbacks. Yet, despite what happened to her, nobody seemed to have the right vocabulary for what she was going through. Someone even said she was possessed by an evil spirit. It was absolute nonsense.

So when I visited Lama in Duisburg in 2017, on a trip to see Redwan, I deliberately opened up about my own mental health problems. I told her I was walking in a world of triggers. Every backfiring car or thunderclap makes me jump out of my skin. If I see a police car, I break into a sweat. I have regular nightmares. The flashbacks come when I least expect them.

I spoke for around fifteen minutes about the symptoms of

PTSD. Lama looked at me throughout, tears pouring out of her eyes. 'Hassan, keep going please. Don't stop,' she said. 'You are describing exactly what I feel myself.' I showed her the definition of PTSD online and she started sobbing in relief. Finally, she had an explanation for what she, too, had been going through.

She is far from the only one. So many of us have been left with these problems. I'm worried that they will be passed on to the next generation. What happened through my work at the hospital was very healing for me, being able to finally effect change and come full circle, but there is more that I need to work through before I have children myself.

I'm determined to use all the tools at my disposal – therapy and treatments like EMDR – to tackle these lingering wounds. I'm such a fan now for talking about things and bringing them out into the open. If you hide things from the light of day they can fester. If I can deal with my own symptoms, I'll be able to advocate that other refugees who have experienced trauma do the same. Therapy is a journey and one I've only just started, but there are other tools for healing too.

I don't want my future children to go through the same things I've gone through. I want them to have a safe life and not endure the level of trauma I had. I want them to live in a world of justice and accountability, much like how I imagined Britain to be before I came here. This is part of the reason that I work so hard as an activist.

I hope that we'll see Assad and his men taken to the International Criminal Court in The Hague for the war crimes they committed. There is ample evidence of genocide. We can't bring the dead back, but we could offer them and their families justice.

From posting the photograph of me in my PPE, to the video addressed to Boris Johnson, to filming the statue of Jen, social media has been pivotal to my activism, altering the course of my life. My story is one of our times.

In the early days of the Syrian uprising, Facebook was crucial for finding out where demonstrations were happening. Citizen journalists like me were so important in disseminating information about what was happening, later revealing the truth about what Assad was doing to his people despite the official denials.

Then, when I was crossing to and across Europe, Facebook groups were crucial for gleaning tips on the journey. That was an advantage that Syrian refugees had on the Iraqis, Somalians and Afghans who had been displaced by war years earlier and tried to cross to Europe to claim asylum here – we had social media, to share information with one another. Which bus stop to go to, where to stay in Greece and Serbia, how best to avoid the police.

When our boat had been sinking, I was able to drop that pin to my friend on WhatsApp, so that she could call the coastguard, which almost undoubtedly saved lives.

And WhatsApp is my constant means of communication with my family. We haven't been under the same roof for so long, so it's our daily way of staying in touch. Our virtual dining table. My mum is always sending me articles – often fake news!

I wouldn't have met the woman I fell in love with if I hadn't started following her on Instagram and slid into her direct messages. It is such a millennial way to have met your partner.

Even before the pandemic, I was using social media for advocacy work, trying to talk about the contribution that refugees make to Britain. Obviously, it stepped up hugely with the video to Boris Johnson, but since leaving the hospital I've continued this strategy. In August, I worked with a group called Led by Donkeys to project a video of me talking about refugees onto the white cliffs of Dover. It was an open letter to Great Britain. I talked about how the white cliffs of Dover had been visible from my refugee camp. How they represented hope. Hope of a safe life and a better future. I mentioned that Britain isn't truly facing a refugee crisis. That of the around thirty million refugees around the world, Britain is home to only one per cent of them. And that refugees are being used as a distraction by an unfit government for the true crises that the country faces.

It was a message of compassion. I firmly believe social media can be a force for positive change. But it can undoubtedly also be used for evil. To spread false information and mobilize hate. So, we need to be very careful. It's a tool and we need to use it to tell the truth, to foster connection and raise awareness about things that would otherwise remain hidden.

As well as advocacy on social media, I would like to continue making films about subjects that matter. I want to keep making documentary films, putting faces on crises. Giving my contributors full agency and support. Collaboration rather than voyeurism.

I also have some political ambitions but I'm not sure what form they will take yet. My willingness to get political here is new. But the government response to Covid has been so disappointing that I feel compelled to try and make a difference.

When the pandemic started it felt – briefly – as if everyone was on one side. Let's beat this thing together. I felt as if I were joining a national effort.

But the government let people down, time and time again and my disillusionment with them is now complete. My radar for danger also extends to corruption, you see. I've witnessed the depths to which an administration can descend in Syria. I know when something is not right.

There have been so many failures and U-turns, such a lack of accountability. I think of all the people I met who showed courage when confronting the unthinkable. Those saying goodbye for the last time through their smartphones. Those working courageously without adequate safeguards or protection. Those so nearly hung out to dry by an administration that didn't see – or cynically chose not to recognize – their value.

And I think of volunteering at the food bank. The lonely old men, harried single mothers, resigned children – all relying on hand-outs to get through the week. Meanwhile, there are reports of consultants being paid 7,000 pounds a day for Track and Trace. The system is in disarray and the poor handling of the pandemic has led to one of the highest death rates due to Covid in the entire world. While so many are left poor and hungry in one of the richest cities in the world.

They deserve better.

WITH HARDSHIP COMES EASE

I'd like to still be living in Britain in five years. Hopefully in my own place. I've lived in so many apartments, I'm tired of moving. I want somewhere I can call home and if I get indefinite leave to remain, I will be able to apply for a mortgage. It won't be the same as our beloved apartment near Maysat Square, it's unlikely to have a balcony, but it will be somewhere to make new memories. Where I can put up pictures and cook for my friends and feel a sense of belonging at last.

I've got used to the taste of the water here now. And although it's nowhere near as sweet as that in the springs around Damascus, it's keeping me alive.

My dream is that my parents will be able to come and visit. To meet my friends. To show them around this country that has become an integral part of me.

I have the trip planned in my head already. I can see the highlights from my imagined iPhone photo reel. (I'd document it in detail, of course I would!) My mother gazing at the flower beds and majestic trees of a London park. She loves greenery more than almost anything, aside from her children. My father, head tipped back to look at an exhibit in one of the big museums. The two of them, walking through a food market, side by side, reminded of Damascus by the clamour and clouds of smoke. Wandering along the ribbon of the canal. Unwrapping paper parcels of fish and chips.

In my mind, I can see the expression on their faces as they take in all of these new experiences and then look at me. Pride and relief. I'm okay. The life I'm building is a good one. After all the worrying and suffering they have been through, the concern that I myself caused them, they can unclench that little bit more.

As it stands, this is all a total fantasy.

Under the current guidelines, it is almost impossible for my parents to get a visa to visit me here. We will have to meet again in another arbitrary spot between where we both live. Georgia, again maybe. Lebanon. Jordan. Malaysia. Sudan. But I live in hope that this will one day change. That they'll come and stay in this city I live in now, so different from the one that they raised me in, that together we called home, but beautiful.

There is a verse in the Quran that translates as, 'With hardship comes ease.' It's relevant for all of us, given not only what this pandemic has done to our lives but also the reality of being a human being. We will all encounter hard things, it's unavoidable. But they throw the good stuff into sharp relief. Experience has taught me how important it is to pay attention to everyday instances of joy, for as long as they last. It has shown me that moments of hope come, when you least expect them.

Throughout the process of working on this book, it has been constantly on my mind that there are still people in detention centres in Syria being tortured. This very minute. In those putrid, terrifying cages, wondering if today will be their last.

There are still so many people risking their lives in the hope of a better life. Drowning, lungs filled with salty water, because they dared to hope for freedom.

There are still families living in makeshift camps in Greece, looking after babies and toddlers in unsanitary and freezing conditions. I don't want to say they have nothing because you can always have dignity, love, pride and the dream of living a safe life, but they have much to endure.

These people are just like you. They just want homes to call their own, work they find rewarding, an education for their children. They want birthday cakes, first days of school photographs, cups of tea, good nights of sleep, favourite songs on the radio, walks in fresh air. The patchwork of everyday lives lived in peace.

It's just an accident of birth, the country named on our passports, which shapes our destinies.

The simple truth is that the refugee population is growing – and will continue to do so. Man-made crises and global warming will displace many more people in the years ahead. This is a simple fact. And the Western world needs to think about how it deals with this. To uphold the values which so many people think it stands for – the rule of law, accountability, humanity and social justice. Rather than degrade itself with racist policies based on fear, such as the violent maritime pushbacks in the Aegean Sea which I witnessed first-hand and continue to this day, the interminable processing of asylum claims and endless rhetoric about people stealing jobs.

Multiculturalism is amazing, the most wonderful gift. Just imagine how bleak and dull Britain would be – musically, gastronomically, culturally – without the successive waves of immigration that have yielded such riches for this country. Imagine what would have happened when the pandemic hit if there hadn't been that army of people, many of them originally from somewhere else, willing to work for minimum wage, changing nappies and holding hands. Scrubbing light switches and spoon feeding. Wrapping up the dead. Approaching their jobs with decency, courage and pride. Day after day.

In my life so far, danger has come close to me more times than I would have liked. I've seen death up close and I can testify that we are all the same as we near the end in that we yearn to be gently touched. To remember the good times. To talk to our families one last time. We dream of home, of safety, of remembered love. Our humanity unites us, surpassing all those artificial and provisional designations. Nationality. Skin colour. Profession. Wage. All of that so easily forgotten when it comes down to it. None of them should matter in the first place.

I hope I've demonstrated just what a person can contribute to the country they decide to make their home. What a difference they can make – indeed, are making, right this very minute.

We're all interconnected. Our humanity unites us.

EPILOGUE

This book is as much a personal memoir of overcoming fear with hope as it is a witness statement to the destruction of my home and country.

At the time of writing, the Syrian conflict is in its tenth year. It has led to more than 500,000 deaths and displaced an estimated 13 million people – over half of Syria's pre-war population. More than 6.2 million Syrians are internally displaced and 5.6 million are refugees, predominantly in Lebanon, Jordan and Turkey. Syria's detention centres still hold tens of thousands of detainees including innocent women and children. The vast majority have been arbitrarily detained for their participation in peaceful protests or for expressing dissenting political opinion. I have attended so many protests in London since making my life here and each time I am reminded of the people back home who are imprisoned for doing the exact same thing. The weight of this double life, of my voice and their forced silence, is hard to bear at times.

The trauma behind the numbers is overwhelming. It's hard to comprehend the collective and individual pain inflicted on so many innocent people. Families have been torn apart and those of us who have survived are forced to navigate a life far removed from what we have dreamed of as kids.

Coronavirus is spreading in Syria, at the time of writing, and it is spreading quickly. The situation is much worse than the regime admits. The official numbers remain low but the likelihood is that these are grossly underreported. With hospitals so damaged, there aren't adequate facilities to treat those getting sick. It's hard to think about what the suffering will be like for so many. And yet, despite the seriousness of the pandemic, Covid is the least of people's worries. The queues outside bakeries and fuel stations are growing. People are struggling to put food on the table as a result of economic collapse and sanctions, which are disproportionately affecting ordinary citizens.

Assad has won the war but lost the country. There are no more widespread protests and most of the cities that were liberated have been recaptured by regime forces, aside from the pocket of Idlib. Assad has – with the backing of Russia and Iran – succeeded in quashing the uprising. But at the most terrible of costs. He now presides over an empire of dirt, riddled with rebel factions. Syria is not the place it was. The infrastructure has been destroyed while many of its ancient monuments have been annihilated. The memory of genocide will endure forever.

Because of this devastation, millions of Syrians are now scattered around the world trying to find truth and purpose in their lives. And despite all they have endured, they are succeeding. They are serving their new communities as teachers, doctors, chefs and frontline workers. They are helping to build lasting connections across families and friendships and neighbourhoods. And although we love contributing to our adopted homes in this way, deep down we hope it will one day be safe for us to return and rebuild our own.

Across non-regime-held areas, civil society has established schools, hospitals, universities, local elections and a free media. What started as volunteer efforts have developed into organizations now supporting four million people in Idlib. This work continues despite years of carpet bombing, missile strikes and chemical attacks.

Recently, Syrian activists have started the long process of holding those responsible for war crimes to account. In February 2021, a court in Germany convicted former Syrian secret police officer, Eyad al-Gharibin, of aiding and abetting crimes against humanity. He was convicted for his role in arresting and transporting protestors nearly a decade ago to an interrogation centre in Damascus known for torture. This conviction gives me hope that Syrian survivors might one day see justice. Justice for the crimes committed won't erase the pain but it will help people be able to live fuller and more complete lives. Justice matters because I don't want any other country to suffer what we did. I don't want anyone to suffer as I have.

As I write, a similar chain of events is unfolding in Myanmar as the world largely looks on and does nothing. It's hard to ignore the feeling of dread in my stomach; surely we all know how this ends if we don't speak up against what is wrong, what is inhumane and what is unjust? Collective silence enables fascism to flourish. If we don't speak up we let others down. If we don't uphold international law we will continue to embolden dictators and fascists everywhere.

At times it is really hard to hold onto hope. Trauma holds you back, it makes you feel like things that have happened could have been your fault. It lies to you. The reality of it all is bleak. What started spontaneously as a peaceful uprising against the Syrian regime was turned into a war by different factions that hijacked it for their own vested interests. But it wasn't entirely a failure because we did succeed in discrediting the Assad autocracy. I don't think any democracy that respects human rights will normalise relations with the Assad regime at any time in the future. That's because of what we did, in holding onto hope and risking our lives to tell our stories. That's what I'm doing in writing this book, too. In telling my story and that of my family, I stand for so many other Syrians. Those whose voices wouldn't otherwise be heard. Those who want the world to know the truth.

Hope, not fear.

RESOURCES

I have crossed paths with some incredible charities during my journey. If you are inspired after reading this book and want to contribute, please have a look here:

Choose Love: @chooselove https://choose.love/

Molham Volunteering Team: @molhamteam https://molhamteam.com/en

Freedom From Torture: @freedomfromtorture https://www.freedomfromtorture.org/

Barts Charity: @bartscharity https://www.bartscharity.org.uk/

Fareshare: @FareShareUK https://fareshare.org.uk/

ACKNOWLEDGEMENTS

Deep down, I know that I would not have been able to survive and write this book if it weren't for my parents' prayers. Mama Rania and Baba Imad, I love you with all my heart, I am grateful to you both and I am so sorry for everything I have put you through.

To my siblings, my nephews and nieces. Despite the distance between us, your love keeps me going.

I'd like to thank everyone at Pan Macmillan – particularly Carole Tonkinson, whose support has repeatedly surpassed the mere professional. Likewise, my agent Rachel Mills, who helped me turn this dream of mine into a reality. And Rebecca Ley, who guided me through the process of writing this book with utter kindness and care. Thank you for the gummy bears, Rebecca.

To my dear friends who have been so crucial in terms of reading drafts of this book and providing feedback. There were times I felt like giving up, you made sure I didn't - thank you, Redwan Ghiba, Sophie Dahl, Josie Naughton, Anna Nolan, Heydon Prowse, Josh Baker, Rachel Mantell and Jen McGeachie.

My heartfelt gratitude goes to the Temperleys, whose farm in Somerset is one of my favourite places in Britain. And to the Howards whose wonderful hospitality has also been such a blessing.

To Dr Hamodi Kayal who has been incredibly helpful in terms of helping me to process some of the events which I have written about here.

Finally, I want to thank all of you who helped me with a smile, by calling me 'mate' or having a friendly chat. You made me feel welcome, and I'll never forget it.